China Love You
The Death of Global Competition

by
Dr. Eric Wu & Geshe Michael Roach

Published by Diamond Cutter Press

ISBN 9781937114114

PRINTED IN THE UNITED STATES OF AMERICA

Table of Contents

Foreword

The two largest economies in the world are now China and the United States—which means that these two countries will have the greatest influence on the state of our planet, for many years to come. If the two nations cooperate economically and politically, then the entire world will see a period of peace and prosperity which it has never seen before.

And yet, surprisingly, those of us who live in these two countries know very little about each other. In each country, we read in our newspapers about the other, but this just gives us a general and often incomplete picture. We don't really get to know each other, and it's possible that we can start to misunderstand each other. Since our two countries are now the two strongest in the world, this kind of misunderstanding can hurt all nations.

One place where normal Chinese and Americans work together every day is in business. When a big international business project throws us together, we begin to spend time with one another—we start to communicate more, person to person—and then the misunderstandings just melt away, often over a dinner table somewhere, because we find out where the other person is coming from and why they act the way they do.

And yet a story of American and Chinese businesspeople working together, and what they have learned from each other, has rarely been told. We are two businessmen—one Chinese, and one American—who began cooperating on a single business project several years ago. As we worked together, we became friends; and as we became closer friends, we opened up more to each other, and learned more about each other's countries and customs and history.

As we learned, we began to understand much better why Americans and Chinese might see the world differently sometimes, and how we can start to bring these two visions closer together. Because there is so little information available, we started to take notes about what we learned from each other; and later we had the idea to do a book together, because we hope that other people in our two countries might read this book and understand each other more—and thus bring the whole world closer.

It's important to say, right here at the beginning, that neither of us is a professional policy maker or political figure. We are just two people who have worked together a lot on business projects, and talked together a lot, and spent a lot of time in each other's countries and with each other's colleagues and family. Thus, much of what we write in this book isn't about government policies or official statistics or anything like that—it's just the personal impressions of two people from two different countries.

As with any two people who are friends, we have preferred to focus on the positive things we can learn about each other; we feel that this should be the first step of any friendship, between people or countries. In time, after we become very close friends, we can be more critical and dive into questioning each other's beliefs and actions—but by the time we do become close friends, we sometimes know so much about each other that this critique is no longer even necessary.

One thing that both of us have always shared is a deep interest in Chinese traditional culture, especially the ancient literature of China. As each of us pursued our separate business lives for years before we met each other, we were independently studying these great books—many of them thousands of years old. Independently, we began to apply the ancient wisdom found in these works to our modern business enterprises and personal lives, with very successful results.

Eric used these principles to build his executive training company, Guang Yao ("Light on Life" in English) of Beijing, into one of China's premier coaching firms, teaching many thousands of people every year. He has also founded cutting-edge medical research centers seeking cures for cancer, diabetes, and heart disease; as well as innovative educational programs for children all around China. Michael helped found Andin International, a diamond jewelry manufacturer in Manhattan, which reached US$250 million in annual sales and was purchased by Warren Buffett in 2009. Michael's book about how to use the ancient wisdom of Asia for business and personal success—The Diamond Cutter—is an international bestseller now in more than 30 languages of the world.

And so while the first half of this book shares insights we have gained that will help Americans and Chinese people understand and appreciate each other, the second half presents a proposal, drawn from the ancient wisdom of Asia, for a new business model which states that the greatest amount of economic success for ourselves comes directly from making others successful.

This is not simply a kind or noble approach (although it is both kind and noble), but rather one which brings greater financial results for those who really understand the details of how it works. In the end, we believe, this model will replace the current world model of competition, which can cause such disastrous results on a personal, corporate, and international level.

And so we hope that our small book will hasten the death of global competition.

Dr. Eric Wu & Geshe Michael Roach
Beijing, China & Sedona, Arizona, USA
October 2016

Preface to the Second Edition

Now, in the cold weather of international tension, it is more important than ever before that we Americans and Chinese try to understand more about each other. This book is a great way for all of us to do this—quickly, easily, and yet deeply.

Not long ago the two of us, Dr. Eric Wu and Geshe Michael Roach—Chinese and American—were sitting at Cricket's Café, a tiny coffee shop in the small town of Rimrock, Arizona, in the western USA. Michael often has business meetings there, because the café has such as friendly atmosphere and is so close to his home. It is also the only place in all of Rimrock where you can get a coffee and breakfast in the morning!

Grace, the long-time waitress at the café, drops by to fill up our coffee cups.

"By the way, gentlemen, we're closing tomorrow!" she says brightly.

Michael groans, but smiles. "You guys are always doing that, just closing up for a few days and running off to your cabin out in the woods to take a break. When will you be back to open up again?"

"Oh no Michael," says Grace. "You don't understand. We're closing closing. Like closing the café. Look at the sign!" Michael looks out the window and for the first time notices a sign near the front walk that says, "After 34 years of serving our community, we're retiring! Thanks a lot!"

Ralph Nye, the master American astronomer who owns the café with his wife Kay, hears the ruckus and wanders over, with that usual huge smile on his face. And as usual, since it's a weekend and he doesn't have to be at the nearby Lowell Observatory fixing huge telescopes, the Cricket's Café coffee pot is glued to his hand, pouring out fresh cups for old friends filling the café.

"That's right, Mike!" he says. "Kay and I are finally retiring!"

"But... what... you can't do that! I need this place! Everybody in this town needs this place!" Michael waves his arm at everyone else packed into the tiny room— mostly elderly folks who really depend on the café as their only source of daily fellowship.

Eric is staring intently as the scene unfolds. This is his first visit to Cricket's, and he can feel the real concern in his close friend Michael's voice.

"Well Michael, if you don't want the place to close," laughs Grace, "then maybe you should buy it!"

Without thinking at all about how much trouble it is to run a café when you don't know a single thing about the restaurant business, Michael yells back, "Well then I will. I'll buy the place!"

Eric says, in his usual quiet way, "Yeah! And I'll help him pay for it!"

"Done!" yell Ralph and Kay in unison, and thus the adventure began.

It's three years later; Michael and his wife Veronica are still trying to figure out how to run a café. The local county has given 34 years of exceptions to the building code for Cricket's Café, since it's one of the few businesses that has ever survived in this sleepy little town. But now the government wants everything brought up to date—a huge investment of time & money.

Crickets, as you may know, are tiny little insects that don't look all that different from those universal pests, the roaches. "Cricket" was Kay's nickname though, and it worked to call the restaurant "Cricket's Café" for all those years. Michael & Veronica have changed the name to "Peach Tree Café," mainly because the website address for this name is still available in the area. But that means we're going to have to plant some peach trees!

Now the town of Rimrock is out in the middle of the Arizona desert, but with patience and care and a lot of (expensive) water, you can grow a tree. And so the new peach tree near the café front door is doing pretty well... but then a strange thing happens.

This February, winter still has a hard lock on Rimrock—yes it's desert, but high desert, meaning that it also snows in the winter! Things are still frozen hard, and this lonely little peach tree does something crazy: it starts putting out flowers.

Michael & Veronica are frantic. Because—for a fruit tree—the flowers are what turn into the fruit, later on: they turn into the peaches! But if the flowers pop out too soon—goodness knows why—then the delicate petals will freeze; fall off; and... no peaches for the whole year! How is Peach Tree Café finally going to open, without any peaches on our signature tree??

We call our friend, the Master Gardener. What's going on? Why is our peach tree acting so crazy?

Master Gardener agrees to stop by for a visit. He walks around the tree a couple of times, hemming and hawing, and then declares, "Desperate measures!"

"Desperate measures?" reply Michael & Veronica. "What do you mean, 'desperate measures'?"

Master Gardener: "Didn't you ever hear of that old saying, 'Desperate times call for desperate measures'? When things get really bad, you have to try something new; something unexpected; something desperate!"

"So what's so desperate with the tree?" we ask.

"Ah!" replies Master Gardener. "Trees know things about the coming weather that humans just never figure out. This peach tree is pushing out her flowers because she sees that she might not get another chance this year—she senses some dangerous weather arriving in the coming months, and she's trying something really crazy to get her pollen supply!"

"What do you mean, her pollen supply?" we ask.

"Look, didn't you know? What you've got here is a lady tree. Lady trees are just like... well, just like lady humans! If they wanna have a baby, they need some pollen supply from a man! You know what I mean!" he says a little shyly.

"Ah... okay, we got it," we both nod.

"And look here," Master Gardener points up into the branches. "There's your bees, a few of them, sneaking out of their hive box early, because they know that Mrs Peach here needs some help!"

We look up in the branches, and sure enough, there are a few lonely bees gliding from blossom to blossom, shipping in grains of pollen on the hairs of their legs. (Did we tell you that we keep bees to help our trees and garden? But it's still winter, and they're supposed to be glued to the inside of their box, keeping the queen warm.)

"That's, errr, how peach trees have sex!" laughs Master Gardener. "The bees carry the boy tree's pollen to the girl tree's blossoms; that gets her pregnant; and then the peaches pop out—her babies! Just like humans, really!

"And it's too early, you see," he continues. "It's way too early for the girl tree to be opening up for pollen. But there's something about the cold; there's a feeling to the cold of this year's winter; and she knows somehow that this might be her last chance to make it happen. She feels —she knows somehow—that storms are coming which might stop her for the whole year to come. She knows she has to make her peaches now—yes it's too cold, but there's a chance, and she has to try."

And this is how it is in the world right now, you see. There is a kind of cold touching the whole world, especially between the nations. A lot of mistrust, a lot of misunderstanding. We've all been staying inside our homes; and we haven't met each other face-to-face for quite a while; and what we knew about each other we've begun to forget, and we've had no chance to learn new things from each other, so far from each other.

Which makes the second edition of this book—China Love You—even more crucial than the first edition was. We hope that you, dear readers, also notice the chill in the world right now, and we hope it will move you to put out a few new, exploratory blossoms, and open up to receive the pollen of fresh ideas and feelings from people of other countries.

And we ourselves hope to be the bees that, with this small but important book, bring you the springtime peaches of cross-pollination—rather than the barren future which is the only fruit of turning inside to our own country, and only our own interests, and descending into competition against the peoples of the rest of our world.

There are new ideas here, ideas that you have never heard of, which can swiftly bring all our nations to great cooperation—and to the mutual prosperity and joy that working together always creates.

With best wishes,

Dr. Eric Wu & Geshe Michael Roach
Beijing, China & Rimrock, USA
February 2022

Part One
Current Issues

1
China Love You

Michael:

Why have we given our book such an unusual name? Any time there's a big change in the global alignment, it can make people nervous. I know that many Americans for example are nervous that China has suddenly become such a tremendous economic power.

This is human nature. When a country is poor, we often don't give it enough attention and help. If the same country suddenly becomes wealthy—more wealthy in some ways than our own country—then suddenly we give it too much attention, and perhaps even feel threatened.

I grew up in the United States; I have spent a long life in this country—over 60 years—and I have seen it go through many changes. During the course of this long life I have seen our country repeat at times some of the same mistakes with other countries and peoples, generation after generation.

Like many Americans, from reading newspapers and listening to the television, I built up a certain impression of China and Chinese people. The impression was often negative: of a very ambitious and even aggressive people, who were difficult to get along with. I heard in our news about internal problems in China that would make an American feel unwelcome if they visited. And so, like many Americans, I avoided travelling to China for many years, until I was forced to do so for my business.

Before my first visit, I was a little nervous. Would these people be cold and pushy? Would I feel uncomfortable with many social restrictions? Would I be coated in terrible pollution?

But in fact, on my first visit I met many business associates whom I gradually got to know better and better. Every time I came back to China, I felt more at home: faces and names became familiar, and people struggled to speak my language. At a birthday dinner for a mutual friend, my host made me a separate, ginseng pizza—to give me a taste of home, he said, with the pizza; and to help me live a long and healthy life, with the ginseng!

I found that all the people around me were kind and considerate; I felt safe; I made more and more good friends. These friends were clear-minded and curious about life, more healthy and more energetic than many of my countrymen in the US. One evening in Beijing, after quite a few business trips to the country, I was alone in my hotel room and suddenly had an experience of strong joy and wellbeing; it suddenly struck me that I had travelled a long road from my initial nervousness about China, to a place where I now felt as if my business associates and I had actually become a single, warm family.

I know it sounds strange to say that about business colleagues in a foreign country, but that's what really happened! I remember that a few weeks later I was back at my dentist in the United States, and mentioned to him that I had just been working in China. He gave me a look of great concern and asked me if I hadn't had a very difficult time.

It was hard for me to remember that I had once felt the same, and looking back I realize that it was because I had just automatically accepted everything I had read in the newspapers, or heard on television, about China and Chinese people.

Which brings me to the title of our book.

A few years ago I was giving a series of seminars near my home, in Arizona, USA. Because I make presentations throughout the world, visitors from other countries sometimes travel to America to attend my local programs. And so I found an older Chinese gentleman there in the back of the class, sitting ramrod straight and trying to catch every word.

Over the course of several days, as the seminars progressed, I realized that he didn't speak a word of English! And so we arranged for a younger Chinese speaker to sit next to him, whispering a quick translation as we went. At the end of the series, the gentleman came up to the lectern, gave me a formal bow, and held out both of his hands, with great ceremony. There in his palms was the middle of a toilet-paper roll—the cheap grey cardboard part—with something written on it.

I tried to be graceful and accept the cylinder, and rolled it over to read what was on it. There, in the shaky hand that you might see from a young child in elementary school, were the English words:

China Love You!!!

Stuffed inside was a bunch of Chinese money, about a hundred dollars' worth.

When I think about it, this little gift says a lot about China-US relations. Our two cultures are *totally* different, and whenever we're together, we probably make small, unintentional mistakes all day long—like handing an American an empty toilet paper roll, which in the US we might sometimes consider a little dirty. The American in turn might accept the gift with only a single hand, which in Asia would be considered less than respectful.

But actually the whole exchange was one of love, and mutual regard, and generosity. Because we were looking into each other's eyes at the moment, and because our hands were touching, we both knew that this is what we each intended.

So it's important for Americans and Chinese people —normal people, not just government leaders—to get together whenever they can: visit each other's countries, try to make personal friends. And it's also important to keep in mind that we *will* make occasional mistakes with each other, just because our cultures and histories are so different; and that we should be quick to forgive, and slow to take offense. If we stay close enough, the mistakes don't matter.

America, China love you. China, America love you.

2
The Middle Kingdom
& The Beautiful Country

Michael:
Eric, I've heard friends say that Chinese people think too much of themselves. I ask them why, and they say, "After all, the very *name* that Chinese people use for their country means 'Middle Kingdom'! They think that China is the center of the world!" What do you say about this, Eric?

Eric:
It is true that the Chinese name for China is *Zhong Guo*, or "Middle Country." But to understand what the expression means, first we have to go back more than 3,000 years to the time of a Chinese leader named King Wen.

There was a period in his life when King Wen was imprisoned by his rivals. During these darkest days, he had a chance to go deep into the meaning of life and the universe. And then he had a realization—he said, "The *Middle* in *Middle Country* is a middle of ideas, not of places." We can put it this way:

> Where do human beings come from?
> They come from their heart.
> Where do human beings go?
> They go to their heart.
> In-between the coming and going,
> Where do they stay?
> They stay in their heart,
> In the balance of all the forces
> Of the universe.

These forces are what we call the elements of earth, water, fire, and wind. Of these, earth holds the middle place, tying together all the others, as our heart holds the middle and manages the body.

So what King Wen is saying is that *Middle* means *Heart*, and in fact in Chinese we sometimes call our heart "the heart of the middle." The Middle is the origin of life itself.

This same word, Middle, also refers to a specific point in Chinese acupuncture. The full name of this point is "Middle of Man," and it is found between the nose and the upper lip. The area just above this point has the nature of *yang*, which refers more to the spiritual world. The area below the point relates to *yin*, and the material world of people.

We use this particular acupuncture point to manage the heart—to balance between the *yin* and the *yang*: the material and the spiritual. In this sense, the goal of our life is to find our own Middle, our own Balance.

We say that finding this balance is no easy thing: the Middle is difficult to find, the Heart is difficult to see. But the mission of our life is to find our Middle Heart. In the quiet of the Middle Heart, we also balance the fundamental energies of the world: earth, water, fire, and wind. This then creates a beautiful world of perfect harmony.

King Wen came to the conclusion that the world had lost its Middle, and he had the idea that we could try to return to this Middle, even as a country. And so he worked to revive even older ideas and practices of light and truth, helping our country to find its Middle.

As the element of earth ties together the other elements, so too do all things ultimately depend upon the earth, or soil, beneath our feet. In ancient times then, soil was considered one of the most sacred things in our world. And so the Chinese word for *Country* is actually tied to the word for *Middle*, and "Middle Country" is a beautiful idea of a country whose people are trying to be balanced in their life, between the spiritual and the physical.

We even take pride in the fact that our Chinese complexion has a bit of yellow color in it, because the richest earth in our country is the yellow soil found in the state of Shanxi, at the middle of our country.

The part of China in which King Wen lived, finally, was called Zhou. It was a land surrounded by mountain chains shaped like circles within circles, and so his people and domain came to be called "Middle Country." In more recent times, as our country has become more unified into a single nation, with a strong center, we have chosen to revive this expression, Zhong Guo, as our name for China.

Michael:
You once told me that there was another meaning of "Middle Country," connected to how we relate to other countries. Can you explain that?

Eric:
Yes, there's another meaning of this name for China. Traditionally, we Chinese have tried to stick to the idea of a "Middle Way"—a phrase that harkens back to our Buddhist traditions. For Chinese people, staying in the middle means steering a middle course: not going to extremes.

In foreign relations, for example, we have tried in the long term not to go to one extreme, where we meddle in the affairs of other countries. And at the other extreme, we have also tried not to shut our country's doors to visitors and ideas from the outside. We have not always been successful at this Middle Way, but we do believe in it as a country, and we feel that this policy is generally going well in modern times.

All this is why, in my understanding, we like to call ourselves "The Country of the Middle." It's certainly not meant as some kind of superiority complex, where we believe that China is the center of the whole world, or that we are better than other nations. Instead, it's a middle viewpoint that we hope can embrace all nations.

By the way, it might interest our readers to know that the Chinese name for "America" is *Mei Guo*, which means "The Beautiful Country". As a people we do admire a great many aspects of American culture, which a lot of us have learned about—as do many people in the world—through the very popular American films.

3
Chinese & American Names, and Saying Them Correctly

Eric & Michael:
One good place to start, in understanding each other, is to get our names straight! Very few normal Americans even know the name of the President of China, or the names of any of the famous Chinese writers who have been producing magnificent literature for thousands of years. Even when we see the name of a prominent Chinese person spelled in English letters, we are often unsure how to pronounce it correctly. So let's touch on that, just a minute, before we go deeper.

People living in America generally use at least two names—a "first" name and a "second" or "family" name—and sometimes even a third one in-between those two, although this name is rarely used in everyday life. The personal name, like "Michael," comes first; and then the family name, such as "Roach," comes second.

In China, the order is reversed. The family name comes first, and then the personal name. So Eric's birth name is Wu Mingfeng, where Wu is the family name. There is a custom in China, nowadays, for young people to pick a Western-sounding name, to make it easier for foreigners to remember. Each person picks their own name, which can be a lot of fun, and we know Chinese young people who have chosen the name of "Cinderella," or "Othello."

You may have noticed that a lot of Chinese have the same family name. This is because about 50% of Chinese share the only some 20 family names, with just three of them—Li,

Wang, and Zhang—shared by over 20% of all Chinese. And that's because Chinese family names were originally given to everyone in the same clan, or same geographic group, or connected in some way to the same member of the royalty.

In America, there are over 150,000 family names!

Until you get to know a Chinese person fairly well, it's respectful to refer to them with their full name—such as Wu Mingfeng—or to refer to them as Mr. or Mrs. or Miss, followed by their family name (the first one): Mr. Wu. The same for an American, but of course the family name comes last: Mr. Roach. Once you become friends, you can just call each other by your personal names: Michael, or Mingfeng, or Eric.

About pronouncing Chinese names correctly, you can get everything right if you just learn a few basic tricks. When the modern method of pronouncing Chinese in western sounds—known as Pinyin—was first developed in the 1950's, the scholars who worked on the project tried to represent each Chinese sound with one or two western letters.

Sometimes though there was more than one Chinese sound that was close to a western sound. So in this case, they tried to use a different western letter—even though the result was to use western letters in a way that they aren't normally used, for example, in English.

The name of the current president of China, Mr. Xi Jinping, is a good example to start with. "Xi" is his family name, and "Jinping" is his personal name. The closest English sound to "Xi" though is "Shi," so it should be pronounced that way.

You will also see this same English sound spelled as "Shi," which is pronounced in a slightly different way in Chinese than "Xi"—but the difference cannot be heard or repeated by most English speakers without training. So here's an easy chart to help you out with some of the most common unexpected spellings:

All the new Chinese letters an English speaker needs to know

1) **ch** and **q** in Chinese words are both heard as **ch** by an English speaker; so for example pronounce "qi"—or "inner energy"—as *chi*

2) **j** and **zh** are both heard as **j** by a normal English speaker, so for example you can pronounce the name of Guangzhou (a southern Chinese city which is in the top 10 metropolitan areas of the world, by population) as *Guang-jo*

3) as noted above, **x** and **sh** will be heard all normal English speakers as the same; so the name "President Xi Jinping" is pronounced President *Shi Jinping*

4) **c** and **z** are both pronounced as **ts,** with a slight difference that most English speakers can't hear; it's impossible to find at the beginning of an English word, but it's there in the middle of "pizza," or when we say "It's a baby!" really fast—so, for example, the word in Chinese for "where?" (which you'd better learn if you're looking for a bathroom!) is *zai nali*: pronounce *tsai nali*

By the way, the main dialect of Chinese has four different tones, and they change the meaning of the same word completely. So if you say for example the word *da* with a lot of emphasis, it means "big." If you say the same word with the tone of a question in English, you might be saying "fight"! So you'll have to study these four tones a little if you really want to say people's names correctly.

4
Individualism vs. Groupism

Eric & Michael:
We've seen how tens of millions of Chinese people may share the same family name, whereas in America the same number of people may have many thousands of different names. This difference between our two countries comes in part from of a difference in how we see the role of the individual in a family, or a company or country. If we can understand how each of us feel about the place of an individual in a group, we can go a long way in understanding each other; and thus prevent mistaken judgments or misunderstandings.

Michael:
American culture places a big emphasis on the individual—on what a single determined person can do. This is very common in the movies, for example, which are a mirror of our culture. In an American movie, say like the *Transformers* series (which has grossed over $3 billion), a single nerdy young man ignores what everybody else thinks and works together with mechanical aliens to save the world.

In a movie like this, the young man will often fall in love with a young woman; the parents on both sides, and society in general, may disapprove of the match—but the two young people push ahead with their relationship and prove all the older people wrong. And oftentimes the parents or society will acknowledge, in the end, that it was right for the younger ones to stick by their independent decisions.

Eric:

Your American movies can be immensely popular in China, but this thing about individualism is definitely not what we see as the best for everyone in our country. For thousands of years of Chinese history, a very big population has had to live together in harmony upon a relatively small piece of land. Over the centuries our culture has developed into one where the individual must not pursue their own selfish aims, at the expense of the group.

In China, if millions of young people decided to go against the system and do something different that they thought was better, it would be chaos—and periods of chaos *have* happened in our country in past centuries, and they have cost the lives of millions of people. So we have learned to live together in a group, and live by the rules of the group, simply out of necessity, for survival—a big family in a small house has to have some rules.

This is how almost all Chinese people also feel about public protests, for example. We believe that it is important for individuals to express their thoughts, and we believe it is important to stand up and speak out if something wrong is going on. But we believe that this is best done through the channels that society has set up. With well over a billion people, our country would be paralyzed if a few million of us decided to block some local streets, for example.

I think it's good if Americans appreciate that normal Chinese people, like myself, understand why more firm rules of society may be more important for China than for the US, and that on the whole we support them and choose to live by them.

5
Creativity & Responsibility

Eric:

Creativity in China and America is tied to this same distinction between individualism and groupism. Michael and I were sitting together in a hotel coffee shop in Singapore recently talking about this, and I pointed to some things around the room: the way the coffee was made; the design of the hotel lobby; the cellphone on the table and even the pop music coming out of the speakers above us.

"All of this has come from America," I said to Michael. "Because you are so little restricted by the ties of the group, then each of you is more free to be creative, and you have been: Your baby country is only 200 years old, but it has come up with all kinds of inventions and innovations that our country—in our 5,000 years of history—hasn't thought of; and we have enjoyed using and re-casting these ideas in our own way.

"As I understand it, an entry-level employee in an American company who feels they have a good idea can feel free to go straight to the vice president of the division, or even to the CEO, and pitch it to them. In China we would have to be more mindful of going up through the chain of command: present the idea to our immediate manager, and hope that they will appreciate it and pass it on up. But of course, in this way, a lot of good ideas die stillborn."

Michael:

After saying all this, Eric was quiet for a minute, still gazing thoughtfully at all the American inventions surrounding us.

"But when you lose your respect for those who are older than you—when that attitude doesn't mean a lot in your country any more—something else can happen too," he said.

"There can come a divide between the generations: each generation focuses on their own needs, on their own dreams, and they lose sight of the needs and dreams of the generation ahead of them, or the one coming up behind them.

"That is, when you create something new, you have to think about how it affects your parents and their generation; and how it affects your children and their generation—there has to be sort of a generational awareness.

"If you create a cellphone or a tablet and hand it out to children to keep them quiet all day, you have to think ahead of time about what that might do to the relationship between these children and their parents: it has to be part of the process of invention, of creativity.

"What will those children be like after 20 years of staring most of the day into a little 6-inch box? How will they treat their parents; when will they talk to them—and what kind of parents will they become themselves?

"And if you strip the earth of rare minerals to produce these electronics, what will there be left for the next generation? If as you create things you feel disconnected from the generation to come, you can leave behind a wasteland for them.

"And so yes, the restrictions on our behavior demanded by Chinese tradition—the connection between generations—can impede creativity, but they can also protect the larger world, the longer history to come."

World Choices #1

Here we're going to start the first of what we call World Choices. Chinese people have a certain way of seeing things; a certain way of doing things. And then American people have a different way. Of course it's important to understand and appreciate each other's views, and that's the goal of this first half of the book, which we've called "Current Issues."

But we have another job here—and that's to decide *which system is better.* Would the world be better off if we all became a little more American, a little more individualistic; or if we all went the Chinese way, and went along more with the group? Or should we go for some kind of a mix?

We're going to come up against these choices more and more as we go through this little book. We'll put each World Choice in its own small box, like this. And then in the second part of the book, which we call "Eternal Issues," we'll talk about a completely new way of dealing with these choices.

This new way comes from an ancient text called *The Diamond Cutter Sutra.* The Chinese edition is in fact the oldest printed book in the world with a date of publication in it.

6

Protecting the Environment

Michael:

While we're on the subject of global sustainability, I'd like to say something about the reporting in the US press about pollution in China, and what's being done about it. I was in Shanghai recently on one of the worst pollution days in Chinese history—we were advised not to go outside without a cloth mask, and walking between buildings at our hotel, it was difficult to see the wall opposite us.

I've also had the experience of taking Chinese friends out to the wilderness in my home state of Arizona, USA, and seen their amazed reaction to the sight of millions of stars blazing overhead, and the miracle of the Milky Way on a clear desert night.

And so I've talked to Eric and other friends about how Chinese feel about the environment, and as usual it's not quite what you hear on the news in the US.

Chinese people are obviously not unaware of the problem, and they obviously care as much as anybody about their own health, and the health of their children. It only takes a few minutes of thought to realize that nobody in the world likes to walk around in polluted air, and of course they will do something about it.

Chinese friends, especially young people, that I've talked to were shocked to hear that they were portrayed in the US news as not caring about the environment. They said that environmental awareness has jumped just as fast as the economy in China; and that their government, for example, has committed to spend $800 *billion* in the next 5 years to clean up the environment.

To understand more about pollution in China, as usual we have to understand more about where people are coming from. Here's a quick snapshot.

Eric & Michael:
It's important to remember that—even until quite recently— China was an extremely poor country and that she still has a long ways to go just to catch up. Here are some numbers to think about:

❖ Homes
The average American has 2 full rooms of living space. The average Chinese has about a third of this, which means that the 2 rooms in China are occupied by an average of three people—not just one—living in them. Naturally, Chinese people would all like to have just as much space as Americans already do.

But this would require building hundreds of millions of new houses. Those buildings will need things like steel and cement, and bringing those materials into the country and building homes with them is going to create more pollution, such as carbon emissions.

So just for Chinese to catch up to what most Americans already have, it will require more mining, more forests, more oil. If Americans say that their Chinese brothers and sisters shouldn't use these resources, then to many Chinese people, what they really seem to be saying is that Chinese don't have the same right to living space as Americans do.

❖ Consumption of the world's resources

The United States is home to only 5% of the world's population. But the US uses one third of the world's paper every year; a quarter of its oil; almost 25% of its coal; and about 20% of many metals such as aluminum or copper.

The highly respected Sierra Club in the US estimates that the average American uses up 53 times more of the world's goods and services than the average Chinese person does. Each person in the US creates more than 3 times more carbon emissions than each person in China, even with China undertaking huge construction housing and road projects just to catch up with the US.

Educated people in China have often visited the United States, and they know that California for example has very tough environmental standards, such as laws on how many trees can be cut down. At the same time, they see the Americans living a lifestyle that requires many poorer countries to cut down their own trees, and send the wood to America to feed its demand for paper.

If we're going to say that everyone in the world has an equal right to live in the same comfort and safety, then obviously China's going to have to use a lot more resources to catch up.

Automobiles

America has 8 cars for every 10 people. China has 1 car for every 10 people. Of course almost everyone in China dreams of following the American Dream, and owning their own car. It's very convenient to own your own car, and it's very inconvenient to stand around waiting for a bus or whatever. That doesn't change, no matter what country you live in.

76% of Americans drive to work *alone* in their car. Only a third of Americans regularly walk or ride a bike to someplace they'd like to go. 75% of Chinese do.

Roads

There is a mile of paved road for every 123 people in America. But in China there is only a mile of paved road for every 615 people. (About ten years ago, before the government began a big road-building project, it was one mile for every 1,200 people!).

So to catch up, China will need to build 500% more roads!

Again, this takes cement and steel, to create the kind of infrastructure America has had for almost 100 years. Chinese people naturally would like to drive places as easily as American do. And that will take more resources and create more carbon emissions.

Airports

American airports have 5,054 paved runways. Chinese airports have less than a tenth of that: 463 paved runways. But China also has almost 5 times the population of the US. Of course, Chinese people would like to fly to another city to see their friends and relatives, just as much as Americans do! To catch up to America, China will have to build over 20,000 more runways. And that will take resources.

Bottom line, it's very important for all of us to realize that—just as Americans have their American Dream—Chinese have their Chinese Dream, and Mexicans have their Mexican

Dream, and Syrians and Nigerians and Ukrainians have their Dreams too. In a way, a lot of these dreams have come from the example of the American one.

Michael:

Whoa, wait just a minute! you might exclaim. When you say that China would like to catch up to the American Dream—that they would like to *follow the example* of the United States, it's important to acknowledge that *with many things that they do that affect the environment, the United States is a* **bad** *example.*

That is, we Americans admit that we are very wasteful, and that we use too much of the world's resources, and that we should change our habits. We don't *want* Chinese people to follow our example in *every* way.

If that's the case, then we need to make ourselves a better example, fast. It doesn't work when you are very wasteful yourself, and then tell your friends not to be. As always, the best way to convince other countries to develop good habits is to be sure that we've developed these habits ourselves. Otherwise, it doesn't seem fair to others, when we demand something from them that we aren't asking of ourselves.

7
Population Control

Michael:
We're going to get another question from some of the Americans here: "On one hand, if China has too many people, it's not fair to count their needs *per person*, the way you've done it above. They should have had fewer people!" And at the very same time a lot of Americans will ask an opposite question: "Does China really have a policy that each family can only have one child? Do Chinese people *like* that policy? Do they support it?"

Eric:
For centuries, China has had a very large population. One reason is that agriculture has obviously been a big priority of our country for many centuries, and much of that farming—of rice, for example, which is our main food—is very labor-intensive. And so farming families, especially the poor ones, would often try to have as many children as possible, to help with the crops.

Michael:
It was that way in America in the beginning too; that's why our schools have always had a two or three-month vacation in the summer, because the children used to help their parents with the farming at that time.

Eric:
Right, it makes sense. And don't forget that, in the past,

China didn't have the public safety net that America did, with their social security for elders, and similar programs. And so in Asia, your children have always *been* your social security program, and you would try to have as many as possible—especially boys, who would do more work and traditionally stay in the parents' house after marriage.

All that began to change as our country became more prosperous, and people already had more financial security. We began to address the overpopulation problem seriously an entire generation ago, in 1980. This is when we created a policy that each married couple should only have one child.

There are some things you should know about this policy. First of all, it only extends to about 35% of the population; for example, people in rural areas, who depend more on their children, and the ethnic minorities in our country may have additional kids. This also applies to over 50% of people whose first child was a girl.

The general policy has been increasingly relaxed recently, especially for parents who are themselves only children. People who break the policy pay a substantial fine.

Michael:
How do Chinese people themselves feel about this policy?

Eric:
You might be surprised to know that the Pew Research Center, one of America's leading think tanks, did a poll and found out that over 75% of the Chinese public supports the one-child policy. First of all, we understand very well what overpopulation can do to our quality of life, and the environment.

That is, we only have a fixed area of land and it can only support so many people. Moreover, if you consider the amount of this land which is farmable, it gets even smaller, compared to some other countries. The US and China have almost exactly the same land size, but the US has nearly 50% more land which is farmable. If we consider the difference in population, than there is almost 6 times more farmland per person in the US.

Secondly, like parents all over the world, more of us are deciding ourselves not to have children, or to have fewer children.

That said, you should realize that children, and family, are usually the most important thing in a Chinese person's life: we love our children so much that there is a special problem called the "Little Emperor Syndrome," where an only child especially is given so much love and attention that they can end up bossing around the parents and grandparents completely.

But a viewpoint is developing in our country that says "quality, not quantity." Like parents in other countries, it is more and more common that both the husband and the wife in China need to hold down a job to make ends meet. This means that we have less and less time to spend with our children.

If we choose to have fewer children, then we can afford a bigger home for them. And we also have enough time to give each one the attention they need to have a great childhood and education. We can spend more money on each one, sending them to better schools and hiring special tutors to help them after school, with things like piano lessons or extra English language classes.

Many of us would like to see our children get some of their higher education overseas, so they can broaden their outlook on life and make more connections for their future work career. But it takes a huge chunk of a Chinese family's income and savings to do this; right now, about $80,000 a year. We do it though, because children and education are a huge priority in traditional Chinese culture: for centuries, the best jobs were given to people who did well on national educational exams.

So for all these reasons, Chinese people care about overpopulation, and we are in a mood to keep doing something about it. It is estimated that—if we hadn't started taking the steps we did 35 years ago—then the population of China would be about 300 million more than it is now: nearly the population of the entire United States!

World Choices #2

It is questionable whether our planet—with global warming, the destruction of the oceans, shrinking supplies of fresh water, and the loss of trees and forests—can sustain its current population of 7 billion people. And the population of the world, according to the UN, still continues to grow at a rate of 75 million people per year: it is thought that by mid-century, we will have 9 billion world citizens, or 25% more than now!

So we come to another World Choice: what do we do about overpopulation? Do we follow the American model of Individualism, and hope that individual people will come to their senses and have fewer children; or do we follow the Chinese model, and set a limit on the number of children that people are allowed to have?

Which one of these two approaches is going to work?

8
Energy

Eric & Michael:

Whatever the population of the world ends up being, we're all going to need energy to live. Energy makes our cars go; we use it to grow our food; we need it to make our buildings. One of the most important places where our two countries will need to cooperate is in how we each get the energy that our people require, just to live. So let's take a look at where each of us gets our energy now, and then think about the future.

Eric:

Our country's energy mix is about 70% coal, 20% oil, and the rest divided between natural gas; nuclear; and renewables like hydroelectric power from dams. Almost all of our coal comes from inside the country, and about half of the oil does too; but we still need to import petroleum and natural gas from many different countries, including other Asian producers; the Middle East; and now Russia.

Coal is definitely not clean, but it was the first major energy source that we ever found in our country, and most of our electric power plants are already set up to use it—we are trying to change that. But like the United States, China has always wanted to use its own energy sources whenever possible, rather than importing supplies, so that we are not vulnerable to disasters like the US experienced during the oil embargo by Arab countries in the 1970.

We can call this "energy security". Energy security is another reason why our country is so sensitive about the status of the oceans off of the southeast coast of our country: the Chinese economy, and therefore the internal stability of our country, depends on imported oil; and that can only reach us through these sea lanes.

It's important for normal Americans to understand that China, more than anyone, really wants to increase our use of renewable energy sources—hydroelectric, solar, and wind. This is because of the same two reasons we've listed above: these sources will reduce our use of coal, which we know is choking our air; and they'll also give us better energy security, since we don't have to depend on other countries to send supplies to us.

We're trying to pump our renewable energy percentage up to 15% as soon as possible (the world average is something less than 3% right now). We are already the world's leader in solar panel research and manufacturing, and in total wind and solar energy production.

Michael:
I can say that I was struck, when I visited China, how almost all the new homes and apartments I saw already have solar hot water heaters installed on the roof. I live in Arizona, which has some of the most hours of sun per day of any part of the world, but almost none of our homes have these heaters—so we are wasting our own oil and coal, in a big way.

There are even neighborhoods here where *it's not allowed* to put up a solar hot water heater on your roof, because it doesn't look nice! I like how Chinese are finding cool ways to *design* their roofs *around* the solar panels and passive water heaters, so that they actually make the roof look chic.

Okay—our country's energy mix is about 35% oil, 25% natural gas, and 25% coal; with the rest divided between nuclear and renewables. America has the largest coal deposits of any country in the world, and we export a lot more than we import. We still import some of our natural gas, but only around 12%. The percentage of oil that we import from other countries has been running around 60%, but it has recently dropped to about 40%. Here's why.

In the last few years, we've produced a lot of our own oil, by using a new method called "fracking"—hydraulic fracturing—where sand or chemicals in a fluid are injected under high pressure into old oil wells, to keep cracks in the underground stone open, so that new oil or natural gas comes out.

We've got so much new petroleum coming out of old wells that we are now the world's largest producer, even more than any of the Arab countries; this has caused the price of oil to drop around the world, which helps the economies of almost all countries (except those that depend on selling oil!).

But—and this is a big but—it's not clear what this technology does to the environment, and in some countries it's even banned, until it can be determined whether we're not creating a new ecological disaster. Fracking uses a huge amount of water, which goes underground, and mixes for example with methane that comes out of the oil deposits. This contaminated water can get into the water table, and thus into our drinking water, and contribute to new cancer cases in a big way.

So it's clear that we Americans have to head the same direction as China, with renewables. Generally, European and North American countries are trying to reach 20% renewables by 2020; and recently the G7 organization (representing 7 major economies of the world) announced that it would try to eliminate fossil fuels altogether by the end of this century—so 100% renewable energy by 2100.

Michael & Eric:

Until we do reach this new world of renewable energy, our two countries are going to be competing for the fossil-fuel energy that's out there around the globe—because we are by far the two biggest users of the world's energy.

Any time there's competition for resources, there's a potential for conflict. If we want to assure a peaceful world for our children and their children, we need to start working right now on ways to make sure our energy competition doesn't get out of hand.

Another thing that China and the US need to do—both out of compassion and for the sake of world peace—is to make sure that when our competition drives up the price of energy, we do something to make sure that poorer countries can still get their energy too, at a price they can afford.

World Choices #3

It seems like we have two choices about how to assure that both our countries get the energy we need—and these two choices sort of reflect how we each run our countries already, and what we feel comfortable with culturally.

Americans have generally chosen to go with the Individualist approach, which is sometimes referred to in economics as the "Invisible Hand." The Invisible Hand means an open market: you just let energy sources come out freely on the world marketplace, and then whichever individual country bids the most for them gets them.

This means that the rich and powerful countries will get most of the oil and gas and coal—and then they will get more rich and powerful, often at the expense of smaller or poorer nations. That's generally been okay with Americans as long as we were the richest and most powerful country. But will we still support this approach if someone else becomes more rich and powerful, and we can't get the energy we need or want?

The other choice is called the Visible Hand—and that's been the basis of the Chinese economy for about the last 60 years or so. That is, the central government is a visible hand that reaches in and decides prices; sets economic and monetary policies; controls production and distribution of goods and services.

This is a kind of Groupism, where we try to make sure everyone is taken care of—which is the real meaning of the Chinese style of "socialism." But then the problem becomes: Who's going to run the group? Who's going to decide how we divide up the energy? We're going to need some kind of Boss Organization that oversees all the world's energy.

So here's another World Choice for us: Invisible Hand, or Visible Hand, for the energy that we all need?

9
Currencies

Michael:

This same question of the Visible Hand vs. the Invisible Hand is also important in how our two countries manage our central banks, and currencies. There's a lot of talk by politicians and newspapers in the United States about how the Chinese government prefers to control their monetary policies tightly—with a Visible Hand—instead of allowing things like currencies to settle at their own "natural" rate, under the Invisible Hand. Despite all this talk, not a lot of us in the U.S. really understand what the issue is; so maybe it's worth a little review here.

Eric:

Just as America has decided to call its money "dollars," China has elected to call its money *renminbi*, which around the world is often abbreviated to RMB. The word *renmin* means "the people of the country," and *bi* means "currency"; so together the word *renminbi* literally means "the currency of the people".

But when *counting* in RMB, we use the word *yuan*, which is an old word with the same root as *yen* in Japanese: it literally means "round"—a reference to the shape of a single coin.

So maybe if you sell some goods from a company in America to a company in China, they might pay you a certain number of yuan, in RMB currency. Nowadays there are between 6 and 7 yuan per dollar, so it you have like 650 yuan in your pocket, it's about 100 dollars.

To add to the confusion, financial markets use the abbreviation CNY for the yuan (it comes from ChiNese Yuan). The same abbreviation is more often used for Chinese New Year, our most important holiday, so it's good to know which CNY you're talking about. The symbol for yuan, like the symbol $ for "dollar," is ¥.

Michael:
So here's the currency question, in a nutshell. Years ago, China was trying to catch up to the more prosperous economies in the world. They saw that most of the countries that had ever succeeded at catching up did so by manufacturing lots of stuff and selling it to other countries at an attractive price.

An easy way to make the prices of Chinese stuff more attractive was simply to use the Visible Hand—central government control. Instead of just letting the market decide how many yuan you could get for a dollar, the government of China set this number artificially.

So let's say that, if the government didn't control things, people in the world were generally willing to pay 1 dollar to buy 5 yuan.

So if you wanted to buy a nice pen made in China that cost 5 yuan, you had to pay 1 dollar. If you want to buy 10 of these pens, you have to pay 10 dollars.

Now the government of China steps in and announces that every dollar spent for Chinese-made goods is worth 7 yuan.

And so suddenly you can buy this nice pen for around 75 cents. For the same 10 dollars, now you get like 13 pens— three extra! So all the big American office-supply stores run to China to buy their pens. Chinese factories get more orders, and more Chinese people have jobs.

Eric:

But when you give more of your dollars for another country's dollars, you obviously have to be losing something somewhere, on the other end. Pens are made of plastic, and it takes oil to make the plastic. Right now, most oil is bought and sold in US dollars; and the price of oil is pretty much the same for everybody.

So when the tables are turned and China has to buy dollars to pay for our oil, we end up paying more, because we already announced that it would take 7 yuan to buy a dollar. So if a barrel of oil costs 50 dollars, we were paying 250 yuan for it before. But after our government changed the exchange rate, now we have to pay 350 yuan.

Michael:

So doesn't it work out the same, in the end? If you end up losing money on one end to make money on the other end, what's the point of messing around with your currency exchange rates?

Eric:

Well, you're right, and we can't keep up these policies indefinitely; sooner or later the yuan has to settle at its "real" value, and in fact the Chinese government has already allowed it do so, in the last few years.

But right away you can see three reasons why the policy was important, and why it worked. Because more office-supply stores bought their pens in China, we could offer them better and better deals for bigger and bigger orders, and we got a bigger share of the world pen market.

Secondly, more US dollars start to flow into China, so we were able to build up our bank account of dollars, which meant we built up some security for when we have to buy things like oil and other raw materials, which we need to pay dollars for.

Finally, we were able to keep our people employed. Now I know that keeping people busy (and well-paid) is also important in your Beautiful Country, and in the end—for the peace and prosperity of the entire planet—we need to achieve that at the same time. But I think it will help both of our peoples if we all understand, given the history of China, how absolutely crucial it is for our country to have full employment.

10
Unemployment

Eric:
When we say that each of our countries needs enough energy to keep it going, we need to talk about what happens if we *don't* get enough energy. I think it's really good if Americans could understand *why* we Chinese feel that we need to keep our country growing at a steady rate, and what happens if we don't.

That is, the American economy has been strong enough for long enough that there is some "wriggle room" built into it. When the world economy nosedived in 2008, and the official unemployment rate in the US crept up close to 10%, it meant that most Americans just had to tighten their belts: nobody actually went hungry, and there were no riots in the streets.

During this same time, the unemployment rate in China stayed below 5%, which is where we feel that we have to keep it. With a country of some 1.4 billion people crowded onto a single limited piece of land, and without a fully developed public safety net, we would have a big problem if *our* unemployment got up to 10%—that's *over a hundred million people* sitting around hungry, bored, and restless. And that could lead to some huge problems inside our country.

Michael:
I think here we Americans need to appreciate a little bit more about the history of the country of China. Any of us who were paying attention in our grade school history classes can point to the big events in our own country's development. Here are the few I remember:

Eleven Most Important Events in US History

- 1492
Columbus "discovers" America, meaning the first white man reaches the Americas on a boat, from Europe

- 1620
Pilgrims, seeking religious freedom, arrive in North America to start a colony, aboard the sailing ship *Mayflower*

- 1776
On July 4, the American colonies declare their independence from the British crown, and create the United States

- 1861–1865
The American Civil War, fought between 7 southern states and 27 northern states, kills over half a million people; and the slavery of black people is abolished

- 1878
Thomas Edison invents electric light bulb; most Americans feel like this is the beginning of electricity in general

- 1903
On December 17, the Wright Brothers fly the first airplane

- 1908
Henry Ford begins selling his Model-T, which Americans treat as the beginning of the automobile culture worldwide

- 1912
Arizona becomes a state, which completes the general shape of the continental United States

- 1914–1918
World War I kills more than 16 million people; the United States joins the conflict in 1917; but there is no fighting on American soil

- 1939–1945
World War II—America joins the fighting in 1941; up to 85 million people die, but again there is no fighting in the continental USA

- 2001
On September 9, terrorists carry out a suicide attack in 4 hijacked airplanes, killing about 3,000 people and destroying the World Trade Center in New York—one of the only foreign attacks on the continental USA

Eric:
Since China is more than 200 times older than the US, we have had a lot more big events in our country! But here are a number which affected the most people:

Some of the Most Important Events in Chinese History

- 2698BCE (almost 3,000 years before Christ)
Beginning of the reign of the Yellow Emperor, which we consider the beginning of the Chinese nation

- 2650BCE
Cangjie is said to invent the first written Chinese characters

- **550BCE**
  Estimated year for the birth of Laozi, who wrote the *Dao De Jing*, basis of Taoism in China, emphasizing a way of goodness and the need to flow in harmony with it

- **551BCE**
  Confucius is born; his *Analects* helps shape a Chinese culture based on family values

- **105CE**
  Cai Lun of the Han Dynasty credited with invention of paper

- **150CE**
  Approximate date of first Buddhist teachings to reach China

- **189–280**
  Three Kingdoms period, a hundred-year civil war with about 35 million deaths

- **618–907**
  Tang Dynasty; flowering of Chinese power & culture, including translation of over 1,000 Buddhist scriptures by Master Xuanzang after a 17-year journey to India and other countries

- **755–763**
  An-Lushan Rebellion, a civil war with about 13 million deaths

- **About 850**
  Invention of gunpowder by Chinese, during the Tang Dynasty

- **About 1040**
  Invention of the compass by Chinese, during the Song Dynasty

- **About 1050**
  Chinese help invent the modern method of making steel

- **1205–1279**
  Mongolian invasion of China, with more than 10 million deaths in China, and about 35 million in the entire region

- **1368**
  Ming Dynasty conquest of China, death of about 30 million people

- **1618–1644**
  Manchu conquest of China, death of about 25 million people

- **1839–1860**
  The Opium Wars, invasions by western countries resulting in about 40,000 casualties; more than 15 "Unequal Treaties"; and a century of domestic chaos

- **1850–1864**
  Taiping Rebellion, a civil war with over 20 million deaths

- **1912**
  Last of the emperors of China gives up his position, and Sun Yat Sen helps found the modern nation of China

- **1921**
  Communist Party of China founded

- **1937–1945**
  Japanese invasion of China, with about 20 million deaths, including the Nanking Massacre in 1937–38 with the rape and murder of up to 300,000 Chinese civilians

- **1927–1950**
  Chinese Civil War, with about 8 million deaths

- **1949**
  Founding of the People's Republic of China by Chairman Mao Zedong

- **2014**
  The International Monetary Fund declares that China has become the world's largest economy

Michael
You can see in just this abbreviated list that more than 150 million Chinese (about half the current population of the entire US) have died during the history of the country, both from foreign invasions and civil war. Less than one percent of this number have died in America from such calamities, and no foreign army has ever conquered American soil.

I think that, from these numbers, it's easy to understand why Chinese people are anxious to keep their country in one, peaceful piece. China is coming up soon on the 100th anniversary of their current form of government, and not long after that on the 100th anniversary of their nation in its modern form. This is one of the longest, most peaceful periods for their country in all of their 5,000 years of history.

My feeling is that the Chinese very much want to keep this period going, and so they are very sensitive about maintaining unity inside their country, by keeping people working— and protection from outside interference, through a strong economy. Part of building this strong economy has come through a strong central government, a strong Visible Hand, setting policies like the currency rates we talked about.

The bottom line is that a certain amount of business, and dollars, have left America to China, to help them catch up, and to keep people working and keep peace inside their country. I think that—if we are going to be friends, and if we're going to work together as two superpowers contributing towards the peace and prosperity of the whole globe—we need to understand and respect this need, and its history.

The ultimate goal, of course, is for both of our countries to have full employment, prosperity, and security. Eric and I will present a proposal for that in the second half of this book.

11
International Relations

Michael:

Eric and I were sitting in a coffee shop one day, and I asked him what Chinese people feel about the very active role that the US tends to play in international affairs—which unfortunately, in the last decade or more, has included involvement in a number of very tragic, armed conflicts. I was wondering how we appear to such an ancient culture, and I was guessing that maybe we looked like some overactive, feisty teenager. Here is what Eric said in reply.

Eric:

There are many facets to the Chinese attitude about international relationships. I have overseas friends who complain to me that China doesn't seem to want to get involved in international problems; for example, when there's a vote at the UN about taking some kind of international action, the Chinese government might often abstain from voting.

To understand this attitude, you have to remember that China is a very crowded country, and has been for many centuries. We are forced to live close together, and we have to get along, more than people in other countries. Most of us live in apartment buildings; if the couple next door is having a quarrel, we will most likely just try real hard not to listen to it. If the argument gets really loud, then we just get up and turn on the TV until it's a little louder than the yelling.

So we don't really have a tradition of getting involved in other people's quarrels, if we can at all avoid it. Keep in mind as well that the United States only has two neighbors—Canada and Mexico—and that you've had almost completely peaceful relations with each other for the entire short life of your country.

China, on the other hand, has 14 different countries on its borders—more than any other nation in the world. We can't get into fights with our neighbors: we have so many of them that it would be a disaster, both morally and also financially.

Michael:
I've also noticed that—just in general—Chinese seem a little wary about getting involved with foreigners. Westerners feel like your country is a little closed off. Why do you think that is?

Eric:
This goes back to a very sad part of Chinese history known as the "Opium Wars". About 150 years ago, products from China were getting very popular with the British people —things like Chinese tea, and our unique porcelain ware. By contrast, our people at that time weren't very interested in any of the products we could get from England, except for silver. So our government asked that when British traders purchased Chinese goods, could they please pay in silver.

This was difficult for the British, since they didn't have any of their own silver mines, and had to bring in tons of silver from places like Mexico, at great expense. And so the British decided that—since they had already conquered India—then they would force many of the Indian farmers to stop growing food crops, and instead grow opium flowers, which is where heroin and cocaine come from. The British thought that then they would sell this opium to Chinese, and charge them silver in return, and thus turn their silver deficit into a silver surplus.

One result of this policy was that an estimated 10 million people died of hunger in India, during a famine in Bengal in 1770.

Our government had completely banned the use of opium since 1799, but the British continued to smuggle it in, and encourage people to use it. It is estimated that opium smuggling eventually provided 15% to 20% of the entire revenue of the British Empire, causing at the same time a complete drain of silver from China.

In 1838, the Chinese government finally decided that the situation had to change, and they seized some 20,000 chests of opium (over two and a half *million* pounds worth) from the British smuggling ships; threw them in a pile on a farm field; and destroyed them.

In response, the smugglers convinced the British crown to attack China: to force our government to legalize their sales of opium to Chinese people, even though within a short time opiates became a controlled substance in England itself, because the same government had realized that they could be very addictive and harmful to people's health. Unfortunately, American traders were also heavily involved with the opium business in China.

This conflict, and another similar one about 20 years later, led to the collapse of our government. The British troops marched in and burned down our Summer Palace (which at the time was something like your own White House), and stole thousands of pieces of priceless Chinese art.

This artwork is still sitting in museums in England and other countries. We have asked for it to be given back, but it has not been. In a way, the artwork represents how we Chinese feel about getting involved with Western countries. These Opium Wars led to a hundred years of complete chaos in our country, with no stable government, and repeated famines and civil wars. We still feel a little hesitant to re-engage internationally; for us, these painful events are still hanging in the air.

Michael:
But that seems strange to me; you see, before a few months ago, I had never even *heard* of the Opium Wars. I mean, there wasn't a word said about it in our classes in school.

Eric:
And you see, that's very shocking to us Chinese. It is perhaps the most important event that ever occurred between your countries and our own—and it is something that is affecting, and will affect, relations between America and China for decades to come, even as the world's two superpowers—and yet no one even thought it was worth teaching you about it in school.

For us to really be friends, to be partners, you need to learn more about us, and we need to learn more about you, about what makes each other tick.

Yes, well...there is a bit more to the story. After the first Opium War, after many of our people were killed, our country was forced to sign a "trade agreement" that quarter of the people were hooked on heroin?

allowed the British to sell opium in our country, unlimited. By 1906, over a quarter of the men in China were using opium. Can you imagine what would happen to the US—to your national productivity, to your national self-esteem—if a quarter of the people were hooked in heroin?

But it doesn't end there, either. We were forced to sign more and more of these agreements, which we call the "Unequal Treaties". In time, the Western governments even demanded that we give them the right to large pieces of land inside of some of our cities, where they could put their businesses and government offices.

The British had also developed a port named "Hong Kong" to help smuggle opium into China, and we were also forced to grant a 100-year "lease" of the entire city to England. So perhaps this will help everyone appreciate why we are so sensitive about what goes on there.

In China, and in Asia in general, a sense of respect— of keeping face—in relationships is absolutely essential. And yet here we were, humiliated, again and again. In fact we have a name for that period in our history: it is called the "Century of Humiliation." It has never been an easy thing to forget.

I think that if Americans, and western people in general, knew more about those years, then they would understand their Chinese brothers and sisters a lot better, and feel more empathy for our hesitation to get involved in international affairs—especially in conflicts around the world.

Michael:

I heard another part of this same story, which might touch a lot of Americans, the same way it touched me. During the height of this opium addiction problem, a large number of Chinese workers—about 12,000 of them, including many who were basically sold into slavery—were brought to the United States as laborers, to perform the most difficult and distasteful jobs.

One of these tasks was to build the railroad across the United States, which took about 7 years, beginning in 1863. Shortly after the work was finished—while many of these workers were just getting settled in America and trying to bring their families over to join them—the US Congress passed the "Chinese Exclusion Act" of 1882.

This was basically the only time in American History that a group of people were prohibited from immigrating into the United States, based solely on their race. Chinese people were harassed for decades throughout the country, and many had to leave for Mexico.

Trained by the British back home, they had brought with them their opium poppies, and their opium addictions. Forced to leave for Mexico, they took the opium there. And thus began a cycle of drug abuse, gangs, and violence that hurts all of North and South America, to this day.

12
Cultural Pollution

Michael:
I don't think a lot of Chinese are much aware of it, but I personally feel that there's another reason for them to be a little wary of an immediate, full-on relationship with the West. When I first started spending a fair amount of time in China, I started to realize that people just looked better—more fit, more healthy.

Then I would get on the plane and come back to America, and immediately in the airport it was super-obvious to me that a big majority of the people in my own country—it is estimated at about 70%—are seriously overweight. In our country, we have been trained to eat too much, and too much of the wrong foods, and it is literally killing our people, and stealing our strength, and our national productivity & creativity.

Then I see companies like McDonalds and Kentucky Fried Chicken opening up all over China—there are more than 7,000 outlets for these two chains already operating there. They are selling huge amounts of sugar and fat and bread and dairy in a country where people just never had the habit of eating these things—I mean, most of my Chinese friends think that a bowl of rice smothered in fresh greens is just the yummiest thing they can imagine.

But then I see those habits changing, and spinach giving way to American pizza and Coke, and at the same time I can see that Chinese people's health is really going to suffer—that in the end, if they keep this up, they're going to be just as overweight and slowed down, and just as damaged in their creative impulses, as my own countrymen are.

And please remember I say all this from a deep love and appreciation for the country I grew up in, which I proudly call my home. I wouldn't want to live anywhere else. But I just don't want to see us be a bad example for the Chinese, or for any other country—or even for our own children. I recently read that one of the world's largest insurance companies is predicting that the change in eating habits of Chinese is expected to lead immediately to a 50% rise in "rich-country diseases": heart attacks, diabetes, and cancer.

And this extends to other things as well. The American media makes a big deal about the fact that things like Google and YouTube are not even allowed in China. But when I talk to my friends there, I start to understand how most of them really feel about it.

That is, one of the biggest uses for the internet in Western countries is for pornography: the word "sex" is in fact the most-searched-for word in the English language. And frankly, most Chinese just don't want to see their kids getting into this kind of addiction. It bleeds away people's energy and focus and sharpness, and it has ruined the spirit of a great many young Americans. I mean, I recently heard that *the average American spends 5 whole hours per day watching television.*

To me (and fortunately I've never owned a TV), this is simply a tremendous tragedy—and I start to understand a country where people really just don't want it. But I also know that these American habits are very tempting, very addicting, and I've seen other countries in Asia where the ghostly blue light coming out of living-room windows has already replaced the evening walk, or quiet family conversation, or gazing at the stars off the porch.

Maybe those of us who are sensitive to this problem need to do more about it, just to help both our countries.

World Choices #4

This question about the influence of US fast-food restaurants and "garbage websites" on the health of the Chinese public brings us to another one of our world choices. Again, it is a reflection of the American spirit of Individualism versus the Chinese tradition of Groupism. That is, what do we do, as a country, if we start to realize that a certain kind of food, or certain types of internet content, are hurting our people, especially our young people?

The typical American might answer that we have to respect individual people's right to choose. That is, it's not the government's job to tell people what they can eat, or can't; or what they can watch on their computer screen, or not. The government can inform people clearly that there are certain physical and emotional dangers to specific kinds of foods or images on the internet, but it's up to the individual to decide what he or she is going to do with that knowledge.

The Chinese approach might be different—and we have to respect those differences. Chinese might say that, just as it's a parent's responsibility to protect their children from things that might hurt them, it's a government's very purpose to help protect their citizens from things that might hurt *them*. And so the government has to take an active role in limiting harmful influences from foreign countries.

So which is the right way here? Another choice we will discuss in the second half of our little book.

13
The American National Debt

Michael:

By the way, Americans have been "overeating" in another way too, and that's with how much money we borrow from other countries. In his career up to now, Eric has worked as a strategist in some big banks in China, and I asked him how normal Chinese people feel about the huge American debt. Before he was a banker, Eric was an MD, having graduated from medical school in both the western and the Chinese styles of medicine. And so the answer he gave me came a little bit from the banker, and a little bit from the doctor too!

Eric:

How do we Chinese feel about the huge American debt? First of all, you need to realize that there is a big difference between the way Chinese feel about getting in debt, and the way Americans feel about it. Family is extremely important to all Chinese people, and a big part of a Chinese person's life is taking care of both their children and their parents.

And so almost 100% of all Chinese are really into putting away as much savings as they can, every week. They feel that they *must* have enough money ready to send their children to a good school when they get older; and they *must* have enough money to take care of their parents in their old age. A Chinese person who builds up a lot of personal debt and then doesn't have enough money left to take care of their parents and children is considered extremely selfish and dishonorable, by everyone who knows them. We would never want to get stuck in such a spot!

Michael:

The feelings you've described seem very clear and noble, but it's just not how most Americans think. Most American parents would like to put aside something to help their children start their own family, but most of us leave home at an early age, and we feel as though we would like to prove ourselves, on our own.

Perhaps this is again that difference between Individualism and Groupism. I myself left home at the age of 18, and made my own way from then. I know that most Asian children would like to have their parents live in their home when they grow old, so that they can take care of them; but in America most elderly people have a retirement pension from their work or from the government—and when it is needed, they go to live in a retirement home with other pensioners.

Because this is the case, most adult Americans spend most of their income on having a family and trying to purchase their own house—not an apartment—because there is still enough land in the US to allow this, if we can put together enough money. Americans are not hesitant to go into debt to get their own house, and this attitude extends to buying a good car or going on a nice trip during the two or three weeks we get from our jobs for our annual vacation.

Because of all this, we easily get into the habit of having a number of credit cards, and maintaining a certain amount of debt, with high interest payments to make every month. I'm afraid that this is just the American way—we would rather have the things we want now, than wait for later; I suppose it's not completely responsible.

Of course all the money we borrow comes from a bank, and of course the money in the bank comes from other people's savings; and when I was younger, it was considered very dishonorable not to pay back these debts in full, and on time. It was also considered very shameful to accept public assistance from the government, rather than working hard to earn our own money.

But I'm afraid that standard has slipped in recent decades, and more and more people see it as acceptable to declare bankruptcy, without thinking of how this hurts the other people who have put their savings in a bank, perhaps to buy a house for their own family, or something similar. And it has become more and more a way of life to accept charity from the government; so much that many people I think have forgotten how to work.

There don't seem to be very strict standards about encouraging people on welfare to try to find at least some small kind of work that they can do, and the result I think is that the American national debt is getting larger and larger—more and more difficult to pay off.

I know that much of the money we have borrowed, as a country, has come from China—and I wonder how normal Chinese people feel about how big and unmanageable our American debt has become.

Eric:
The first thing you have to remember is that Chinese people *do* want to save money, to help their parents and their children; and they would like to make sure that these savings are safe, and that they can make as much interest on their savings as possible. So Chinese people are always looking for some safe place to make their investments.

Many Chinese have visited America, and we know that your country has a strong rule of law, and that in general you try to keep your promises. America has a reputation as being a stable country which is not going to change suddenly, and the American dollar so far has also been stable.

And so when a Chinese person, or even the Chinese government, wants to make an investment, we have purchased bonds from the American government—which just means that we have loaned your government the money we have set aside for our children and our parents. And then your government has used this money for various purposes like roads and bridges, or public assistance to people who are not working, or to care for the elderly; and recently, unfortunately, for a great many expensive military actions.

Michael:
Yes, but how do normal Chinese *feel* about these loans?

Eric:
As I said, our goal in loaning America the money in the first place was to protect our savings, and to make at least some modest interest on them, so that we could take better care of our parents and children. So far, this has worked out very well—your government has paid the interest on time and responsibly, and we are happy that we made the loans.

Michael:
But in recent years, the debt has gotten so large that it seems possible that we will no longer be able to pay the interest on time, much less return the amount of the original loan. And as you know, America has come dangerously close to defaulting on our loan—which just means declaring bankruptcy, but as an entire nation.

Eric:

We're aware of this problem, and we're watching it closely. You know, Michael, that I was trained as a doctor. Suppose a patient comes to the doctor and says they have a bump somewhere on their body. The doctor checks the bump and perhaps even does a biopsy, to see if it is cancerous or benign.

I would say that—to many of us in China who have invested our money in America—we see that your country has grown a bump, and we're watching that bump carefully. As long as it doesn't get malignant, we feel that both you and us can live with it—we can manage the debt. But if it does look like you would decide not to pay the loan back, then that would create a crisis which would permanently damage both the United States and China.

From our side, we would lose all the money we had saved up to help our children and parents, which again is an extremely important part of every Chinese person's life. From your side, people would suddenly stop loaning you any more money, and they would pull out of America whatever investments they could. The whole American way of life would suddenly be put in serious jeopardy—imagine your children and grandchildren suddenly living like a poor country, without roads, without jobs, without any hope for the future.

We Chinese people have so much of our savings invested in America that it would be a total disaster for us too. And we recognize very well that if something serious happened to the United States, it would really hurt not only China, but every other country in the world too. We all depend on you!

So we are hoping that America will try to be more responsible about borrowing money; and we are hoping that your people will recover their old pride and commitment to hard work.

Michael:

That will require a big effort, I think, to reverse this slide that America is in—not just financial, but in our work habits. I feel really afraid that the average American is stuck in sort of a dream world, spending more and more of their time watching movies and worthless TV shows, or fiddling with the internet and their cellphones. And I also feel afraid that our bad habits will spread to other countries, who still look to the US as an example of what to be and how to live.

World Choices #5

So we have one more example of Individualism vs. Groupism. Which is better? Should we take the money we've earned and spend it pretty quickly? Doesn't it stimulate the economy, when money flows faster? The person from whom I'm buying something will have to work to make the thing that I'm buying; and when they get my money for their work, then they will buy something from somebody else, who will have to work to make it, and then everybody wins.

Could it even be *compassionate* then, and *more* responsible, for me to even *borrow* money to buy more and more things, and keep more of my fellow countrymen working, and making their own money to buy more things?

Or is it more responsible, and more kindness, to slow that money down—to set it aside, and hold it, for the day when my parents and children are going to need it?

Which choice is the right one?

14
Beyond Materialism

Michael:
Something's been on my mind, as I make a lot of trips to China, and it's something I want to say to my friends there.

Up until this current generation, China was a very poor country. Things like a car, or even a refrigerator, were beyond the reach of most Chinese even just 25 years ago.

Suddenly, all that has reversed itself. The first time I ever visited Beijing, almost everybody was riding a bicycle to get to places—I had never seen so many thousands of bicycles on the street before! Now when I go to the same city, I almost never see a single bicycle at all, and I'm amazed at all the new cars. Sitting and watching traffic go by on a highway is like watching a bunch of TV ads for every beautiful new car you can imagine.

I'm also amazed that Americans don't really recognize this incredible achievement by their Chinese brothers and sisters. I very rarely see any news show in the US that congratulates China for this incredible turnaround, or rejoices in the new prosperity and security that has been handed to hundreds of millions of people. Rather, there can seem to be some kind of resentment, or jealousy, or even fear, that someone else's country is doing as well—or perhaps even better—than our own.

I see though in China that some people are going beyond this comfort and security, and reaching farther, for luxury—and then more luxury. I think there is a time and place for luxury, and I also think that every human being in this world has an undeniable right to try to reach this luxury, if they would like to. That should be open to everyone.

But I'd like to say something about why so many American people are *not* trying to reach for luxury—why they have decided that a modest house, and a modest car, and even a modest job, is enough for them.

This reflects an ideal that is also part of the American Dream, and it is deep in our American bones. We have had a prosperous way of life in our country for long enough to realize that having more money and more things, beyond basic security and comfort, *does not make us more happy*. That is, many people in America have come to the realization that increasing the number of outside objects we possess does not translate into a corresponding increase in the happiness and satisfaction that we feel.

At some point in life, if we have a chance to reach as high as we want and make as much money as we can, then we begin to understand that it's not outside things that make us happy.

I have a friend who climbed to the top of Mt Everest, the highest mountain in the world, at the cost of great physical suffering and personal loss—comrades on the climb dying around him. And yet, he was extremely happy. I have also had many other friends—for example, in the diamond business—who possessed extraordinary riches: who married their children in stadiums with 60,000 people in attendance, or whose toilets were literally made of gold. But some of these were so unhappy that, in the end, they committed suicide.

So I can say with certainty, from my own experience, that happiness does not come from outside things, from accumulating more and bigger outside things. In fact, outside things don't seem to have any more than a very brief effect on how we feel on the inside.

I think that modern American culture is sort of a reflection of this truth. I mean, there *are* lots of people in America who, in my opinion, have gotten just too lazy to work hard—who have been put to sleep by their televisions.

But there are also a lot of Americans who *do* have the talent and drive to get rich, if they want to; but who choose to do something else with their life. I suppose that to get to this place, you have to grow up in a country where everyone for many generations before you has already had a car and a refrigerator.

But once you do have them, it often happens that you begin to look for deeper and more reliable sources of happiness. People in America, more than in almost any other country, spend their money to help other people in the world who are suffering—even those in faraway countries, people whom they will never meet. Not a small amount of the military action we take as a country—mistaken as it may be—is motivated by a sincere desire to help other nations in trouble, even at the cost of the lives of our own sons and daughters. Hundreds of thousands of Americans, who could be working late to earn themselves a bigger car or a bigger house, leave their office in the evening and go to donate their time volunteering to build homes for the poor, or to serve the dying at a local hospice.

I think it's crucial to have your material dreams, and to get a chance to fulfill them—this is a human right, and everyone has to try it. But after you reach these goals, you may find—as I think many Americans have—that a complete dream goes beyond just the material.

World Choices #6

So will we go the Chinese way, or the American way? In a way it was the Americans who started this big emphasis on material success: a big house, a big car, a big salary. And now it's the Chinese people's turn. But which one will make us happy? Should we try to live more simply, and be successful inside; or should we focus on the outside, and build up the security of our family, and the success of our country? Which way is better?

15
The New Global Alignment

Michael:
Despite its old reluctance to get too involved with international issues—and now we Americans can understand more about that reluctance—China now has the largest economy in the world, and she has begun stepping up on the world stage.

We see Chinese businessmen in almost every country of the world, buying natural resources or selling the products they create with those resources; we see Chinese rockets carrying the world's satellites out into space; we see the Chinese army growing stronger, and equipped with new and ever more sophisticated weapons; we see China creating new alliances with nations all around the world—for example, just recently with the Asian Infrastructure Investment Bank (AIIB, a huge new financial institution on the level of the World Bank or the International Monetary Fund (IMF, with member countries not just from Asia but from the West as well.

Of course there is a natural envy that people of any country feel when someone else outperforms them; but along with that, there is a real concern about China's intentions in this new global alignment. So Eric, I'd like to ask you a question: Where does China want to go with all this? What will the new world look like? Is there any reason for Americans—or Europeans or Latin Americans or people anywhere else, for that matter—to feel nervous?

Eric:
Michael, you've heard about the dynasties of China, each one centered around a different emperor and their descendants.

That is, we don't so much date things in our history the way you in the west do, by a number of years. When we want to say when it was that something happened in Chinese history, we just mention the dynasty: This happened during the Qin Dynasty, or that happened during the Song Dynasty. And then everybody knows what time period you are talking about. In our history there are some 20 dynasties, stretching back some 5,000 years.

Starting about 1400 years ago, there was a special dynasty that we call the Tang Dynasty. This dynasty lasted for most of 300 years, a period of exceptional prosperity and culture in our country. During that time, the capital of China was located in a place we now call Xi'an (pronounced *Shi-ann*). They say that, in those days, Xi'an was the biggest city in the world.

This was also a time when China had cordial relationships with many different countries of the lands around us. They even maintained embassies in Xi'an City, and there was a great deal of harmony and sharing between us, about all kinds of the technology of those days—such as the secrets of making our very fine Chinese porcelain, which even today you call "china" in English.

These relationships developed with the help of the Silk Road, which was an ancient trade route that stretched from China to Europe. It was along this road that—six centuries after Xuanzang, our famous wanderer—the Italian explorer Marco Polo reached Beijing, and wrote his fascinating description of our country, its products, and its progress.

This is the kind of vision that we Chinese have in mind, when we think of the place we would like to take in the world today. Our society hasn't traditionally been one which is interested in conquering other countries: even today, we have a very strong army, and there are many smaller countries surrounding us that we could take over if we wished; but we have not, because we don't feel this is our way.

What we would like to achieve, internationally, is to be an example of a country that can live in peace and cooperation with other nations—to try to be one of the leaders that brings the world to a new level of prosperity, and freedom from war. We would like to go back to the days of the Tang Dynasty.

That's why we are reaching out to engage other countries in peaceful projects—such as the bank you mentioned, which has the goal of helping all the countries in Asia develop a modern Silk Road: a zone of free trade and travel stretching across the entire of Asia and Europe, contributing to the prosperity of almost half the population of the world.

Michael:
There was another extremely important event during the Tang Dynasty, and that was the life of Xuanzang, the explorer you just mentioned, who I know is a favorite of yours, Eric. Can you tell us about him, and what he means to China?

Eric:
Sure. Xuanzang (remember to pronounce this as *Shuen-Tsang*) was a Buddhist monk who was born around 600AD—about the time that the Middle Ages were getting going in Europe. He had a lot of tough questions about the things he was being taught in the institutions of the time, and he felt that the answers he was getting weren't good enough. So Xuanzang decided to take a trip down to India, which is where the Buddha had lived almost a thousand years before, to see if he couldn't find what he was looking for.

Now you have to realize that Xuanzang couldn't just hop on a plane, the way we do nowadays. He was walking, on his own two feet! As the crow flies, it's about 2,000 miles from Xi'an to central India; and even then, there is the problem that the Himalaya Mountains are sitting in the middle of the road, and you have to go around.

Anyway, in those days a lot of what we now call Pakistan and Afghanistan—and the area north of them, and almost all of India—were part of one huge spiritual empire, and Xuanzang was happy to take the long way around, so he could pause in each place and look for the answers to his questions.

It's hard to believe, but Xuanzang walked over 10,000 miles total, and for *more than seventeen years!* He visited some 138 different kingdoms; learned many of their languages; and even went as far south as Sri Lanka, an extra 4,000 miles.

But Xuanzang's greatest achievement was that he came home with over 600 books of knowledge: the cream of the wisdom of Asia in his times. When he arrived, the emperor of China in those days—whose name was Taizong—had the great foresight to build him a beautiful, traditional Chinese tower, and to hire a huge team of translators, so that under Xuanzang's direction they could make all of this knowledge available in our own language.

It took them some 20 years, but he and his team finished the job, and some of the world's greatest wisdom became part of one of the greatest dynasties of China. When we think of what we would like China to be in the modern world, it is not just a political power: we would like to be a wisdom power, someone to help the world understand why all of us came into this world, and what great good it is that we are meant to do during our time here together.

Part Two
Eternal Issues

16
The Diamond Cutter

Eric and Michael:
Among the hundreds of precious texts that Xuanzang carried back to China was one which, we feel, could contribute a valuable new world-view to go along with the new world-order we've been talking about in the first half of this book.

That work is known as *The Diamond Cutter*. It was first spoken by Gautama, the Buddha, some 2500 years ago; and later it was written down. Xuanzang and his team translated the *Diamond Cutter* into Chinese in the Tower of Xi'an; and about 200 years later it was carved onto blocks of wood that were used to create the oldest printed book in the world with a confirmed date.

Coincidentally, both of us came to this work in our younger years, and each began to use it in his adulthood, as sort of a guidebook for personal and business success. The *Diamond Cutter* is considered one of the great books of all Chinese traditional culture, and so naturally Eric grew up with it, and with the story of Xuanzang's epic journey.

Eric:
When I was a kid, I was fascinated by a long-running series on Chinese TV called "Journey to the West." This is the name of the most famous version of Xuanzang's story—it is a later adventure tale based upon his own extensive record of his trip, and is one of the most popular novels in all of Chinese history. In this version, Xuanzang is accompanied on his travels by a magical monkey, a feisty pig, and a reformed water monster.

I seem to have some connection with this Xuanzang. After my medical training, I worked in banking, with quite some success. I attended a number of management training courses, and the teachers were impressed with my insights. Eventually, the owner of a large food-products company asked me to give his staff a coaching session. I had this idea to build the entire program around Xuanzang's *Journey to the West*, along with the seed principles that are found in the *Diamond Cutter* book that he brought home with him.

Michael:
How did that first training work out?

Eric:
Well, the owner of the company really took to the ideas I presented, and he put them into practice with great enthusiasm. And now he is worth more than a half a billion dollars! Naturally he recommended me to many of his friends; and that's how I've built my own very successful training company, which is called Guang Yao, or "Light on Life."

This name also refers to a great love for humanity, and a wish to make other people successful. Even as a child, I used to dream about doing something to help the world in a bigger way. From a very early age I had this strange habit of closing my eyes whenever I was walking outside and the wind passed around me: I always made a little prayer that whoever was touched by that same wind afterwards should suddenly feel happy, and see all their dreams come true.

So this is how the ancient *Diamond Cutter* made my own life successful; I think Michael's story is similar.

Michael:

Right—I think most people know the story: I spent 25 years in a Tibetan monastery, and my teachers challenged me to create a company based on that same *Diamond Cutter* book, to prove that I understood the principles found inside. And so I went to New York City and helped to start a diamond company which eventually grew to $250 million in annual sales, and was sold to Warren Buffett in 2009.

In fact, I used much of the money I earned from this business to support a project to help save the ancient Asian books of wisdom—many of the same books that Xuanzang brought back from his journey. Later on, I wrote my own book about how anyone can use these same principles for success in their own home life and career—and I even decided to give this book the very same name: *The Diamond Cutter.*

That book has now sold hundreds of thousands of copies around the world, and has been translated into more than 30 languages.

Eric & Michael:

So you can see, we've both used these ancient principles to achieve success in our lives, already. What we want to do here in the second half of the book is to see if we can use those same ideas from the oldest printed book in the world—the cream of Chinese literature and thought—to chart out the future of the relationship between our two countries, China and America.

17
Subhuti's Question

Eric:

Much like the teachings of Jesus which are so familiar to many Americans, a great number of our most ancient books in China are records of conversations between some great teacher and his or her students. These often begin with a question asked by the student—and then the teacher's answer becomes the book.

This is how the *Diamond Cutter* was written as well. A student of the Buddha's named Subhuti approaches him at the beginning of the book, and starts off the conversation by asking three questions:

How should we live?
What should we do?
Where should we keep our focus?

The answers to these three questions give us a roadmap for the future relationship of our two countries: they help us make the right decision with the Six World Choices we talked about in the first part of this book. Michael, I think it's best if we start with the answer to the last question, and then work our way back to the first.

18
Focus on Emptiness

Michael:
Well, the Buddha tells his student Subhuti, "You should keep your focus on emptiness." There are *so many* wrong ideas running around about this idea of emptiness that I thought we could pause right now and get it clear, since it's at the core of our new proposal for China/America relationships.

In fact, clearing up this idea can be done quite easily.

So I was in a car in Singapore recently with my friend Tee Peng driving—he was playing some of his favorite songs for me. This really good song called "Endless Love" came on, in Chinese, and immediately I went crazy over it. We were stuck in heavy traffic, and I begged him to play the song over and over again. It's from a popular movie called *The Myth*.

Tee Peng bet me ten dollars that I couldn't name the singer, and he won of course, because I don't know any Chinese singers at all! Except that it turned out that I *did* know this singer, because it was the famous actor Jackie Chan—I learned from my friend that Mr. Chan was trained as a Chinese opera singer before he started busting heads in action films.

Back in the USA, I played the song for my friend Maria, and her reaction was pretty bad; you know how people say "Oh, that's *interesting!*" when you play them a new song that you're excited about, and actually it sounds terrible to them, but they want to be polite—so they just say *"Interesting!"*

Eric:

Yes, so you see, that's a very clear and simple example of emptiness. To get to emptiness, we start out with the question: Is the song coming from its own side, or is it coming from my mind?

Of course normally we would say that the song is coming from out there, from the car stereo. After all, the song starts playing when we turn the stereo on!

But there's also something about the song which is obviously coming from us. That is, if the song were *good* from its own side, then it would sound good to everyone who ever heard it. Same thing if the song were *bad* from its own side. So there must be *something* about the song which is coming from us!

Michael:

Right, and you can go even deeper on that. I mean, to a dog for example the song might very well sound like how a police siren sounds to us. So on one level, the song is *not even a song* from its own side. Even its *songness* is something that's coming from us. But how?

19
A Seed Splits Open

Eric:

What the *Diamond Cutter* says is that—in the very moment that you reach out your hand to turn on the car stereo—a tiny seed splits open in your mind. That seed has been sitting down there in the unconscious section of your mind for a while; and then like a watermelon seed waiting under the ground, its time suddenly arrives, and it splits open.

When the seed opens, a tiny sound or image emerges into the conscious section of the mind. Technically this is only a millisecond of a sound, but a whole bunch of seeds in your mind go off quickly, one after the other, and so you hear a whole song in your head.

As the sounds "go off" in your mind, the mind "throws" them—millisecond by millisecond—into the outside world. So the impression we have is one of an entire song unfolding out there, from the stereo; but actually the song is emerging from our own seeds. And that's why Maria hears a different thing, and that's why the dog hears something even worse: their seeds are different.

Michael:

If that's really where a song on our car stereo comes from, then we have to ask the question of how the seed got into the subconscious part of our mind, in the first place.

20
How Seeds Are Planted
in the Mind

Eric:
Well that's the interesting part. Here's what the ancient books say. Now suppose that the week before I listened to the song on the car stereo, I was sitting in a restaurant with a couple of friends: Fred and Sue. Suddenly, another mutual friend—call her Ellen—walked by our table.

Now unknown to Sue and myself, Ellen had just had an argument with Fred a few hours before. So when she paused at the table to greet us, Fred attacked her very unkindly, saying a lot of unpleasant things.

I was surprised at Fred's reaction to a simple greeting, and so I took a few minutes to say some nice things to Ellen—telling her how great we thought her last project at work had gone.

Each time I said a word to Ellen, she heard it; and I myself heard the words too, even as I spoke them. You can picture the sound of each word arriving at my eardrums, and then being transmitted to my conscious mind. From there the word made an impression upon my subconscious mind as well, similar to the way that an imprint is left on the palm of one hand when you press it hard with the thumb of the other hand.

During the days following the conversation at the restaurant, this impression on my subconscious mind slowly turned into a seed, sitting there, waiting to split open and start the song on the stereo. In fact, the old Sanskrit word for this seed is "a karma"—and this gives us a better idea of what "karma" really means.

And because I was trying to make Ellen feel better—because my intention was kindness—then this was a "good karma": a sweet seed was planted. So when the seed split open in my mind a week later, the song that I heard on the car stereo was a *good* song.

21
The Emptiness of Jackie Chan

Michael:
So that's where the emptiness part comes in—because when I played Jackie Chan's song for my friend Maria the next day, it sounded terrible to her.

You can think of Jackie Chan, and his song, as being like a blank white movie screen. When the seeds in my mind split open, the sound that came out and got "glued" to him and his song by my mind was wonderful. When the seeds in Maria's mind split open, they "projected" a terrible sound onto the same person, and the same piece of music.

But if you take away how *my* seeds made me hear the music, and you take away how *Maria's* seeds made her hear the music, then all you have left is the blank white movie screen: the screen in the theater ten minutes before they turn the projector on.

Eric:
Right. So that's what this ancient word—"emptiness," or *kong-shing* in my language—really means. It's really just sort of that empty or available space which is out there waiting to get filled in by the song that my particular seeds make me hear.

And if Fred happens to be sitting next to me in the car when I turn on the stereo, then that same empty space is going to be filled by a *lousy* song since, remember, he was yelling at Ellen the week before—in the restaurant—and therefore planted a *lousy* karmic seed.

So now that you understand what "emptiness" really means, you can see it isn't at all some weird thing where you focus on a black color in your mind; or you try not to think of anything; or you think of everything as an illusion.

Michael:

So let's go back to the question that his student asked the Buddha: *Where should we keep our focus?* And the Buddha says, "Focus on the emptiness of things."

So what's the point? How is that supposed to help us resolve those Six World Choices? How is emptiness going to help China and America create a safe and prosperous world together?

22
The Dragon Master

Eric:

For about seven centuries after the discussion in the *Diamond Cutter*, these ideas about the world being like a blank white screen—and seeds being like projectors inside of our heads, playing the movie of our life on that screen—started to get lost in our part of the world. I mean, you can easily guess how confusing it could get to talk about "emptiness," if you didn't have a clear and simple explanation like Jackie Chan's song on the car stereo.

And then along came an Indian thinker who was so extraordinary that he is sometimes called "The Second Buddha." His name was Nagarjuna—which literally means "Master of the Dragons," for it is said that he undertook a journey to the land of the dragons to recover great and ancient books of emptiness, and became the dragons' favorite forever after.

Nagarjuna wrote a number of famous books, including one which is considered the greatest work ever written about emptiness; its name is simply, *Wisdom*. This book in fact became the foundation of several of the greatest schools of thought in Chinese history. The entire text is written in poetry, and the opening lines are themselves the essence of the work:

> Nothing starts,
> Nothing stops.
> Nothing fades,
> Nothing stays.
> Nothing comes,

Nothing goes;
No two things
Are separate,
And no two things
Are one.

Wisdom then is a book about deciding between choices, and it will serve us well in resolving our six World Choices. Let's see how.

23
A World Where Nothing Starts, and Nothing Stops

Eric:

The first of the Six Choices was a very basic one: we had to decide whether, globally, it would be better to go the American way, and focus upon the rights of the individual; or whether we can make more progress by following the Chinese tradition, of surrendering to the interests of the group.

We were thinking that, on one hand, an individual like Steve Jobs who breaks away from the limitations of the past is free to be more creative—to come up with the Next Big Idea, something like the iPhone.

But it's also true that a whole society of individuals might cut themselves off from past and future generations—from the needs of their parents, and their children—and exhaust all the world's resources just to make those iPhones, without thinking of the needs of the groups to come.

Michael:

We can make this choice by turning again to *The Diamond Cutter*—to Subhuti's second question: *What should we do?* We already know that the solution has something to do with emptiness; for example, the fact that "nothing starts, and nothing stops" is supposed to help us here somehow. That is, what should we do—focus on the individual, or focus on the group—in a world where nothing starts, and nothing stops?

Eric:

Before we decide what to do, we need to talk about exactly what it means when we say that nothing starts or stops. It obviously doesn't mean that nothing starts: we know, for example, that the first iPhone was released on June 29, 2007—sales *started* on that day. Telephones with a rotary dial, where you spin the number dial with your finger, basically stopped on April 21, 1962, when a phone with touch-tone dialing was unveiled at the Seattle World's Fair.

So things *do* start, and they *do* stop. So what is Nagarjuna talking about?

Michael:

This question has caused trouble for 18 centuries. When you first hear the word "emptiness," it's tempting to think it means that nothing exists, or that somehow the whole world is unreal, just an illusion. But that doesn't *help* you when you're trying to decide whether—in the new Chinameran world—we should focus on the individual, or on the group.

It also doesn't help you to say that nothing starts, or nothing stops. Or does it?

Think back to where the song on the car stereo came from. It looks like it's coming out of the stereo, but now we know that it's coming out of a seed in our own mind—a seed that was planted when we heard ourselves speaking kindly to someone the week before.

In that sense, then, we can say that the song *didn't start* (coming out of the stereo, on its own) and *didn't stop* (on its own, when we turned off the stereo). And in this sense, *nothing* in the world ever starts, or stops.

So how does that help us make a decision, between global individualism, and global groupism?

24
Decisions that Make Themselves

Eric:

If you think about it, those famous words from Master Nagarjuna—"nothing starts, nothing stops; nothing comes, nothing goes," and so on—are all talking about decisions, choices. Choices between two things: starting, stopping; coming, going; one or many.

But when we talk about choices, it's absolutely important that we remember one thing.

Which is that there are many choices in life that are just made *for* us, *before* we have to make any decision. There are many decisions that *make themselves.*

Suppose, for example, that you've been looking for a new job. One company has made you an offer where you have a lot of time off, but the pay is not so good. Another company has made you an offer for a position where the pay is great, but you have very little time off.

And then before you can really start to sweat over a *decision* about which job to accept, a third company comes and offers you a position with better pay and more time off than either of the other two positions. *The decision is made for you.*

Now what if we could take all the tough decisions in our life, and do something to them, to make them decide themselves, before we have to? That's what Nagarjuna is talking about.

Michael:
So let's look at how that works. We're trying to make a choice between the individualistic atmosphere that creates a Steve Jobs; and the group atmosphere that prevents the Steve Jobses of the world from denying future generations their share of the world's rare-earth minerals, or creating a culture where children live on a cellphone and forget their parents.

So in this example, we're basically trying to make a decision that will give us the best chance of making sure that *both* of two good things happen: (1) our world culture gives birth to lots of super-creative people; but at the same time (2) we leave lots of minerals for the next generation, in a world where our kids pay attention to the rest of us at the dinner table.

In short, we don't *want* to be forced to make a choice between these two. We don't *want* "one or the other." We want a third possibility—a third option—to happen. *We want a decision which gives us both choices.*

And if possible, we want both choices to happen *before* we need to make a decision. We want the choice made *before* it becomes a choice.

25
Option 3

Eric:

There's a special expression in the ancient books of China called "Option 3." This is where we should go with the Six Choices, Michael.

We use Option 3 when we're faced with two choices—doing things for the group, or excelling as an individual—and we decide we don't *want* to decide: we do what we have to do, to make *both* choices happen.

So going back to where the song came from, it's obvious what we have to do. Instead of struggling between the two choices, we just plant the seeds to make *both* of them happen. And that's Option 3—like getting a good salary, *and* a great annual vacation, both.

In fact, if we were Nagarjuna, we'd probably be saying, "There aren't any single creative individuals, and there aren't any groups of happy generations." Meaning that *there are*, but not *from their own side*—only if we *plant* them. And then there are *both*.

An important point to notice here, with all this talk of emptiness, is that these ancient wise men and women are trying to shake us up: they're trying to get us to *think*. So when they give us advice, they say crazy things like "Nothing starts, and nothing stops."

So let's get down to the seeds for this particular Option 3.

Goal #1
A world which fosters individual creativity

Our first goal was to see a culture in the world—in the new world where China and America are helping to set the global tone—which fosters individual creativity: where the environment is ripe for the rise of a new Steve Jobs.

Now there are special seeds for "planting" a specific environment; they are presented in an ancient teaching called the Four Flowers. We need to understand these four, if we're going to see the new world that we want.

26

Creating a New World
with the Four Flowers

Eric:
When we were kids and we first heard our mom talk about the word "karma," what we understood was that *if you do something bad to somebody else, then something bad will come back to you.* And the same for something good.

Now this kind of "get back the same thing" is, indeed, one of the ways in which a seed in the mind behaves. In the example of the song, we spoke sweetly to someone else and then that seed opened up a week later into a melody that we found pleasing.

But there are actually four different ways in which any single seed opens; and in Chinese traditional culture we call these the "Four Flowers". When you say something nice to another person at a restaurant, it's not *just* that you're going to hear a nice song come out of the car stereo the next week. Three other good things are going to happen too.

Michael:
So let's look at these Four Flowers. The first one is easy. Suppose I work for a software company, and my boss has asked me to come up with a new idea for a smartphone app that will help people lose weight. I spend a week looking at all the weight-losing apps that are already on the market, and I absolutely can't come up with any idea for anything better. Which is to say, the Steve Jobs type of creativity is just avoiding me, completely.

Eric:
Right, so the seed to plant is obvious. To plant a karmic seed, a mental seed, we *always* have to do something for somebody else. So to get my own creative juices flowing, I just have to help somebody else think up a new idea for *their* boss. When the First Flower opens, the new idea that I've been looking for will "just" pop into my head—actually, it's emerging out of my subconscious mind into my conscious mind, as the seed from helping that other person splits open.

Michael:
The Second Flower is not something you might think of right away. Basically, we're just not hard-wired to think that we need to help somebody else get what they want, if we want to get what we want. I mean, how many of us rush out to find someone else who is having a creative block, and help them through *their* block, in order to get through *our* creative block?

At some point in some people's lives though, they hear about—or they figure out on their own—this revolutionary idea that *to get what I want, I must help someone else get what they want.* The ancient wisdom traditions of China—and actually those of America and a lot of other places in the world—would say that, in this case, the person has actually evolved to a higher life form, in the same way that a human's intelligence has evolved to a higher state than that of an insect.

But the truth is that the whole thing is just really counter-intuitive: I have to help *you* to help *myself?* The only way it's going to happen is if we get over our resistance to the idea, and try it once. When we do try it once, the seed we plant has a Second Flower, which is that it becomes easier for us to try it the second time; that is, every seed plants a habit.

This is true of good seeds *and* bad seeds: once we tell a lie to one person, for example, it becomes easier for us to tell a lie to another.

Eric:
Let's skip to the Fourth Flower, and then come back to the Third. Now you have to understand that seeds in your mind act just the same as seeds in nature: an acorn that only weighs 10 grams will grow into an oak tree that weighs over 2 million grams; that is, it multiples 200,000 times! The ancient books of China give a very simple formula: a seed planted in the mind will double in power every 24 hours.

That means, for example, that if you say 1 minute of nice things to your friend in a restaurant on Monday, you have enough seeds to hear 2 minutes of nice music on the car stereo by Tuesday. The good news is that by Sunday, while you're relaxing on your day off, the seeds have multiplied enough for you to enjoy a whole hour of music.

Michael:
Now the ancient texts also say that we use up seeds at the rate of 65 per second. That is, a single second of music that you hear coming out of the car stereo is actually made up of 65 good seeds firing in rapid succession, like a machine gun.

But if everything you say to everybody in your life is planting seeds that double every 24 hours, then you don't have to be a genius at math to realize that we're piling up a lot of extra seeds all the time: Just the minute that you took to tell Ellen that she did some good work at her office is going to create almost 4,000 seeds—and in just eight days those seeds will be very close to a million, which is enough seeds to create 4 minutes of your life.

Now on the day that you talked to Ellen for a minute, you probably talked to other people for hours. The bottom line is that we're constantly planting more seeds than we can possibly use up before the day we die.

Eric:
There's another thing you need to know about seeds— which is that *nothing can destroy a seed*, until it destroys itself, by opening: that is, the growing of an oak tree from an acorn always destroys that acorn, as the power of life passes from the seed to the tree.

If you think about it this makes a lot of sense, because even just in the physical world it's a law that, as Newton put it, "For every action there is an equal and opposite reaction." If you do help someone in the next office come up with a cool creative idea, then it's inevitable that the universe will reward you with some creative ideas of your own: that's just justice.

If you could ever *help* someone in the next office and have *nothing* come back to you, then somehow that would break all the rules of the universe—somewhere down inside us, we all sense that.

So now what happens if we're piling up all these indestructible seeds and our body suddenly dies? The ancient sages of China say that the seeds will survive the body—and that inevitably, no longer how it takes, conditions will come together again that will make them open. This in fact is why we say that people always live again, after they die.

Michael:
So that leaves us with Flower Three, which is the one that we were looking for, to change the general environment around

us: to create a world where the creativity of the individual is honored and fostered. When we have spoken kindly to another person last week and that seed opens in our mind this week, it not only creates a beautiful song coming out of the car stereo, but it also helps create the world around us, and the people who live in that world.

That is, we will begin to see more creativity all around us: new inventions, new music and art, more enlightened laws and policies, innovative traffic signs. We will also see more creative people around us, and an atmosphere of creativity.

We'll even see more people trying to get creative by helping others be creative—which is the most creative thing of all!

The Four Flowers:
How a Seed in the Mind Opens

1) *You get back the same thing that you do for someone else.*

> If you want to get a creative idea, help someone else get a creative idea.

2) *Try this new system a few times, and it will start to become a habit.*

> Who could have guessed that helping someone else, be creative is the reason we have new and creative ideas ourselves? Try it once or twice; you'll succeed; and it will become a habit.

3) *When mental seeds open, they also ripple out to create the world and the people around us.*

> Helping another person be creative causes us to live in a world where people are creative, and individual creativity is honored.

4) *Because mental seeds multiply quickly inside the mind, their effects ripple far out into the future.*

> The effects of how I treat others today might very well ripple out even beyond my own lifetime.

27
Planting Powerful Seeds:
The Four Coffee Shop Steps

Michael:
Okay—so we've got half of what we wanted: our new global perspective respects the creative needs of the individual—allows the new Steve Jobses all the room they need to do their thing. Now we have to take care of the other half: We need to make sure that the individual geniuses of the world don't ignore the needs of those who have come before them, and those to come after.

Goal #2
A world which respects the needs of the group

Eric:
The second goal of our Option 3 here was that—even with the invention of a new smartphone by our classic Individual— the interests of the group should not be compromised: in this case, we want children who are wise enough to put their phones down during dinner and share some warmth with their mom and dad—with the generation that has sacrificed a big part of their life to bear and raise them. And we want moms and dads who are wise enough not to let their hunger for a new smartphone outweigh the need to leave lots of natural resources for the generations to come after them.

Creating wise and considerate children in our world is going to take some powerful seeds. So it's time to learn exactly how to plant a powerful seed: it's time to learn the Four Coffee Shop Steps. These four steps were put forth by an Indian master from the 4th century named Vasubandhu; works by him and his brother, Asanga, are some of the most popular in 5,000 years of traditional Chinese culture.

How to plant considerate children with the Four Coffee Shop Steps

Coffee Shop Step #1
Decide what you want
The first of the Four Steps is always to define to yourself, clearly, what you want to achieve. In this case, we're quite clear: We want to see a world where—even if a super-Individual creates a great new smartphone—children will have the sense not to bring it to the dinner table, ruining the warmth between them and their parents.

Coffee Shop Step #2
Choose someone who's trying to achieve the same thing, or something similar

Karmic seeds are sort of like an echo, or a basketball—to plant them, we need to "bounce them" off someone else. That is, we need to find what we call a Karmic Partner: someone with whom we can plant our seeds.

As we say things to this partner; or interact with them; or even just think about them, we are also hear the words we say; see the actions we take; and listen to the thoughts we're having. As we saw in our conversation with Ellen, the impressions that these words and actions and thoughts make upon our conscious mind become—within a few hours—karmic seeds within our unconscious mind.

When we select this Karmic Partner, we choose someone who wants the same thing that we do, or something similar.

In this example, we are looking for someone who perhaps is having trouble connecting with their children. At first, we might think that it's difficult to find such a person; but if we really start looking, we can always find many people around us who are having exactly this problem. We just never paid that much attention to them before!

Coffee Shop Step #3
Help this person for one hour, once a week

Now that we've chosen our Karmic Partner, it's time to plant some seeds with them. Once a week, we commit an hour of our own precious time to helping them—and again, every single word we say to help them, and every single action we take, and every thought that drives these words and actions, serves to plant the seeds in our own mind.

Now we could invite this person over to our house, or we could invite ourselves over to their house, but they might find this uncomfortable: "Hey! I hear you have trouble with your kids! How about I come over on Friday and set you straight on how to raise children?"

What works better is a neutral space, and a neutral approach: "Say, I'm having some problems with my kids acting up. I know you might be going through the same thing, and I thought maybe you could help me. Could we get together on Friday at the coffee shop down the street, and compare notes for a bit?"

When we meet our Karmic Partner at a neutral space, like a coffee shop, they don't feel like they're somehow obligated or trapped—if they want to get back to the things they have to do today, they can just stand up and excuse themselves easily.

It's good to meet your Karmic Partner for the same length of time, and the same day, each week: we strongly recommend an hour on Friday afternoon, since for many people this is a relaxed and pleasant time, just before the weekend starts.

This way, planting seeds with them becomes a regular habit—which is what it's going to take to plant enough seeds to see a change in the world. Remember, our goal here is to plant a Flower Three: we want to create powerful seeds on a personal level—with children and parents close to us—that will ripple out and create a change in our larger world.

Coffee Shop Step #4
Do your Coffee Meditation

Michael:
The fourth of the four steps is the most important, and the most fun! You see, the first three steps serve to *plant* a seed. But there's something you have to understand about these mental seeds: If we don't water them, it could take *years* for them to grow and create the change we want to see in our world.

In fact, that's why for example we see generous people who never have any financial success; or people who reach out to lots of lonely people but can never seem to find a partner for themselves. They have planted lots and lots of seeds— and, as we've seen, those seeds are also doubling down in their subconscious mind, every 24 hours.

But it's like keeping a packet of watermelon seeds in a drawer: if they just sit there, you can wait for years and you'll never get that delicious burst of watermelon taste inside of your mouth. So you have to "water" the seeds.

The way we do this is Step Four. Every night, just before we fall off to sleep, we lay down on our bed—maybe even prop your head up on your hand. From this quiet place, we begin to think about all the nice things we've been doing this week; especially with our special Seed-Planting Project.

In our present example, we start to replay the video of how we took our friend out to the coffee shop to talk about the kids. We try to bring up every detail of the meeting: which table we sat at; what kind of coffee we each ordered; exactly how the conversation went.

And then we make a *very conscious* effort to *appreciate* what we did: the help that we tried to give to our friend. You don't have to worry about this appreciation descending into pride: We're not thinking, "I'm the very nicest person in our whole city! Nobody can help people like I do!"

Rather, we are taking a clear and honest pleasure in the kindness we were able to show to another human being. At the same time, it's important to feel the same pleasure *for the fact that we are trying a whole new method of changing the world*—that we are trying to making the world a safe and prosperous people for the children of both our countries, China and America.

There's a long story about why Step Four is called "Coffee Meditation"; for now, let's just say that the idea is that we're not sitting in some tight, formal meditation posture, with our legs tied up like a pretzel. Instead, we just relax and get our mind into a good mood, for reviewing the good things we've done today.

In fact, you can go further and add a nice little Dessert Meditation to the Coffee Meditation, just by thinking about all the nice things you've seen *other* people doing lately, especially for their children. This will also water the mental seeds of your Coffee Shop Project to help your friend.

Eric:

So what happens if we plant this seed with the Four Coffee Shop Steps, and water the seed well? As the seed splits open and world-images start to pour out of it, I will see my own children, and the children of my family and friends, start to behave towards their parents with more warmth and respect—even to the point of putting down their cellphones at the dinner table!

After that, Flower Three begins to kick in—and even the children of people we don't personally know begin to act with this same kind of consideration; because (believe it or not even kids on the other side of the world, if we are aware of that side of the world even in a peripheral way, are also coming from our own seeds.

The Four Coffee Shop Steps: Purposely Planting Our World

1 *Decide What You Want*
> In a single sentence, say what you would like to achieve.

2) *Choose Someone to Work With*
> Choose another person who wants the same or a similar thing.

3) *Help This Person for One Hour, Once a Week*
> Once a week, for an hour, take your Karmic Partner to a neutral space where you can both feel comfortable—like a coffee shop. Spend that hour helping them to achieve their own goal.

4) *Do Your Coffee Meditation*
> The first three steps plant the seed; but it won't open unless you water it. To water the seed, do Coffee Meditation: with your head on your pillow, just before you go to sleep, think carefully about all the good things you're doing to help this other person succeed; and how happy you feel to use this new system, where you succeed by helping someone else to succeed.

28

The Four Powers:
Getting Rid of Old Bad Seeds
to Fix a Problem in Your Life

Michael:

Okay, we're almost there! We've got a world full of brash creative individuals; but still the children in that world respect the wishes of the group: the generation that came before them. Now we have to make sure that this older generation itself cares about leaving enough natural resources for future generations—we don't want to see selfish people in our world. Once we have this last element in place, we've got a world with the best of *both* Chinese and American culture.

When you have a positive goal that you want to reach, then you need to plant a strong, positive seed with the Four Coffee Shop Steps. When you want to *remove* something from your life or your world that is negative, then you need to use the Four Powers.

The Four Powers are an ancient teaching that began with the Buddha himself, in a book that still exists in China, called *The Sutra of the Four Powers*. These powers are four steps that we take to remove the old bad seeds that are making our life unpleasant. If we have a problem in our world that we see selfish people stripping the entire globe of resources that future generations will also need, then we can rid ourselves of this problem just by using the Four Powers.

And that's because the negative things and people that we see in our world are coming from old bad seeds in our mind. Again because of Flower Three, these bad seeds are creating people we see who are so obsessed with the next new smartphone that they are ignoring the needs of the generations that come after them—who will also need access to resources such as the rare-earth metals required for smartphone components. Let's see how this works.

Using the Four Powers
To Get Rid of Bad Seeds
That Make Us See Selfish People in the World

First Power:
Take a Few Minutes to Think About
Where the World is Coming From

This is easy—you can just take any simple object and think about where it really comes from. I like to use a pen.

Now it's common knowledge that the way the eye works is that there are cells—called "rods" and "cones"—at the back of the eyeball; and these cells are good at detecting colors and shapes. And so if I pick a pen up off of the table and look at it, all my eye can do is see a cylinder-shaped object that has a sharp point and maybe a black color.

That is, my eye can't recognize this object as a pen: as far as the eye's concerned, the only thing in my hand is a thin black cylinder. The eye just sends this information on to the brain, via the optic nerve. My brain then goes to work and interprets the data it receives, and decides that the object is a pen.

Looking at this process in a more precise way, on a karmic level, my eye is picking up clues—shapes and colors—and then my brain is laying an image on top of these clues to organize and explain them. The image that my brain chooses is the one which emerges at that moment from a karmic seed; and that seed has been "cooking" in my mind since last week—when I offered my friend a pen to sign something. Seeing myself hand them the pen then made an impression on my conscious mind, which subsequently became a seed in my unconscious mind.

Just going through this train of thought is all you need to do for Power One, the first step in removing an old bad seed from your mind.

Power Two:
Understand the Urgency and Make a Decision

For the second power, we focus on the thing out there in our world which is causing a problem: in this case, people who are so selfish that they would use up all the resources of the world, for what they want for themselves.

Because we just went through the exercise of thinking about where things in the world are coming from, we immediately remember that these selfish people are also emerging from seeds in our own mind. And those seeds were planted when we did or said or thought selfish things ourselves, perhaps a week or two before.

And now we also understand that—during that week or two—those seeds have been *doubling every day.* A single seed that we planted a week ago to see a single selfish person in our world has now become a seed to see 64 selfish people. We have the option of either getting rid of this seed today, or waiting until tomorrow—when it might suddenly decide to open into *128* selfish people surrounding us. Needless to say, we should rush to dispose of the seed today!

When you feel this sense of urgency about getting rid of a bad seed right away, and make a decision to do something about it *today*, then you have mastered Power Two.

Power Three:
Make a Commitment to Stop

Eric:
Once we've reviewed what a bad seed can do in our world, and how fast they multiply, we're motivated to actually get rid of the seed. For this, the third of the Four Powers is by far the most important.

For this power, we simply make a commitment not to repeat whatever we did to plant the seed in the first place. In our example here, if we are seeing selfish people around us it means that we most likely have some personal habit of selfishness, in some aspect of our life. Maybe we make decisions about spending the family money without consulting our wife or husband; maybe we make decisions about what we're all going to eat at a restaurant, without even showing the menu to the other people sitting with us.

For Power Three, we review our life carefully and try to pick out the single biggest negative habit we have which might be planting the seeds to see what we're seeing. And then we make a commitment: "I promise I will stop this bad habit I have, of making major purchases using our family funds without consulting my spouse beforehand."

Incidentally, it might be the case that what actually *planted* the negative seed here was something much longer ago—a selfish act that you don't even remember doing. That's okay; if you make a commitment to stop any selfish tendency in your mind stream right now, that will also function to remove the seed.

Michael:

By the way, there's an old oral tradition here which you should know about. Some of the negative habits we have are so ingrained in us, and so easily acted out, that it would be a mistake to promise we will never repeat them for the whole rest of our life.

For example, we might detect that the most prevalent selfish habit we have is interrupting other people who are trying to say something *they* want to say. For most of us, a habit like this is not something we're going to be able to shut off completely, for the rest of our life, within a single day. If we make a commitment today never to interrupt another person for as long as we live, we are almost certain to break that commitment—probably within a few hours, or a few days. And then we will have planted a *new* bad seed.

So there's a custom here to put a time limit on our commitment, if it's not something we can reasonably expect to honor for the rest of our life. In the case of not interrupting other people, we could for example commit not to do it for the rest of this week—and then remain very vigilant for that length of time, relaxing this vigilance a bit after that.

Power Four:
Do Some Kind of Make-Up Activity
to Balance the Karma

Eric:
Notice that the third power involves making a promise *not* to repeat the kind of activity which planted the seed that we're trying to get rid of. Power Four then involves making a promise *to* do something, to balance the karma of the mistake we made before.

If for example we've been interrupting people constantly during conversations, we might make a promise to make a phone call this week to two people that we know are lonely, and need to talk to someone. This unselfish behavior "cements" our battle against the old bad seeds, much in the way that Coffee Meditation—the fourth of the Four Coffee Shop Steps— "cements" or waters a good seed.

Michael:

Traditionally, there are two indications that tell us we've been successful in eliminating an old bad seed. The first is that we start to feel better about ourselves and our life: we begin to feel a deep sense of wellbeing, and we have the sensation of letting go of a burden that we've been carrying around for some time. It's kind of like carrying a heavy backpack around for two or three days, and then suddenly setting it down and taking a pleasant walk on some cool green grass amidst beautiful trees.

Eric:

The second indication that you've succeeded in removing a bad seed has to do with how bad seeds are actually "removed." You see, we can't simply cancel a bad seed anytime we want, because that would contradict a very basic law of the universe— perhaps the most basic law that there is. This law says that anytime you do something to hurt another person, you *must* undergo a painful experience in return; and anytime you do something to help another person, you *must* undergo a pleasant experience in return.

That is, the entire universe runs by a certain absolute kind of justice, and there has never existed a force—nor will there ever exist a force—which could contradict this justice. We always get exactly what we deserve, good or bad, and there are no exceptions, ever. Thus, say the ancient books of China, a seed—until the day it opens, and thereby destroys itself—cannot otherwise be destroyed.

So what good does it do, to use the Four Powers?

Picture what happens to a watermelon seed if you set it down on the concrete floor of your car garage, and keep it warm, and keep it wet. In time the warmth and moisture cause the seed to split open, and a small sprout emerges.

But because there is no sunlight in the garage, and none of the nutrients in the hard cement that you might find in the fertile loam of your garden, the sprout will live only a short life, and then naturally shrivel and die.

The same thing happens to your bad seeds, when you have applied the Four Powers to them. They open prematurely and—like a child that has left the womb far too early—cannot survive. What happens then is that you undergo some much smaller version of the karmic result you were supposed to experience.

Our *Diamond Cutter Sutra*, in fact, describes this phenomenon: a seed that was supposed to open as a fatal car accident, or a malignant cancer, opens instead as that little watermelon sprout—meaning as a brief, violent migraine headache.

Which is still a lot better! So that's what we mean when we talk about "taking out" an old bad seed—and still maintaining that cosmic justice. In our example here, after doing the Four Powers on our old bad seeds from selfishly interrupting people for years, our boss at work might selfishly force us to work overtime for an entire week; and then slowly but inevitably, we begin to see fewer selfish people in our world: and the vision of Option 3 is fulfilled.

The Four Powers:
Getting Rid of Old Bad Seeds

1) *Take a Few Minutes to Think About*
   Where the World Is Coming From
   Sit and look at a pen or a cellphone and
   understand how it is coming out of seeds in your
   own mind, and not from its own side

2) *Understand the Urgency and Make a Decision*
   Think about the fact that seeds already
   imbedded in your mind double in power every
   day; make a decision to get rid of your old bad
   seeds, quick!

3) *Make a Commitment to Stop*
   Make a commitment to stop doing negative
   actions like the one that planted your bad seeds.
   If necessary, set a time limit during which you
   will stop.

4) *Do Some Kind of Make-Up Activity*
   to Balance the Karma
   Make another commitment to *start* doing
   something: a kind and positive action which is
   the opposite of the negative one you did before.

29
Who Wins,
When Titanic Meets Iceberg?

Michael:
So let's just see what it looks like when our Option 3 is fulfilled here. Because I helped another person with their own project to make a new phone app—and because Flower Three ripples out to all my outside world—I now have the seeds to see individual creativity flourish, and be honored, all around me. The American ideal perseveres.

I also have the seeds to see the younger generation honor the generation above them, tucking away their cellphones at the dinner table, and actually enjoying a conversation with their parents: the Chinese ideal. I have removed as well the seeds in me to see, in my world, people who would deny the resources of Mother Earth to the generation to come after.

Eric:
But there's a basic problem here that's been here all along, and it might look as though we still haven't taken care of it. If I plant the seeds for a highly individualistic colleague who possesses the creativity to invent a new kind of smartphone, that smartphone is *still* going to require rare-earth metals. And if he or she is *really* creative, then that smartphone is going to be wildly successful, and there will be a tremendous demand for it, and people are going to run out and dig up whatever rare-earth metals they can find to produce more of the phones, to meet that demand—regardless of what that does to the planet, and future generations.

On the other hand, if I plant seeds to see people who are extremely sensitive to the needs of their parents and their children and *their* children, then there will be this unstoppable force in the world which drives the usage of smartphones—and the mining of rare metals—down.

And it just doesn't seem like these two opposing forces could ever coexist in one and the same world. Something has to give. In my heart, it feels like the Titanic approaching an iceberg: The irresistible force of an extraordinarily creative person, and the fantastic product they create (both titanic) is approaching the immovable object—the massive iceberg—of a culture where people will not give up the good of the planet for their own selfish desires.

It seems like when these two collide, only one will survive, and the other will have to be destroyed. This was the basic, unsolvable problem that we began with, in the case of each one of the Six World Choices. We *can't* have a world which is both Chinese and American too, at the same time.

Michael:

This is of course the dilemma of this whole book—the dilemma we started out with. If Chinese culture and American culture are so different from each other, and each country's influence is expanding out into the larger world, then sooner or later they will crash into each other, with painful results, just like the Titanic and an iceberg.

The solution here lies in one fact: it was *seeds* that created both the Titanic *and* the iceberg. And it was *seeds* that created China in the first place, and America too. *Seeds can do the impossible, because seeds already do the possible, which was impossible yesterday.*

To put it another way, it's not that seeds—and the things they produce—need to accommodate the universe, the things that are already possible. Rather, the universe itself has to scoot over when seeds come to sit down on the bus—because the seeds are the boss: they run the universe, and not the other way around. The universe has to accommodate your new seeds, and it always will.

In practical terms, this means that if you plant all the seeds that we've talked about so far, then there is no choice: In some way or form—in a way none of us can yet imagine, nor need to now—the culture of extreme individual creativity *will coexist with* the culture of extreme consideration for the needs of other generations.

Somehow, in a way we cannot now imagine, smart individuals will be cranking out new smartphones, and we will produce millions upon millions of them, and there will be plenty of rare-earth metals reserved for future generations, and children will revel in the warmth of an evening meal together with their parents, uninterrupted by electronic irritants—all at the same time.

How can that be? Because what is now, is.

30
Strategies to Prevent
an Overcrowded World

Eric:

Then it's time to resolve our second World Choice; that is, in the new global alignment, do we go more the "group" way and set an official limit on the number of children a couple can have, or do we go more the "individual" way and leave it up to people's personal good sense to help with overpopulation?

This is a crucial question, I believe, not just because we will soon run out of space, and food. The way I see it, clean water will become a problem long before anything else. The United Nations says that within 15 years, the world's supply of clean water will fall short by 40%; the World Economic Forum rates water shortage as the greatest danger in the world, above terrorism, war, and disease.

Already, 1 out of 10 people in the world have no access to clean water—and 1 out of 3 people have no access to a toilet. By 2050, the world population will increase about 30%, to over 9 billion people—instead of the 7 billion that we have now; but the *amount* of water that *each* person uses will actually increase even more. If we cannot control our population, we will see millions of people dying from lack of water; and wars fought over the water that remains.

Michael:

Let's go back to Master Nagarjuna, where he says that "Nothing fades, and nothing stays." When we apply this to the world population, what he's saying is that it will never decrease, nor even stay the same, only because of outside actions that humankind decides to take. Policies to reduce the population will work only if the deeper causes for them to work are present; and those causes are inner—they are the seeds within our own mind.

From a practical point of view, we can see that the reduction of childbirth rates in Japan, for example, has led to a dangerous aging of the population, and a weak economy. And experts predict that the economy of India, for example, could in the next few years overtake that of most other countries, due in part to the younger workforce, driven by a high birth rate.

Is it possible to *control* the birth rate; *maintain* a strong and healthy economy; and *assure* enough water and resources for the entire world, all at the same time?

Eric:
Sure it is, in a world which is emerging from the seeds in our own mind—because as we've seen, we can just plant the seeds to make what we want happen on each side of what seems like an irresolvable dilemma. Then the universe will wiggle to accommodate the combined results of all the seeds we have planted.

So let's look at the seeds for the first outcome we seek: controlling the birth rate.

We want a world where people are content to see only enough babies being created to keep the population at a number which can be sustained by the resources of our planet. This will mean that the needs that people feel will change. In societies where large families have been desirable, people will begin to decide that less children is fine.

This will come about through a combination of two types of mental seeds.

First, the economy of the world has to improve to where people no longer feel that the only security they will have as they get older is the children who will support them. Income levels have to be sufficient to set aside more than enough to cover a very comfortable retirement; and the average citizen of the planet has to be considerate enough to take personal responsibility for not overloading the world's resources for future generations.

Michael:
So let's look at these two outcomes. The first one is easy; again, we just use the Four Coffee Shop Steps.

Coffee Shop Step #1
I would like to see a world where every single person has sufficient   income to cover the needs of a very comfortable retirement.

Coffee Shop Step #2
We need to select a single person who is worried about having enough money after they retire. If we help them amass this much money, then we ourselves will have more than enough savings for our own retirement. And then because of Flower Three, the effects of this seed will ripple out into the entire world, and we will see people all around us having more than enough for their golden years.

Coffee Shop Step #3
We spend one hour a week helping this person with strategies to set aside enough money for their retirement.

Coffee Shop Step #4

On our bed at night—just before we fall off to sleep—we take a few minutes to really appreciate the nice things we are doing for our friend. On top of that, we take some time to appreciate this amazing new approach we are taking to helping the whole world, just by planting our own seeds.

Eric:

Next we have to plant the seeds to see the level of consideration in the world change dramatically. People will have to be so considerate of future generations that they are willing to have much fewer children.

This will be doubly difficult because of the intense attachment that people have towards *their own* children. Because we have used our own bodies to create the body of our new child, and perhaps in a large part simply because our own child *looks like* a combination of the two of us, men and women are very, very strongly attached to *their own* children, and will go to extraordinary lengths to care for them and protect them, without taking anywhere near the same effort to care for and protect *other people's* children.

If we can plant the seeds to see this bias change in the world, we'll go a long way towards solving the population problem. The only way to remove this bias is if we can get large numbers of people to understand that it's mistaken.

And it's not mistaken just because *it's not nice* to spend an incredible amount of time and effort to take care of one child who lives in our home, and almost completely ignore the needs of a very similar child who happens to live in the house next door. People already know it's not nice, but their attachment to their own children is so strong that they can't and don't want to change this behavior.

The only way that people are going to treat other children with the same intense love that they treat their own children is if they come to realize that these other children *are* their own children.

31
Your Child Is My Child

Michael:

We all love our own children, and it might seem unreasonable to expect that people will *ever* love other people's children as much as they do their own. But such a change is possible, if we understand why your child is my child.

To do this, we need to separate what we see from what we know is true.

Let's take the case of feeding our own children breakfast. Suppose I have two kids. When I go to the grocery store on Saturdays, I have to buy enough food to feed both of them (and my spouse) for the next week. It seems like I *don't* have to make sure that our *neighbor* has enough food to feed *their* children, if I want to feed *my* children.

Their children, and *their* children's mouths, live over in the house next door, and are separated from *my* children, and *my* children's mouths, by about 100 feet. And that means that *their* children can't *be* children of *mine*. I can feed all of *my* children's mouths without feeding any of *their* children's mouths, so *their* children can't *be* my children.

But we've already proven that this is simply not the case. The food I buy in the store is not coming from the money I get when I work, or from the labors of farmers who live outside my city. According to a higher truth, the job where I work, and the farms in the countryside, are *both* coming from seeds in my own mind.

The *reason* there is food in my local grocery store; and the *reason* I have the money to buy it, is that I possess sufficient seeds within my own mind to *see* the food and the money. If I *didn't* have these seeds, then in my city or in my country there wouldn't *be* enough food for everyone to eat, and there wouldn't *be* enough jobs for everyone to do—and indeed we can see many places where this is the case.

Moreover, the only way to plant the *seeds* for food and money *is to help someone else get food and money*: for example, to make sure that the person next door has enough money to buy enough food, for *their* children.

So from this point of view, in the long term *my* children will never have enough food if I don't make sure that *my neighbor's* children have enough food. And by the way, if your children have had enough food so far in your life, without your making sure that the kids next door had enough food, that's just an illusion, and you are fooling yourself. You are living off of older karmic seeds, planted either consciously or by simple good luck in the past, and one day they will run out. You *have* to learn how to plant new seeds anytime you need them, and not trust that your bank account of old seeds is going to last forever.

Eric:
So we have to divide what we see from what we know is true. Visually, the mouths of my children are separated by some number of feet from the mouths of my neighbor's children. Most of us humans tend to believe our eyes over our understanding—and so we think our neighbor's children aren't our children.

Functionally though—in the way things really work—food can never enter the mouths of my children unless I do something to make sure food is entering the mouths of the children next door. In this sense, which is a more *real* sense, the mouths of my neighbor's children *are* the mouths of my children—and so *in reality*, my neighbor's children *are* my children.

This is not wishful thinking; or grand intention; or even some kind of compassion. In a very practical sense, my neighbor's children *are* my children, and if I don't work hard to see that they get fed every day, then in time my own children will not have enough to eat.

32
We Can Only Save the World
If We Have Already Saved the World

Michael:

So I suppose there has to be some grand plan of educating the whole world, of proving to people that *other* people's children are actually *their own* children. And then if there are only enough resources to feed two children, and your neighbor already *has* two children, then very naturally and without any fuss you and your spouse would decide not to overload the system by having two more of your children inside *this* house.

Eric:

That's right. And so far we've been calling it "consideration": you would be so considerate of the needs of others that you would avoid having more children than the planet can support.

But really we can see now that it's *not* consideration, because the very word "consideration" implies that you are thinking of others and not doing things that would hurt them, or make them unhappy. In our new understanding, we aren't letting go of having more children of our own because we want to make sure that there is enough space and food in the world for other people's children.

Rather, we understand that other people's children *are* our children, and we are just taking care of our own children when we decide not to have children of our own.

In the end, human nature is so strong—the power of self-interest is so strong—that we will only make decisions to save the world for others' children if we realize that those children are our own. We can only save the world if we have already saved the world.

33
Gifting an Oil Company

Michael:
So we've stabilized the number of people on the planet, while still making everyone happy with the number of children they've had; and we made sure the economy remained strong at the same time, so that fewer children wouldn't mean less security for the parents. The only thing we have left to do now is to make sure that the world's resources—water and the rest—will still be enough even for this lower population. Here's a story, to explain.

A few years ago, a Chinese organization offered to buy an American oil company. The Congress of the U.S. was concerned that a foreign country would gain control of resources that were strategically important to the U.S., and began an official debate the question. At the same time, I was invited to give a talk to a convention of several hundred architects, in Florida.

I mentioned the issue facing the Congress: Should we, or should we not, approve the sale of an American oil company to China?

And then gradually I went into an explanation of how our world is coming from seeds in our own mind; and how to plant these seeds by using the Four Coffee Shop Steps. I was careful to emphasize the "boomerang effect," meaning that the only way to get the things we want is to make sure that *someone else* gets what they want.

Now almost all of the architects present were from the southern states of America, and so a good number were quite conservative politically. They were people who most likely believed the stories in the American news that say Chinese people are trying to take over America—when they are actually just trying to make extra money for their children's education by purchasing U.S. bonds.

So when I asked the architects at the end of the talk, "Now do you think our country should sell our oil company to China?" I wasn't sure what they would say.

But one gentleman stood up and stated, "If the ideas behind the Four Steps are correct—and they certainly *sound* correct—then of course we should sell them the oil company."

"Why?" I asked him.

"Well, one of the goals of any country is to make sure they have enough energy supplies for everything their people and their companies want to do. So we can say that's Coffee Shop Step #1: America wants sufficient supplies of energy, far into the future.

"Next we have to choose somebody who wants the same thing, and of course China—which has been playing catch-up with the more prosperous countries in its standard of living—is going to need a lot of energy. So they are the perfect Karmic Partner to choose, for Coffee Shop Step #2.

"Step #3 is easy: we just have to sell them the oil company that they're asking for. And Step #4 is going to be interesting, because instead of doubting whether we should have sold the company (which I have a feeling slows the seed down, instead of watering it), we're going to constantly think about what a noble and helpful thing we have done for someone else's country."

"Bravo!" I said. "And you can also think about the great seeds you are planting just by *using* the seed system! That's the very best kind of Step #4."

I was amazed that a group of nearly a thousand hard-nosed business men and women would arrive at such a beautiful place after only an hour's introduction to the seeds. When that kind of thing happens, it reminds me how *logical* this whole system is; almost everyone senses it right away.

Eric:

So what's going to happen if one country helps another country get enough supplies of energy? The people of that country plant a *collective* seed. Now it's not possible for one person to give another person a seed, no matter how much they might want to; that's because a seed is planted by our own self-awareness that we are helping another person.

But it *is* possible for us to plant seeds *together*, and to reap the results together. If the people of one country agree—through a vote of their elected representatives—to sell an oil company to another country to help that country, then as a nation we ourselves experience the collective result of that kindness.

Once again, the universe will have to adjust itself to accommodate our new seeds. This means that somehow—in a way we may not even be able to guess—new sources of energy will suddenly appear for our own country.

Michael:

Perhaps it's just a coincidence—if there were such a thing—but not long after the Florida talk, in the America in *my* world, a new method of extracting oil was developed, and the United States suddenly became one of the largest producers of oil in the world. In fact, we even *export* oil now, to countries like...China!

34
The Expanding Pizza,
or: The Death of Global Competition

Eric:
So we've solved the question of whether or not the world should go the way of setting a limit on the number of children that people can have. We decided that instead we wanted a win-win, an Option 3: the birth rate remains low, at a sustainable rate, because people's idea of "my" has expanded; economies still stay strong; and the world's resources are protected, all at the same time. We planted three kinds of seeds for three things we wanted, and the universe was forced to cooperate.

But the good news is better than that.

The new sources of oil created by the seeds of helping another country secure energy supplies really are *new*. It's never the case—when we use the 4 Steps to get something—that we are *taking* something from somebody else. So it's not as though somebody else *lost* oil when America gained her new oil.

This is *new* oil in the world. The world's oil production was around 90 million barrels per day before America's seeds ripened; and now that they've ripened, the world's production is 100 million barrels per day. Nobody lost any oil: the total system just has 10% more barrels of oil in it every day—after America's seeds ripened.

Michael:

So look—if that's true, and the seeds open into *new* oil—then something important is going on when you use the Four Steps.

In the past, all of us were thinking of the world, the resources of the world, as being like one big pizza. And the pizza has just 8 slices to it, and no more.

The economic relationship between countries then boils down to competing over a limited number of pizza slices: if China takes 5 of them, then only 3 are left for America to choose from—and if America wants more, they're going to have to figure out how to *take* them from China.

And so *taking*—reaching out your hand, touching what somebody else possesses, and wrapping your fingers around that thing and pulling it in towards Me—becomes the global model. It defines relationships between people, and football teams, and countries: I will need to work harder, and smarter, to take as many slices of pizza as I can from the whole pie, for Me.

Now imagine what happens when we change the model to *giving*, with the Four Coffee Shop Steps. Our hand reaches out, and we open our fingers, and we release an apple—or an oil company—into the hands of another person. When the seeds open, *new* apple trees—or new *oil*—emerge from the seeds.

In terms of pizza, the whole pizza expands. If it was 12 inches across before, now it's like 30 inches in diameter. So instead of getting more pizza by *taking* slices from another person at the dinner table, I get more pizza because the seeds from sharing my slices *made all my slices get bigger*.

And their slices get bigger *too*. So there's no reason for either one of us to try to take slices from the other: If we just keep *reaching out* and *giving,* then the slices we have just keep on expanding, infinitely faster than I'm "losing" slices by giving them away.

Eric:

So think about what this could mean for international relations—for example, with the relationship between China and America. Every time America needs to increase their energy supplies, they just help China secure more energy—and of course, America works very hard to do Step #4: to be happy that they have helped another country; and *very importantly* to be happy that they are trying this new, enlightened system for guaranteeing their own energy supplies.

From my country's side—from China's side—we do the same thing: whenever America needs more energy, we're there to help you get it. From both sides of the dinner table, the pizza is just getting bigger and bigger.

When we keep this up, then everyone has more pizza than they can possibly eat. It doesn't even occur to anyone around the table to try to take slices from someone else at the table—there's just no reason to do it.

On a personal level then, there is no reason to compete with another person. There is no reason for one company to try to out-perform another company, to "take" market share. And what happens on a personal level, between individuals and groups of individuals, starts to spread to a national level—and then no country has any need to compete with another.

Globally, the entire idea of *competing*—the entire idea of *taking* what you want—dies. And with it dies want, and conflict, in the world.

35
Who Is Taking Advantage
of Whom?

Michael:
The third of the World Choices that we had to make was between the Visible Hand and the Invisible Hand, in the regulation of markets and currencies by a national government. We mentioned two examples: policies for setting the prices of energy supplies that will make them equally available to the rich and the poor; and manipulating currency rates to help one country "catch up" to more prosperous countries—as well as to keep their people employed, to help keep their society prosperous and peaceful.

Since we've already solved the world's energy problems with the Expanding Pizza, let's go on to the idea of what happened when China changed their currency rates to help keep their people employed.

I think the biggest problem, for most Americans, is very simple: Every time a job moved to China, one less American had a job. And when that happened enough times, it created a hardship not just for that one American, but for the whole US economy.

Eric:
There's an important new idea here that I think is going to help us solve this problem. And that's *intention*. Intention is crucial when we're talking about planting mental seeds.

Like, I often get this kind of question. A friend of mine was having trouble getting along with his wife's mother. He decided to buy her a gift to try to patch things up. He went to the department store and found a nice bath mat: the kind you put on the bottom of the tub to keep from slipping.

So he picked out a mat that had nice pictures of roses all over it, bought it, had it wrapped, and presented it to his mother-in-law.

The first time she used it in the bath the mat slid, and she fell down and banged her arm. So now she's more angry with my friend than she was before!

The question is, did he plant a bad seed or a good seed, by buying her the bath mat?

The ancient books of China say that he planted a *good* seed, because *intention* is 90% of a mental seed. In fact, whenever we give a gift, we can't be sure that the person receiving it will like it at all—that depends on how nice *they've* been to other people the week before. Of course this doesn't mean we should never give anybody gifts again! It just means we should never get discouraged in our gift-giving, if things don't work out the way we hoped.

Michael:
So I guess you could say that there are three possible intentions, when we do something nice for somebody else. One is that we want to make them happy. One is that we want to make them happy *and* by making them happy we very consciously hope to plant a good mental seed for the future.

The third kind of intention is just sort of neutral—something happens that helps somebody else, but we didn't really intend for it to happen.

We don't take ownership of it, and we definitely don't do Step #4 about it: we don't think, as we lie down to sleep, how nice it was that we created a job for somebody in another country, even at our own expense.

But *was* it at our own expense? Maybe yes, and maybe no. It depends upon our intention.

How does that work?

So it's a fact that the Chinese government changed their exchange rates in order to keep their people busier and catch up, economically, with the developed countries. And it's a fact that this caused jobs to move from America to China, because even *American* office-supply stores started going to China to buy their pens.

And it's a fact that the Chinese economy got stronger because of this; and more people in China were employed; and because of this there was greater peace and happiness in Chinese society.

Now if I'm an American and I *take ownership* of the fact that our country helped China to catch up—if I actually take the time to *be happy* that we helped Chinese people be peaceful and happy—then there is a lot of *intention* there, and so I plant a lot of good mental seeds.

What will happen when those seeds open? I will see my own country—and my own family, and myself—become more prosperous and peaceful and happy.

As we said before, seeds are the only place where success comes from. There is no success in the world that can ever occur without trying to make someone else successful. That's just a law of the universe. And even if we don't know about that law, or we don't believe in it, it still works on us.

Every success we have had so far in our life has come because of that law—because we helped someone else be successful, whether we knew what that would bring us, or not.

Eric:
The way you put it, Michael, it sounds like we should be *grateful* that someone else is giving us a chance to give them something—it's almost like they're the ticket for our own success.

Michael:
Exactly. I was sitting with some business people recently in Germany, and going over these ideas with them. One of them raised her hand and told me, "I don't know. Every time I try to follow this Diamond Cutter system and try to be successful by making someone else successful, I can't shake the feeling that they are taking advantage of me. I mean, you can just see what would happen if I really bought into this system: people all around me at work and at home would be coming up and offering to let me give them something, so I could plant a good seed!"

I laughed and told her, "Personally, I always feel the opposite! If someone gives me an opportunity to plant a seed —if I get a chance to give somebody something, or do something for them—then I don't feel like they're taking advantage of me; instead, I feel like I'm taking advantage of them!" She got it right away, even before I finished the sentence, and we both burst out laughing.

Because it's true. And yes, it's going to take some time for each of us, and for our whole planet, to get used to this way of thinking. Again, it's the difference between taking and giving.

As a planet, as the people in the world, we've tried the *taking* system for many thousands of years—we've tried *competition* as a system, for the entire length of human history. And where did it get us? Worldwide war, worldwide poverty—sickness and death.

Because the competitive model is simply flawed. It doesn't work.

Maybe it's time to give this new model a chance. Maybe it's time to *give*–give even our own job, so that a person in another country can have a job. If this new system is correct, then the only result of such an action (if we are truly *happy* about what we have done, and *own* it, instead of being *angry* about it) is that we are assuring *ourselves* employment and success, for our whole country, for the rest of our life.

36
Surface Causes vs. Deeper Causes

Michael:
So I don't know if you've noticed it, but we've just taken care of our third World Choice. It boils down to this: If we use strong central government control, the Visible Hand, to set market prices or the value of our currency, we plant a *good* seed if our intention is to help others.

If we ignore the needs of others as we take the very same actions, then we are planting a *bad* seed; and eventually that action will hurt us, and our country.

Same with the Invisible Hand. If we let market forces go their own way, without trying to control them, we plant *good* seeds if we are doing that because our intention is to help others. If we *ignore* the needs of others and let prices and exchange rates float at their natural rate, then we are planting a *bad* seed—with the very same action.

Eric:
So now we can move on to the fourth of our World Choices. Again, it was basically a choice between the individual and the group.

Our specific example was foods that are known to hurt people—like a single can of soda which we know has more sugar in it than a child should consume in an entire day: starting a lifetime habit which will almost certainly end up giving them diabetes, ruining their life and creating a burden on their family.

Or a single hamburger or a piece of fried chicken which already has more cholesterol in it than anyone should eat in an entire day: keep this up, and you will very likely end up with a stroke or heart attack, again ruining your life and your family's finances.

In fact, there is a famous saying in China that says, "If you spend to overeat before the age of 40, you will spend on the doctors after 40."

So if big American corporations show up in China and begin opening thousands of fast-food outlets that feed these dangerous foods to people, should our government treat it as cultural pollution and ban them from the country? Or should we instead give individuals the freedom to eat what they want, even if it hurts them?

Michael:
I think we have to go back to that idea of making a problem not a problem before it ever becomes a problem. Like we don't have a problem in the world right now of people trying to eat other people, it just isn't the way our world society does things. So we have to look at trying to make eating these bad foods a problem that just never becomes a problem.

To do that, there's one simple rule; and it's the same rule that has been so successful in the last few centuries, as science tries to cure diseases and create new inventions like cars and airplanes.

We have to find the cause that makes something else happen. To go back to our friend Nagarjuna, "Nothing comes, and nothing goes" without a cause.

Okay then, what's the cause for diabetes and strokes?

Eating unhealthy food, like the hamburgers and fried chicken that American fast-food outlets are selling in China.

Alright, so what's the cause of these fast-food outlets?

The people who own them, and who build them, and operate them, are thinking a little bit too much about making money, and they aren't thinking enough about what might hurt other people's health and family.

Eric:
So let's go deeper. Now we know the surface causes: bad food, places that sell the bad food, and the people who build those places. But what caused *them?*

What's the deeper cause? Because we know, in life, that we always have to go down and find the deeper causes, if we want to fix something. If our roof leaks when it rains, and that makes a mess on the floor of our house, we can put a bucket on the floor to fix that mess in a shallow way.

Or we can go to the deeper cause, the cause behind the cause: we can fix our roof, once and for all.

Now why, in my world, do I have to see people who are selfish in this way, who care more about what they want, than they care about the health and happiness of others?

Do you remember the Four Flowers that we talked about before? The four ways that a mental seed opens? The third flower is that—when mental seeds open—they ripple out and create the people and the world around us. We said that's why we saw people in our world who would use up all the rare metals on the planet to make their own cellphones—and not leave any of those metals for the next generation, to make *their* cellphones.

The seed that made us see these people, we said, was planted when *we ourselves were being selfish*—we gave the example of spending the family money without consulting our spouse ahead of time.

When we took that bad seed out of our own mind, by using the Four Powers—which mainly boils down to stopping the habit of spending family money without talking to the family beforehand—we stopped seeing (and therefore *having*) people in our world who would strip our planet of resources needed by those who come after us.

So now we're getting closer to understanding what to do about the restaurants selling unhealthy food.

37
Everything Comes in Cycles

Michael:

The idea of cycles—breaking bad cycles, and triggering good cycles—is one of the greatest achievements of the traditional literature of China. Dealing with unhealthy food is one of the most important questions in the modern world; especially in my own country, America, where two people out of three are literally killing themselves by eating poorly—which also drags down the productivity, creativity, and happiness of our whole nation. To stop this ongoing disaster, we have to understand the cycles involved in it.

So let's say someone hands me a donut. They do it because they love me, and they want to make me happy.

But a simple American donut is a time bomb. If I decide to put it in my body, the fat will add one more tiny layer of gunk to the inside walls of all the arteries running through my body, and eventually I'll have stroke: I won't be able to get around on my own, and my family will have to spend maybe decades of their life taking care of me.

The sugar will cause just a little more stress on the cells in my body that make insulin, and eventually they will just give up, and I'll get diabetes. That will kill me slowly, and in the meantime use up a lot of my whole family's resources and time.

So there I am looking at the donut that my friend handed me: it's in my own hand now, and I have a choice to either pop it into my mouth, or set it down quietly, and never eat it.

Eric:

If I pop the donut into my mouth, it's because I've weighed the pros and cons of eating the donut, and I've decided that my own selfish, immediate pleasure is more important than my family, my friends, or even my own country—and even my later Me: the one who will have the stroke, the one who will get the diabetes.

Flower One says that people in my own family will be selfish to me, as the seeds I just planted open.

Flower Two says that I will start making this selfish decision more and more often—I will have less and less self-control around junk food, as the seeds open.

Flower Three says that I will live in a world where more and more people and countries live by a selfish life-model: a world where the companies from one country feel no hesitation to hurt the citizens of their own country, and those of another country, in order to make money for themselves.

Flower Four says that the negative seeds I plant will feed upon each other, and build up, until I hold a vast "bank account" of them in the last days of my life. Since seeds cannot be destroyed, then any seeds still left unopened in my mind on the day that I die will open somewhere else later—in a world where selfishness is the planetary norm.

Michael:

And so you can see how downward cycles get started, just by taking a mindless bite out of a donut. *My own seeds create the companies that build fast-food outlets that sell me junk food; and my own seeds make them build one of those outlets near my home; and my own seeds make me want to eat their junk food again,* **which plants seeds for the companies to expand into other countries,** and the cycle just starts again.

So how do we break a cycle?

38
Breaking a Cycle

Eric:
By definition, cycles are almost unbreakable. That's why an addiction to something like alcohol or smoking or gambling is almost impossible to break. The Four Flowers are always at work, making people offer me donuts; making me make the wrong decision about eating them; making me live in a country with lots of donut shops; even making me be born with a taste for donuts.

The ancient wisdom books of China say that they only sure-fire way to stop a cycle is to *understand* the cycle.

In the end, if I truly *understand* where donuts and donut shops come from—where hamburger and fried chicken outlets come from—then, and only then, will I have a chance to break the cycle.

Michael:
I think what Eric's saying is related to *blaming other people.* You can see good people in my country, in America, who blame big companies for building the fast-food outlets that sell the food that makes so many of our country's people unhealthy, and even threatens our security as a nation, as we get softer and weaker.

But in this system, the Diamond Cutter system, we always keep in mind that there are deeper causes behind the surface causes. Yes the fast-food chains are selling the sugar and the fat, and yes the sugar and the fat are hurting people in America, and now in China.

And so it's easy to blame the big companies. But those are just surface causes. A sign that a cause is just a surface cause is that *we can't, as an individual, do much about it.* If huge corporations that make billions of dollars (McDonalds netted US$25 billion last year; KFC netted almost exactly the same) are the ones who decide whether or not China will have thousands of new junk-food outlets in the next few years, you can bet that there's not much any of us can do about it.

Eric:

But every surface cause has a deeper cause below it—*and deeper causes always have to do with the individual, and they always have to do with how we, as an individual, treat other people.*

In the end, the only one to blame, for *anything* in our world, is always—ourselves.

So let's go back to the decision I make when my friend hands me the donut. It's one thing to put it down, and let it go this time—don't eat it—because I know it will make me fat and unattractive.

It's another thing to put it down uneaten because I'm thinking about how being overweight might give me diabetes, or a stroke.

It's yet another thing to put the donut down, untouched, because I know how much of a burden I will be on my family and friends if I get diabetes or a stroke.

There's even a higher place, where I put the donut down because I don't want to contribute to making my country weak and stupid.

Michael:

And there's even a higher place than that—I can break the donut-eating cycle for even a higher reason.

If my friend hands me a donut and I just pop it into my mouth, then I'm sending a message to my friend that eating donuts is a good thing. *By my example*—which is the strongest form of encouragement there is—I am encouraging *them* to eat donuts; and ruin their health; and hurt their family and their country.

If I control myself *for this reason*—because eating the donut *will hurt someone else* right here, right now—then I can truly break this downward cycle.

That is, the only chance we have of breaking a downward cycle that is hurting ourselves is to do it for someone else. To do it because we don't want to hurt someone else—especially someone who might take us as an example.

Eric:

And there's something even more interesting here. When we break a downward cycle, a personal bad habit, for the sake of someone else that we care about, then the same Four Flowers kick in, **and we trigger an upward cycle.**

Let's review what that looks like.

Flower One says that if I refuse to eat a donut because I don't want to be a bad example for the person next to me, then people will stop handing me donuts. They will start handing me carrot sticks instead, and those carrot sticks will taste better than a donut to me! Wow! Seeds are *powerful!*

Flower Two says that if I can just refuse a donut once, forsomeone else's sake, then the second time it will be *much, much easier* to refuse the donut. Third time even easier, and eventually very easy, very natural, to turn down food that hurts me.

Skipping to Flower Four, I can actually do something about the tendency I was born with, of enjoying unhealthy sweets; or chicken or burgers with crazy cholesterol counts.

Michael:
But here's the thing, and *here's the solution to our fourth World Choice.* Flower Three says that if I start refusing junk food, **then big companies will stop *making* junk food— and they will stop exporting it to other countries.**

Without any Visible Hand, and without any Invisible Hand—that is, without government intervention in the rights of the individual to eat junk food; and without encouraging individuals who decide to hurt themselves and their families by eating it—we have resolved the whole problem. A perfect Option 3, if you will.

We see people and countries make decisions, almost automatically, to stop using or selling things that hurt them—the opium trade that we spoke about before, which caused so much pain and misunderstanding between our countries in the past, is something that now everyone understands was wrong and harmful to us all.

With seeds, we can come to the same place: we can look forward to a future when these big companies enjoy making food that is healthy for their customers; and customers who decide, as individuals, not to eat anything else.

39
Branches in the Wind

Eric:
I've watched Michael give talks in my country, China, and one of my favorite parts is where he asks the crowd, "Do you want to go deeper?" And then everyone goes crazy and yells back, "Yessssss!"

That is, in China, we grew up with this wisdom tradition in our veins. If you scratch a Chinese person, you find a philosopher underneath. I know you Americans also like cool new ideas, so here's another one, along the lines of what we were just talking about—with surface causes and deeper causes.

Now it looks like we can affect these big companies by talking to them—by showing them calmly and logically why what they are selling hurts the people they are supposed to serve. Or we could go to our government, and try to convince them that they should take some action to protect the citizens who eat this food. Or we could go directly to the people themselves, and try to convince *them* not to eat this stuff.

Now we all know that each of these approaches *might* work, and they might *not* work.

Here is a very basic principle of the ancient wisdom of my country: When any action we undertake to make something happen works only sometimes, then that action is mistaken. It means we haven't found the real cause behind something—the *deeper* cause.

It's like being surprised that the roof is still leaking, when all you've done to stop the water is to put a bucket under the place where it's leaking. If we find the deeper cause, we can *always* make something happen.

Michael:
The idea that Eric is talking about is sometimes called "Branches in the Wind." And it's pretty incredible, because if it's correct, it means that just about everything all of us do all day, every day, doesn't work.

But if you think about it, that leaves a lot of room for improvement! And what happens then if *everything* we do works, *all the time?*

So here's the idea.

Let's say you have a fruit tree in your front yard—a plum tree. You wait all year for the plums to appear, and then just when you're about to pick them, there's a big windstorm.

During the storm, one of the branches of the tree rubs against another branch of the tree, and some of your plums fall down.

Now why did you lose those plums?

The *surface* cause—the obvious or apparent one—is that one branch banged against another branch, and knocked the plums off. In this metaphor, we are the one branch; our country is the other branch; and people who sell food that hurts citizens of our country are the plums. Talking to those people, reasoning with them, asking them to have some compassion and stop selling things to people that hurt those people, is like one branch banging against the other.

Sometimes some of the plums might fall off—the companies might agree to stop selling bad food (which is very much like the opium sold to China by western countries 150 years ago), and take it back to their own country and their own people. But sometimes they will just ignore what we say and keep selling the bad food, or even increase their overseas sales.

This means that our approach—logical and reasonable talking—didn't work. And that means that this approach didn't reach the *deeper* cause; because if it had, it would always work.

Eric:
Now what's the deeper cause? It's something amazing even to think about.

If you look at that plum tree, and ask yourself *where the two branches came from,* then your eyes go down the trunk of the tree to the ground, and in your mind you see the plum pit—the seed—that years ago started the whole tree in the first place.

That is, the *real* cause for *both* the branches was the seed that gave birth to the tree.

Get this: The cause for *both* branches is the same thing. It may *look* like one branch is affecting another branch, and blowing against it and knocking down plums. It may *look* like the one branch is the reason why the plums on the other branch fell down.

But if you look at the bigger picture, the *deeper* picture, you can see that the original cause of one branch is exactly the same original cause of the second branch.

Which is *to say, it was the seed of the tree that caused the plums to be on one branch in the first place, and it was that same seed's fault that the second branch ever existed, to knock the plums off the first.*

Michael:
Now let's see where this takes us with junk food. We can try to talk to the big companies and ask them to help, but that might not work. We need to go to the deeper cause that *created* the big companies, and *created* the fact that they sell hurtful food.

According to everything we've learned in this book so far, the *deeper* cause why we see a chain of junk-food outlets around us, in our world, is that there is a *seed* for them, inside of our own mind. Those fast-food restaurants are coming directly out of a seed in my own mind.

And if I understand how I *put* the seed there in the first place, then I can take it out, and the junk food will go away, or it will change to healthy food that makes people bright and strong.

How I put that seed in my mind, at some time in the past, is very simple. I was a bad example, myself! When my friend handed me the donut, I popped it right into my mouth, even though I know perfectly well how bad it is for me, and the trouble it might cause to everyone I love, later on.

My own *awareness* that I was (inconsiderately, to my loved ones) popping the donut into my mouth made an *impression* on my mind, like the imprint left behind when you press your thumb hard into the palm of your hand. Within a few hours, that *impression* reverberated in the subconscious mind below, and created a *mental seed.*

And that seed doubled every single day—became more than a million times stronger just within the next three weeks. And *that* created enough seeds for me to see all the many actions that a company has to take to come to my country and set up a junk-food restaurant that hurts me and everyone around me.

Because they *haven't* hurt me. I've hurt *myself*.

And I can stop doing it. I just have to be a good example, myself, quietly, surely, in my own home. Stop planting those seeds. Stop eating the junk food myself, and stop being inconsiderate to my friends and family.

Go to the deeper cause; the real cause—which is to start being a good example for others, yourself.

40
How to Speed Things Up

Eric:

Alright then, we've solved our fourth World Choice, about how to deal with restaurants selling bad food. Now it's time to tackle our fifth World Choice.

The fifth one was, again, whether we should as a planet go the Chinese way or the American way: should we encourage people to save money, so they can have enough to send their children to a good college, and take care of their parents when they get older; or should we encourage people to spend more, so that money doesn't get "stuck," and the economy flows better: more transactions, more movement of money between the makers of things and the buyers of things—a more robust economy for everyone.

Which is better? They both sound good. What we should *do*, of course, is to listen to the last part of that cryptic verse by Master Nagarjuna: "No two things are separate, and no two things are one."

That is, we shouldn't see these two goals as separate from each other: even the fact that one thing is one, and two things are two, is coming from us. And if something is coming from us, then we can change it.

In a world where things are coming from our own mind, then 1 + 1 *can* = 1. We can stash away money to send our kids to college and care for our parents in their old age; and at the same time we can spend money: buy things and services from our neighbors, at a good price, to keep the economy strong and vibrant for everybody.

I mean, it's that simple! Let's make enough money to do *both!*

Michael:
How we're going to make that much money is something we've already learned about in this book. Just use the Four Coffee Shop Steps: decide what you want (enough money for both goals); choose someone else who has the same or a similar goal; help them for an hour once a week; and then do your Coffee Meditation before you go to bed: lay your head down on your pillow and very purposely think about all the good things you're doing for this person, to plant the seed to serve your family and your community, with college money and retirement support and shopping trips!

But look—we've been planting seeds, without really realizing what we were doing, for our whole lives: you literally can't count all the times you've helped other people. In your life, you've definitely planted enough seeds by now to be ten times richer than Warren Buffett or Jack Ma. And we already know that *once you plant a seed, it can't be destroyed* until it opens and brings you back your just reward. Otherwise there wouldn't be any justice in the universe—and there *is*.

So what happened? It's just that those seeds weren't planted with enough understanding—with a clear intention—and they didn't get enough water, and so they haven't cracked open into the good life you want.

So let's take a look at some different things you can do to make seeds like this open stronger and faster. Because the fast-food chains do have one thing right: we want delicious things to happen to us quick—we don't want to have to wait.

Eric:

The single most important thing you can do to make your seeds open faster is the Coffee Meditation that we talked about back in Chapter 27. If your Coffee Meditation is good, you will be successful. If it's not, you won't. It's that simple.

So let's see what we can do to crank up our Coffee Meditation. Here are four very effective suggestions:

1) Do your Coffee Meditation every night

The first thing of course is to do this meditation *every single night*. It's not going to be a chore, because you don't need to light some incense and put your legs into a pretzel shape and sit for an hour on the floor. Just make it a habit that when you go to bed—just before you fall off to sleep—you very purposely turn your mind for a few minutes to the good things you've done today for other people.

The problem is human nature, and our human nature really gets in our way. Human nature is that—just before we go to sleep—we are tired! Duh! And because we are tired, we tend to worry about things more than we should.

In fact, the word "meditation" in the ancient languages just means to *fight with your mind*, to make it think what you want it to think about. This isn't something that anybody ever taught us when we were young, but it's one of the most important skills in a human life.

So naturally, when your head hits the pillow, you will start worrying about how your boss criticized you this afternoon;

or what your spouse complained about over dinner; or—yes—whether you're going to have enough money to send your kids to a good university *and* take care of your parents *and* buy that pricey dress with the nice flower print that you saw in the store window on the way to work this morning.

When the worries start to fill your head, *fight them.* Push them out of your mind and very purposely, and consciously turn your thoughts to the good things that you did today.

If you think about it, worrying is mostly worrying about what came out of your bad seeds today—and when you get upset or thrown off balance by what came out of your bad seeds today, you're just very likely to plant *more* bad seeds. So fight your mind, make it think about the *good* you've done today.

Michael:
Our second suggestion for toning up your Coffee Meditation has to do with expiration dates!

2) Be happy about good things you did a long time ago

So okay, we told you that when you do the Four Steps you should help out this other person once a week for an hour, at a neutral space such as a local coffee shop. But what if you took that person out on Friday, and now it's Monday, and you've already been doing Coffee Meditation on the happy details of your meeting for two days already, and it's getting a little repetitive?

Or what if you got busy and *didn't* take them out this week?

Well now that's a big mistake, and if you keep that up you will definitely never get on track to make any kind of progress in your life. Skipping a week of helping your Karmic Partner is just another way of saying that you don't really believe in this system, and you're not serious about changing your life.

I mean, you rarely skip breakfast, because you *believe* in it, right? You believe breakfast is why you're not hungry after breakfast, and that's why you're committed to eating it! (By the way, if you really think about the Branches In The Wind, you might come to an amazing new understanding of that breakfast—but you figure this out on your own.)

Anyway, sometimes we put our head down on the pillow and we just have trouble thinking of anything amazing that we've done for someone else, in the last few days. If this happens to you, then there's a very easy and powerful contemplation that you can do instead.

Make a little challenge to yourself that you will think of the biggest help you have ever given to someone else, in your whole life, about the thing you are doing your Four Steps for. That is—if you are doing the Four Steps to increase your income to where you can both save *and* spend bigtime—then think back on your life and try to remember the times that you really helped out someone else who needed money.

Now to really appreciate this form of Coffee Meditation, you have to realize that mental seeds have no expiration date. I mean, if you go to the grocery store to buy a can of mushrooms, then you should look at the expiration date on the can, to make sure the mushrooms haven't gone bad.

But mental seeds aren't like that. Once they get imbedded in the subconscious mind, they just stay like that—fresh and ready to grow strong—for as long as it takes for them to split open and send forth their little sprouts into your life. *There's no expiration date on a sweet seed that you've planted.*

So we know that you have piles of old good seeds waiting to open, and we know that thinking about them—enjoying how you helped your cousin make the rent payment on their apartment six years ago, when they were changing jobs and didn't have enough money—is how you water those seeds, and get them to open.

So without any sense of pride or self-importance, when you put your head down on your pillow, go back in your life and think about all the times, even years ago, when you helped someone financially. And by the way, if your goal is something like finding a partner or getting healthy again, then you can do your Coffee Meditation about times in your life when you brought comfort to a lonely person; or to someone who was very sick.

Eric:
That sounds great, Michael, but what if that old seed *isn't* still in our mind? I mean, how do we know it hasn't opened already?

Michael:
Well, for one thing (as we've said already) if all the good seeds you've ever planted in your life in the past—even just by accident, before you knew about seeds at all—had opened, then you would *already* be a very rich person!

But more importantly, there's a cool trick about good seeds. *When you are happy about a good seed you've planted in the past—even if that seed has already opened—then you plant **new** good seeds, just by being happy about it!*

That is, doing your Coffee Meditation every night doesn't just water the seeds that are already there in your mind—the

Coffee Meditation *itself* always plants *new* seeds: the seeds you make just by being happy about goodness in the world, which are very strong seeds indeed.

Eric:
And that brings us to another way of boosting your Coffee Meditation to a whole new level. That is, these seeds of being happy about goodness spreading in the world are themselves very powerful and easy to plant.

3) Be happy about good seeds you've seen other people plant

That is, when you lay your head down on your pillow, you have the option of being happy about the seeds you've seen *other* people plant today, or back at any point in your life up to now. This happiness in the good seeds that other people have planted works to plant new good seeds in your own mind.

And what's cool is that the ancient books of wisdom in China say that—the more powerful that other person's seeds are—the more powerful the seeds you plant when you are happy about the seeds *they've* planted. These books even give a specific "interest rate" on this happiness investment!

That is, if someone we know has saved a family member or friend from a major and very embarrassing bankruptcy, for example, and thereby planted thousands of good seeds; then we can get 10% of the number of those good seeds for ourselves— new seeds—just by doing some good Coffee Meditations about the wonderful thing they have done.

In this case, it's really smart for us to dedicate our Coffee Meditation time—2 or 3 times a week—to thinking about *the very best and kindest* things we've seen *other* people do. This is a

178 | CHINA LOVE YOU

great way of piling up good seeds in your mind; and as you can guess, it makes you a really happy person too.

That is, instead of going to bed with grumpy, worried thoughts about your life, then you go to bed with fresh, inspired thoughts of appreciation. These thoughts circle around in your mind all night; you sleep well, and wake up happy.

Michael:
Alright, those are three great suggestions for being a super successful, and super happy person. But there's one more variation on Coffee Meditation which is the Granddaddy of them all.

4) Be happy that you are finally using a system that really works,   and which also makes you a good example for everyone you know

I mean, it's really important for us to keep looking at the bigger picture, at the bigger thing going on here. We have to ask ourselves the question: What will happen in our country, and what will happen in our world, if people start using the Four Coffee Shop Steps to get enough money to take care of children, parents, and themselves too?

What will happen if everyone makes their money by *giving*, and not by *taking*?

And that's what we've been saying all along—it's even what we chose for part of the title of this book. If everyone starts using this ancient wisdom of China, this Four-Step method, then *everyone* will have more than enough money. People will start to understand that competition for money and resources is just old-fashioned, something that never did work very well —like riding a horse to work instead of taking a car, or travelling from China to America on a sailing boat instead of a jet plane.

And then in our lifetimes we will see the Death of Global Competition. A world where *everyone* in *every country* has more than enough, to send their children to the very best university; to provide their parents with a very happy and comfortable retirement; and at the same time get the house and car and clothes that will make their own life, and their own spouse's life, happy and fun.

So when we lay our head down on our pillow and drop into that Coffee Meditation on the good things we did this week, or ten years ago, or saw somebody else do, then we need to throw in the biggest Coffee Meditation of them all:

I have changed the way I live my life.
Instead of taking to get what I want,
*I am **giving** to get what I want,*
*And **it works a lot better than taking.***

This new way of living
*Is going to make me **very** successful,*
And then people will start to copy
My example.

And then others
Will copy their example,
*Until **everyone** is successful.*

And so I am the virus
Which is going to make the whole world happy.
*Now **that's** something to be happy about!*

41
Let's Be Both,
Together

Eric:

That last kind of Coffee Meditation, the strongest kind of all, is sometimes called "Infinite Meditation" in the ancient books. And that's because—in time—our good thoughts and actions ripple out to touch an infinite number of people. There's no need to say how powerful a seed is planted, when we try to touch and help this many people.

Alright then, it's time to complete this journey, and solve the last of our World Choices, the sixth. Should we try to live more simply, and be successful inside; or should we focus on the outside, and build up the security of our family, and the success of our country?

Which goal is more important? Inside happiness, or outside happiness?

Well you know the answer by now. There's simply no need to choose between the two. We can go back to the Diamond Cutter Sutra itself; to where Subhuti asks his three questions of the Buddha:

How should we live?
What should we do?
Where should we keep our focus?

We started with the last of these. So if you've read this book and thought about it carefully, and someone comes up to you and asks, "Where should we keep our focus?" then you should answer: "Keep your focus on emptiness!"

Almost for sure, this is going to get you a confused look from the other person. But you have to keep your cool and say, "Well now hold up your first finger."

And they will.

And then say, "Point to something in this room that *isn't* coming from a seed in your mind—from something you did to somebody last week, or last month." (If they *haven't* read this book, then you might have to explain to them how seeds are planted, and how those seeds open into everything and everybody we ever see in our life.)

Of course then they won't be able to point to anything. Pop them a smile and say "*That's* emptiness!" Nothing more difficult or mystical than that.

And the *fact* that everything is empty means there's *room* for seeds to project the pictures that pop out of them when they split open.

Michael:
Now the next question was, "What should we do?" We were trying to figure out whether we should concentrate on the needs of the group, or the rights of the individual.

And what we found out is that there is always a third choice: an Option 3. If we understand how the world really works—if we understand it is coming from our own seeds—then we can create solutions which satisfy the needs of the group *and* honor the rights of the individual. We can make both the group and the individual happy—ultimately happy and successful.

Which brings us finally to the first question: How should we live? Is the goal of our life to find inner peace and fulfillment, or is the goal of our life to build an outer society which is prosperous and harmonious?

Eric:
And yes, the answer is that we no longer need to choose between the two. As you Americans say, we can have our cake and eat it too: We can live by the American ideal, and live by the Chinese ideal at the same time.

That's the whole point of this book. If we take advantage of the ancient wisdom of China, the wisdom of the seeds, then as individuals we can find inner peace *and* outer prosperity; and as countries—as the two biggest superpowers of the world right now—we can come to this same kind of harmony, inside our own countries and between our two countries.

Again, this is because—with seeds—we can all evolve beyond the outdated model of personal and global competition. Competition always involves mistrust, tension, and the intention to outdo—to harm, in effect—the other side.

In this new system, we think beyond the way the world has thought for tens of thousands of years. We see that *when we give*, we plant seeds for our own future prosperity—and we realize that *this is the only way to prosperity*.

When we *take*, we are only using up the old seeds we planted by *giving*. When we *give*, we no longer need to *take*, because the things we want will just come to us, more than we ever wanted or imagined we could have, as the seeds open.

So we can see, ahead of us, a world where China and America can lead the planet to a place where *every* country has more than they ever dreamed of, and where there is no longer any reason for competition or conflict.

And the *way* that we come to this New World is by this greater knowledge, and this greater sharing between us. When you achieve your outer prosperity *by sharing with each other*, then automatically each of us—no matter where we live—becomes peaceful and joyful on the inside. A happy path to happiness.

So it's no longer a question of whether we should be successful on the outside, or successful on the inside.

Let's be both, together.

184 | CHINA LOVE YOU

Afterword

Eric:

Michael and I have our own version of a favorite story from the Silk Road days, when China and the West were connected by a camel road for almost two thousand years. We thought we'd just put it here at the end as dessert, to give you more emptiness—one more way to use emptiness in your own life. Because maybe you'd like to own a nice car; maybe everybody would.

A Story of the Silk Road
or: *Where a Good Car Comes From*

More than two thousand years ago, a young man named Alexander—just 20 years old—set out from his home in Greece with an army of 50,000 men. He marched east and conquered many of the great nations of his time, defeating some say armies of millions of soldiers.

In time Alexander and his men came to the border of India, fighting all the way. But here they stood against an army with hundreds of elephants trained to kill, and the young man was badly wounded. His troops rebelled, and demanded that he turn around, and take them home. "Besides, we are close now to the edge of the world," they said; "perhaps we will fall off!"

So he started back, and died on the road. But he left behind generals, to rule the lands he had conquered. Some of these became the Kings of Bactria; and among the greatest of them all was Menander, who lived two centuries after Alexander. The Indians heard his name as "Milinda."

Now in ancient times, kings would seek out the wisest subjects of their realm, and sit down and talk with them, to get advice on how to run the country. Alexander himself was a student of Aristotle; and Aristotle was a student of Plato; and Plato was a student of Socrates.

From these three sages—Socrates, Plato, and Aristotle—came many of the ideas that created western civilization, the culture of Europe and the Americas: government, science, philosophy.

King Milinda heard there was a wise man in his kingdom, a Buddhist monk named Nagasena, who lived in the mountains. And he went up to ask for ideas.

"May I ask your name?" said the King.

"My name is Nagasena, but Your Highness should understand that there is no Nagasena—and that's why I'm Nagasena!" said the monk, with a sly smile.

Now there were 500 Yonaka soldiers on hand, to protect the King. And of course everybody knows that "Yonaka" is the ancient Indian word for "Greek."[1] The King asked his Yonakas to listen, and bear witness, as he questioned Nagasena.

"If there is no Nagasena, then it must be that there is no King Milinda. Am I right?"

"Right you are," replied Nagasena.

"Well if there's no Milinda, then who is it that helps the people of this country?

---

[1] More specifically, the ancient Sanskrit word "Yonaka" comes from "Ionian," one of the four major tribes of the early Greeks.

"Who are the people that I help? Who is it, in your system, that does good? Who meditates? Who reaches the goal of a human life?"

Nagasena said nothing, not yet, and simply gazed at the King. And so the King said more:

"And who is it that kills a person? Who is it that steals? Who takes another person's wife or husband; who is it that lies?

"If Nagasena is not Nagasena, and if Milinda is not Milinda, then right is not right, and wrong is not wrong.

"And then, in your system, nothing comes back to those who hurt others; and nothing comes back to those who help others."

Nagasena said nothing still, and the King perhaps became impatient, seeking to understand.

"Nagasena, are you saying that your head is not Nagasena?"

The monk answered at last: "No, my head alone is not me, not Nagasena."

"Well then are your arms Nagasena, or are your legs Nagasena, or are your chest and your back Nagasena?"

And to each of these Nagasena said, "No."

And so the King said the obvious: "Are all the parts of you together—your head and arms and legs and chest and back; are all of these together Nagasena?"

Nagasena said, "No."

The King was quiet for a while, and then asked, "Well then, is there something outside of all those parts that is Nagasena?"

Nagasena shook his head.

Milinda looked over to his 500 soldiers, and said, "It seems that this monk has no idea what he is talking about." (And the Yonaka guards snickered in agreement.)

Suddenly the monk said, "I'm sorry to hear that your mind is so disturbed."

"My mind is not disturbed!"

"But it is. I think it's because your feet hurt!"

The King looks at Milinda like he's crazy, and says, "Why do you think my feet hurt? My feet don't hurt!"

"Well that's amazing," says Nagasena, "because if I had walked all the way up this mountain, my feet would hurt for sure."

"But I didn't walk," says the King. "They drove me here, on my chariot!"

"What chariot?"

"*My chariot!*" roars the King.

Nagasena looks confused. "What chariot are you talking about, Sire? The chariot that is the four wheels, by themselves?" (At this point, some of the sharper Yonaka guards begin chuckling to themselves, because they can see where this is going.)

"No, no. The four wheels are not the chariot, by themselves!"

"Oh, so you're talking about the chariot that's the seat of the chariot, right?"

"No, no, you fool!" yells the King. "The seat alone is not the chariot—you can't ride one wooden board up this blasted mountain!"

"So which chariot are you talking about?" asks Nagasena innocently. "Is it all those parts of a chariot, laid out on the ground, in one big pile?"

"No, no," the King shakes his head. "You can't stand on all those parts in a pile, and expect to get up a mountain like this!"

"Well," says Nagasena, "then is it *all the parts put together*, into a chariot, that you rode up this mountain to see me?"

"Yes, sure," says the King.

"Okay. So if you took all these parts, and put them together, and showed them to somebody who never saw a chariot before, would *they* see a chariot?"

"Yes," says the King. "I mean, they may not *recognize* it as a chariot, but they would be looking at a chariot."

"Can you *look* at a chariot and not *see* a chariot? Can you not *recognize* it as a chariot?"

"Sure," says the King. "You can look at a chariot and not *see* a chariot, if you have no idea what a chariot is."

"And how do you recognize something as a chariot, when you look at a chariot?"

"I don't know. Maybe when you're young, a chariot passes you in the street, and you ask your Mom what it is, and she says, 'That's a chariot,' and then after that you recognize one whenever you see one."

"And does a dog see the chariot as a chariot?" (Yonaka guards are all shaking their heads.)

"No, I don't think so. I mean they *look* at a chariot, but maybe they don't *see* it as a chariot. Maybe they see it as something big and dangerous, like a lion."

"So can we say that there's no chariot coming from the chariot's side?"

"Why do you say that?"

"Because if the chariot was coming from the chariot's side, then it would look like a chariot to the dog."

King Milinda thought for a moment. "Okay, that makes sense. If the chariot was coming from its own side, then it would look like a chariot to the dog; but it looks like maybe a lion to the dog. So a chariot can't be coming from its own side."

"So when you see a chariot," said Nagasena, "could it be coming from *your* side?"

"I guess so," said the King. "But how is that?"

"Well that depends," said Nagasena. "How do you feel about the chariot? Do you like it, or not?"

"I like it!" said the King. "I'd sure rather ride up here in a chariot than walk!" (Yonaka guards with sore feet nod to each other.)

"Okay then," said Nagasena. "You were just talking to me about good and bad: good people do good things; good people meditate; good people reach the goal of a human life. And then bad people hurt other people.

"And *if there is a Nagasena,* then when he does good things, good things come back to him; and when he does bad things, then bad things come back to him, right?"

"Right," said King Milinda.

"So if you have a good thing, like a chariot, did it come from doing something good, or doing something bad?"

"Well it must have come from doing something good."

"But *how* does it come back to you?" asked Nagasena.

The King shrugged. "Well to tell you the truth, I never really thought about it. I mean people talk about karma: When you do something bad to somebody, something bad happens to you—the same with good stuff. I'm not really sure *how* it all works."

"Well then," said Nagasena. "Suppose your friend has to go visit his Mom, but she lives far away. He tells you he's got to take a few days off to walk to his Mom's house, but you offer to loan him your horse."

"Okay," said the King, "that sounds reasonable."

"And suppose that—as you make the arrangements to get your horse to him—you hear the words you say, and you see the letters you send. And suppose these sounds and these shapes make an impression on your mind."

"Alright, I can imagine that. Those are the impressions that help me remember later where I sent my horse, and who took it, and for how long."

"Exactly. And now suppose those impressions create little seeds in your mind, and those seeds sit in your mind for a few weeks, or a few months. And suppose that when these little seeds open, inside your mind, little pictures come out of them."

"What kind of pictures?" said the King.

"Well, since you were helping somebody get a ride, suppose the little pictures are pictures of things to ride! Suppose pictures of a *chariot* come out of the seeds in your mind!"

"I can imagine that," said the King.

"And now imagine that all the parts of a chariot, even when they're put together, are *nothing from their own side*: suppose *they're so nothing from their own side* that a human can see them as a chariot, and a dog at the same time can see them as a loud and frightening animal."

The King turned his head to the side and looked off into the distance and said, "Well, when you say it that way, that's exactly what's happening. The person looks at the parts of the chariot and their mind glues those parts together into a chariot. And when the dog looks at the same parts, then *their* mind glues them together into something dangerous, like a lion."

"Exactly," said Nagasena. "So if that's what's really happening, and you *like* your chariot, because you don't want to walk up mountains on your own two feet, then *how can you keep your chariot going?*"

The King frowned, and then his face brightened. "Well then, I would have to *plant more seeds* to see chariots. I would *have to give more people rides in my chariot.*"

"That's it!" exclaimed Nagasena, and he stood up from his seat, and walked outside to the chariot. And King Milinda gave him a ride down to town to buy some rice, and the 500 guards from Greece cheered the wise King, and his wise companion. Because only a King who never came from his own side could ride in a chariot that didn't come from its own side with an advisor who didn't come from his own side. (That's why Nagasena said there was no Nagasena, to start the whole conversation! And that's what *emptiness* means—and it doesn't mean anything else.

People who heard this conversation wrote it down as a book, and called the book "The Questions of Milinda." Over the centuries, the book made its way up along the Silk Road, to China, where it was translated into Chinese; part of a great labor of translation that took hundred of years, all the way up to our friend, the unstoppable traveler Xuanzang.

The book connects us all, all the world, along the New Silk Road: it connects our East and our West, the great ideas of ancient Asia and the Greek thinkers who got Western civilization started.

The treasure of ancient books that survive in present-day China, tens of thousands of manuscripts in languages such as Tibetan and Chinese, is one of the greatest resources in the modern world. We can easily see how this wisdom can contribute to the death of global competition, and a new era of peace and prosperity.

Because you can't have a car, if you don't give people rides.

About the Authors

GESHE MICHAEL ROACH is an honors graduate of Princeton University and has received the Presidential Scholar Medallion from the President of the United States at the White House. He is the first westerner in the 600-year history of Sera Mey Tibetan Monastic University to be awarded the degree of Geshe, or "Master of Philosophy." Michael is the founder of the Asian Classics Input Project, which has digitally preserved thousands of ancient Asian books by training and equipping poor people in many countries during the past 30 years. To pay for this work he helped found Andin International Diamond Corporation of New York, which reached US$250 million in sales and was sold to super-investor Warren Buffett in 2009. The Diamond Cutter, his international business bestseller, tells the story of how he used ancient Asian principles for success; and he has founded the Diamond Cutter Management Training Institute for spreading this message to over 20,000 people each year, in more than 20 countries of the world.

DR. ERIC WU was born in China and graduated in both western and traditional Chinese medicine. He then worked in the Chinese national banking system, before founding his own management training company, called Guang Yao ("Light on Life") Cultural & Educational Institute, of Beijing and Xi'an, China. This firm seeks to extract the essence of Chinese traditional culture and to bring it to the modern world, based on a concept Dr. Wu calls "The Power of Seeds." This system has proven very effective in increasing business profitability and sustainable corporate development; and has been applied as well in the fields of addiction treatment; youth education; and the enhancement of the quality of life for senior citizens. In recent years, Eric has also founded advanced medical research facilities which are making significant progress in finding cures for cancer, heart disease, and diabetes. He is a popular speaker worldwide, and has developed innovative educational programs for children throughout China. Eric has a deep interest in the preservation of Chinese traditional culture, and through his Golden Silk Road Foundation has sponsored many projects such as the Silk Road Classics Online Library, which offers thousands of manuscripts from the languages of the ancient silk road, free of charge.

RESOURCES FOR LEARNING MORE

Websites

For business and success seminars by Geshe Michael Roach worldwide, see the Diamond Cutter Management Institute website at *DiamondCutterInstitute.com*.

For more information about the ancient spiritual classics of Asia, see the Knowledge Base website at *TheKnowledgeBase.com*.

For programs by Dr. Eric Wu, especially in China and in the Chinese language, see the Guang Yao Traditional Chinese Culture Center website at *GYDHP.com*.

Other books by Geshe Michael Roach

If you want to start a business, or for reaching financial freedom:
> Read *The Diamond Cutter: The Buddha on Managing Your Business & Your Life*

If you're managing a business or a group or part of a company:
> Read *Karmic Management: What Goes Around Comes Around, In Your Business & Your Life*

If you want better health, more energy, and to feel young:
> Read *How Yoga Works* (even if you don't do yoga!)

If you want a better relationship, or to find a partner:
> Read *The Karma of Love: 100 Answers for Your Relationship*

If you want to go deeper into your spiritual life:
> Read *The Garden: A Parable*

Letters for Paul

Letters for Paul

Anu Kumar

MapinLit
AN IMPRINT OF
MAPIN PUBLISHING

For
Krishna Raj
and
Shama Futehally....
They made it possible.

First published in India in 2006 by
MapinLit
An Imprint of
Mapin Publishing

Mapin Publishing Pvt. Ltd.
31 Somnath Road, Usmanpura
Ahmedabad 380013 India
T: 91-79-2755 1833 / 2755 1793 • F: 2755 0955
E: mapin@mapinpub.com • www.mapinpub.com

Text © Anu Kumar
Front Jacket Illustration by Geetha Kekobad
Author Photograph © Ajay Kumar

ISBN: 81-88204-67-6 (Mapin)
ISBN: 1-890206-42-3 (Grantha)

Designed by Janki Sutaria / Mapin Design Studio
Printed in India

Contents

A BAD BEGINNING

L ong before I became aware of Newton's third law, it was Thamma, my grandmother, who told me that action could have many ramifications. Every action or deed, Thamma believed, led into another action or deed, not necessarily into Newtonian opposite or equal reactions.

The smell is all I remember of Cuttack that first night. The night that lay like a thick compress over sleeping houses and the car purring with relief as it eased away from the station road onto the Cantonment Road. The whiff appeared, faint at first, of damp earth, trapped water, leaves rolled up and dying, and overlaid soon, by another smell, easily placeable. Of things foetid and best flushed away, not left scattered, to rot on their own beside a stale river.

We heard the driver's murmured apologies, the squeal of glass as he cranked the window up. "No problem, the Circuit House is very near now." It was obvious he had served up this explanation before, to other important government officers and their families he had received at the railway station. We listened to him, our noses crinkled, "Two crossings only, then the Circuit House. So sorry about this."

The smell, wrapped up in spanking-clean sunshine, caught me the next morning within minutes of my stepping out into the balcony. It made its way forward, from over the blue expanse of the river Mahanadi, with the same hesitation of the night before. A quarter of a century ago, in 1956, Pandit Nehru had inaugurated the world's largest earthen dam on this river, but now the river lay somnolent, like the buffaloes that dotted its even blue surface. A breeze from somewhere toyed with the leaf-fronds hanging loose from tall heavy-with-fruit palm trees. When the breeze tired and fell on its knees on the low sandbanks, the smell rushed in, in the manner of an over-effusive neighbour. It spread itself everywhere, at short notice. And inching towards the balcony's rails, I only had to look down to see the smell for the first time. Belonging to men in variously designed lungis, who trundled out or into the Circuit House backyard, holding on to used vegetable oil tins. And to those who sat on their haunches, examining the ground. They waited, others took their time, making their own measured decisions. The odour thickened, the blue face of the river shivered and broke away; as I did too. I tore away from the balcony, towards the two french windows in the front of the house.

The french windows held back a verandah but were always kept tightly closed. Mohanty, the orderly, had convinced Ma that this was in everyone's best interests. There had been, to the best of his knowledge, two recent occasions when naughty children had thrown themselves over the verandah, impairing themselves for life. The closed windows overlooked the driveway, followed it all the way to the Cantonment Road. It was here I took to sitting in the afternoons, enveloped in musty smelling curtains, waiting for the postman. If I had not decided on this course of action, shifting from the balcony to the windows that is, I would never have witnessed the incident that was to leave a lasting impact on my life.

The postman came anytime between two and two-thirty but that afternoon he was already running late. Inside the curtains, the heat had swelled like a boil around my nose, while the sweat stamped itself over my back and in places I hated it to gather, my armpits and between my thighs.

By the time I first spotted the postman, the old clock in the hall was already at three. The clock had been a present from the chief minister when he came to inaugurate the Circuit House 30 years ago and by now it was too tired, its pendulum moved in an arthritic manner, reluctant to register time. Once every week, Mohanty would wind it up, fetching the gardener's stepladder to reach it. Mohanty set it 35 minutes in advance because it lost five minutes every day and only when the time came for him to wind it up, did the clock actually deign to show the right time.

There were still four days left to go for Mohanty's winding up session. That meant three days had also elapsed since my letter to Paul. Whether he had received it or not depended on the efficiency of the postal services;

but postmen had become considerably slower than they used to be, and they also complained a lot.

This postman, the one I was waiting for, was a persistent complainer. For much of that week, he had been showing us his sack. How heavy it was, with people still sending each other New Year greetings though we were already ten days into the new year. That day, his sack had spread itself over the back seat. His postman's torso was stretched over the front rod, urging his bicycle on, but the fat sack sat tighter than ever, drawing angry glares, impatient horns from those behind. This was the place where the Cantonment Road was at its narrowest. Vendors and shop-owners had freely helped themselves to the road, displaying their wares invitingly and the roadsides were perpetually laden with vehicles – mainly rickshaws – especially towards afternoon. This was the time, when for lack of passengers, rickshaws would pull up in an obedient line behind each other, draw up their shades, like village women hiding behind their veils, and fall forward into a short repose.

The postman would first pedal past the glass-panelled showroom of Das and Das – opticians since 1936, pass the hardware store after it, and then turn right at the Circuit House gate. Sometimes, he would stop by at the opticians' with a letter or two for old Mr. Das who sat at his counter, waiting for him, fingers drumming on wood, ticking off one busy thought after another. A few shutters away from the opticians' was the Murphy Radio shop. When its owner put on the song he always played this time of the day, the postman's delay became a confirmed and inexcusable one.

Come on, here. Come on here, my darling. Oh-h-h Noorie. N- – n-oorie.

Because he played it so many times, putting it on a while after the postman's rounds, I knew every detail of the song. It began with a flood of orchestral music that subsided for the man to take up a plaintive wail, calling for someone called Noorie. When the orchestra flared, then faded away a second time, it was the turn of his ladylove to call for him, in a somewhat faraway voice. *Come on, here. Come on here, my darling.*

But that afternoon the lady never responded, instead, the music stumbled, and broke off with a shriek. The interruption in the song affected the postman in a very strange manner. He shook himself off his bicycle and used it to nudge his way forward into the small crowd, now collecting with rapid ease in front of the hardware store and the garment shops next to it. In the front windows of these other shops were displayed garish sari collections and dress materials, also plain-looking ladies undergarments, puffed up with sharpened pencils. People were always milling around these shops, looking their fill, exchanging notes and comparing sizes.

But this crowd was not the kind that loitered. It didn't even move ahead but seemed to grow in the sudden hush. Like drops of water that coalesce into a puddle before snaking into something bigger, eating into all available floor space. Rickshaw bells tinkled, they waited, before converging to a halt. And the postman, not caring in the least for an anxious girl waiting for him, her nose pressed against a windowpane, was soon lost in the growing bubble of people.

Soon, other rickshaws meandered in; small two-wheelers also nosed in. The crowd took on the quivery look of badly set jelly. In minutes, over the street, balconies that usually held everyday washing, filled over with people, butting and shoving, trying to elbow into the crowd two-three floors below.

The greedy, growing silence provided no answers, instead it spread itself out like an old quilt, and pressed hard against the Circuit House windows. Mohanty rose from the bench where he had tucked himself away for a quick snooze. He took in the scene unfolding outside, realized it merited some looking into, and quickly buttoned up his shirt. Then, like the postman before him, Mohanty too trundled off to find out "kya ho raha hai", rearranging on the way, the towel-sized handkerchief on his shoulder.

In the silence Ma materialized beside me and together we watched Mohanty depart, his white shirt billowing behind like a ship's wind-laden sails. But Ma was upset because Mohanty had not asked for permission, "Ask Mohanty, where does he think he is going?"

Taking a deep breath, I cranked open the old french windows. The heavy afternoon air hit us like an iron plugged in for too long. The silence churned in the cauldron of heat, stirring up inchoate murmurs, half-coherent shouts, before the piercing whistle of a police van siren thrust itself into all this. Seconds later, the van itself appeared in the wake of the siren; it moved jerkily past Mr. Das, who did not join the crowds, but stood crotchety and curious, outside his shop.

Evincing not the least interest in the action unfolding outside, a rickshaw made a sprightly entry through the Circuit House gates. It made with haste for the portico, its two occupants, our ground-floor neighbour Tiwari's two sons, looking set to erupt with an important announcement. They were gesturing frantically with their hands towards the crowds falling away behind them. I tried to look away, but considering the circumstances, it was difficult. Earlier that week, they had refused my request to include me in their game of cricket. You are a girl – had been the unanimous verdict. Even Bhai, my brother, had agreed.

They jumped down from the rickshaw and stood to attention, their faces swelling in degrees to take on a look of terrible importance. Then they spoke, excitement coating every word like icing.

"A woman . . . she was . . . attack-ted . . . ," and they turned to point out the Circuit House walls, beyond which rested the road and the crowds.

"What happened? . . . How?" – the three of us asked the questions simultaneously. Mrs. Tiwari had also appeared, looking elegant in a China silk sari though it was afternoon and no one could possibly be around to see her in it.

The boys stood to attention again, "Someone there . . . attack-ted her . . . "

And then they switched off their broadcast, looking at their mother and then up at the first floor, unwilling for the attention to die away. But the sound of Mohanty returning, panting and sweating profusely, drew all eyes away. Mohanty said nothing the first few minutes, instead his eyes searched for the most important person he could break his news to, but Kennedy's appearance stayed his options. Kennedy lived in the single-storey quarters within the Circuit house compound. He worked in the night shift at the telephone department and slept through the day. The announcement had winged its way into Kennedy's sleep, pushed tentacles into his subconscious. Shaking off sleep, he now tumbled out of the gates, and into the scene of action. He shook Mohanty by the wrist, "Kono hela? What happened?"

Like the boys before him, Mohanty's trembling finger pointed wall-wards. The police were now waving everyone away. Their khaki-clad figures formed a tight circle at the centre, their batons held high in a warning to all trespassers and also in a welcome to more policemen who had appeared in a second van. "A girl going in a rickshaw . . . someone threw acid."

Mrs. Tiwari shrieked, she pushed a corner of her sari into her mouth, gulping back other sounds that remained. Ma stepped away from the railing, but they let Mohanty speak on. "A girl, she was in that rickshaw. And then suddenly, someone came up, just when it was there. . . ."

Once again he pointed towards the rapidly graying, once yellow, walls of the Circuit House. The walls bent over in old age and by the efforts of countless, desperate bladder-heavy passers-by, also tilted closer to listen. "Someone in a cycle . . . who came up, right there. . . . A boy, no one could see who . . . so many of them always moving about like that . . . "

The afternoon air stayed sombre, giving Mohanty a wide berth. "She was screaming. . . her rickshawala didn't first understand. Only when there were shouts all around, and she fell, making a big noise and remained half-in, half-out of the rickshaw, did he fully stop."

Mohanty rubbed his hands over his scrawny, hairy arms, then over his face, "The sari was coming off . . . I saw . . . then her skin also. It was falling away." He scratched his arm harder, making sure we really understood, "Just coming off, from her arms, her chest, . . . leaving her with nothing on, nothing."

Mohanty crossed his arms around himself after he had finished, shuddering at the power of his own description. He was applauded by the sound of muffled giggles. The boys were choking back laughter into the backs of their hands. Mohanty began again, indignant now, "They are saying . . . it was a quarrel." But Mrs. Tiwari, wiping her face with her sari end, was readying herself for departure. She gathered her sons towards herself, rearranged her sari, then waved her hand in an aimless gesture, of withdrawal or wishing away all that had just happened, "All her clothes going off . . . ," she murmured, ". . . just like that, in front of everyone." The afternoon heat had returned and her retreating steps were heavy with the enormity of recent events.

I chose to remain with Ma for a while on the verandah. But I caught Ma's last words as she too turned away from the verandah, drawing Bhai and me away with her. She spoke very softly, her words meant only for herself. "How could it happen . . . how shameful. . . . What is the world coming to?"

Inside, the room lay swaddled in a comforting darkness. The last I saw of the road before Ma shut first the door and then the french windows, one after the other, was the policemen cooling themselves. They blew into their open shirtfronts, or fanned themselves with newspapers picked up from a nearby shop, obviously without paying. Finally, Ma drew the curtains too.

Ma tried hard to restore the day to everyday ordinariness. But I had begun thinking of the letter I had to write Paul. I could not run away from this smelly, horrible place as I had first confided to him I would. I was going to stay put, to find out what really had happened that afternoon. It might upset Paul that I wouldn't miss him so much.

By the time evening came down fully, the road had sorted itself out. I would have preferred it to stay disorganized a while longer. Through a slit in the curtains, I was memorising the way it looked, because Paul had to be told about it. It didn't look the scene of a major crime. Once the police van left and the ambulance followed, the interest folded up. The street settled down to everyday routine, like a dog lying down again in a much-loved, terribly inconvenient place.

The noise, the smells lifted themselves, first in odd bursts. Some people tried to hold on to the excitement. Mr. Das moved his chair back inside his shop. He was scared of being right out in the street and now sat next to the cash counter to keep a watch over everything – especially the cashier with his quicksilver hands counting out money. It was the song that came to life last. The flautist began on a timorous note but soon took to the air in a bold burst of confidence. When the vigilance office siren bellowed out the closing hours, the streetlights also came on. Once the evening gave way to darkness, the insects would emerge, running into the lights and everywhere else, even the eyes.

When we heard Father's official blue Ambassador grumble up the driveway, we arranged ourselves in suitable news-breaking positions – Ma in the lounge-chair in the verandah, Bhai on the balustrade overlooking the stairwell, I lingered by the door.

"A girl was attacked in the streets today," Ma announced. Father only nodded. Being in the police, he must already have been informed of the incident. But Father's response was muffled as he bent down to take off his shoes. "The house will take a few more days. Durgamadhab wants to wait for a few more days before they shift to Calcutta. His niece is getting married . . . "

Whenever he had unwelcome news, Father looked for ways to avoid looking at Ma. "And then it will be his nephew who will want to get married, then a cousin, then his son's thread ceremony – he does not seem to want to leave," Ma completed for him.

My ears closed up at this point. For some time, conversation between my parents had moved along very predictable lines. The administration was still delaying allotting us a house but every second day, Father would keep reassuring Ma, this would happen soon, very soon. Till that happened, we would keep getting in each other's way. Bhai's books and cricket posters were tangled up in mine, as was Ma's shopping pad. My pencil stand stood shoulder to shoulder with Thamma's snuffbox, and Father's night snoring disturbed everyone in equal measure.

Because Ma was upset at Father's inability to push the administration, even the conversation at dinner stood threatened, though Father strongly believed food and conversation did not go well together. At every meal, Father would meditatively munch on every morsel, his eyes closed in an effort to guess what it was he was consuming. But Ma began soon enough, "Why isn't Durgamadhab moving away? He is behaving as if it is his father's house."

Perhaps it was to stop Ma from going on in this vein that Father chose to speak up that night, "You must be careful going out anywhere."

I looked up to see that the straight line that ran parallel between Father's hair-line and his eyebrows had appeared again. The presence at this point in time of Father's line of worry indicated his high tension levels.

"A girl was attacked in the streets today," Father said thoughtfully, repeating like a well-rehearsed lesson, what Ma had only told him a while before. It was a ploy to buy time, he was thinking of what really to say. But by now I could easily tell him more than what Ma had said anyway.

"She wasn't attacked. She was burnt. A man threw acid at her."

Dinner took time out as everyone stopped to stare at me. "How do you know" – Father was looking down at his plate.

"I read up Barrons. It explained in more detail what happens when acid is thrown. It eats away your skin, quickly and silently, so that it doesn't even pain at first and you can even watch it peeling off. Like orange skin and even your skin looks. . . ."

But I was not allowed to complete my explanation, or the other details I had culled from *Barron's Everyday Science Problems Explained*. Ma put the daal hurriedly down on the table and retreated into the kitchen. Father concentrated on arranging the rice into a careful mound at the centre of his plate. He was marshalling his thoughts for my benefit.

"Yes, yes, I know . . . you must be careful . . . "

"Why?" I had to ask. All this while I had done pretty much as I liked. Stomping back from school in Delhi, just as soon as the bell rang; in the afternoons I played cricket with the boys, though I was usually the umpire or the fielder placed somewhere on the edge of the field. And nothing had happened to me to be careful about.

"Anything can happen . . . it is not safe for girls here."

"Why?" I had to insist. *I hated being reminded I was a girl.*

Father looked me straight in the eye, "Why . . . why? You will stop asking your whys once you know why?"

Then he spoke quickly, as if he was explaining the obvious, "That girl, she was going back home from college. Someone who knew which road she took everyday, must have followed her. He knew when he could throw the acid at her and then run away. It could have been anyone, a stranger who had followed her or even a boy she knew."

My lips opened, another question had just suggested itself but the words did a u-turn and stayed in my throat. Father went on, "There is too much crime everywhere. Not just robberies and dacoities, but worse. And women are at even more risk. Girls your age, especially."

He didn't say anything more and I still didn't have any answers. The window looking outside had three bars, straight, black and horizontal, holding back the dark terrors of the night. The coconut fronds grazed past the balcony as the wind pulled them by the ear and waved at my discomfiture. And far away in the river, a boat sailed home unconcernedly, its lights flashing a rare orange warmth. On the other side, the road was emptied of all the home going crowds. The thelawalas selling bread and omelette or potato and onion fry, with sticks of chilly standing out like a sore warning, had dimmed their gas stoves, waiting for night to take over. In the kitchen, pots, pans, plates and spoons huddled together in an untidy heap. For the rest of the night, they would cower close to ward off the darkness. I felt alone, the weight of Father's words seeped in through every pore of my skin. It coalesced into a giant snowball of fear and dread, in a region somewhere around the chest, immovable.

Words briefly appeared but soon took on a jumbled-up and fuzzy appearance and I knew I no longer wanted to ask Father the question that continued to bother me, "Why had they poured acid on that girl?" Maybe it was I who didn't understand.

I could tell what Father would say anyway. "It's because she was a girl. Must have done something . . . who knows." And his statement would remain hanging in the air, and still have that air of finality that brooks no further questions.

What was it about being a girl that invited trouble?

I stood before the mirror and it showed me nothing that could tell me apart from a boy, except for those, those big, heavy lumps on the chest. Of late, they had begun heaving each time I breathed with great force, and especially if I jumped hard. I hated them because there was very little I could do with and about them. They hung out in such a vestigial unnecessary way, marking out my status to everyone. A girl, *a girl.*

The weight of fear that Father's warnings had added on sat heavily inside me; it jolted at times, shifted slightly, but did not dissipate. Instead, it nudged the memory, and I remembered the first time I felt pain *there* – a sharp, stabbing pain that I traced to that dark brown circle with two strands of hair trailing out, somewhere to the left of the chest. I kept touching it, hoping to soothe the pain away, but it throbbed with a greater vengeance. In school, the pain rose to a throb, beating a loud tattoo inside my chest. Very near tears, thinking I was having a heart attack, I excused myself to go to the bathroom.

In the bathroom, I pulled the shirt out of the waistband of my skirt, then the slip that I had to wear below it. Gently, slowly, I kept reminding myself. Then I looked down anxiously, a prayer on my lips. But the pain was located somewhat higher and to lift the shirt higher, my other hand, clamped tight over the nose, was forced to come into use. The smell of urine, phenyle, and rotten eggs swamped me like a tidal wave. I touched myself gingerly, poking and prodding at the place that appeared to be the epicentre of pain, but found nothing unusual. It clearly wasn't a heart attack but my worries only grew. It had to be something else for which neither I nor Barrons had a name yet, and that was scarier.

Once I was home, I broke the news to Ma gently. "I think I have to be admitted to the hospital . . . ," I began but the pain rose like a sob in my throat and broke into tears. To my horror, I was crying, holding a hand to my chest, where the pain was now spreading in circles deep inside me. Ma yanked my hand away and I heard her impatient snap in my ears, "Don't touch that part, ever."

"But it hurts. . . ." I was wondering when someone would understand.

"It will. It's your breasts, they have to emerge sometime now." Ma didn't take long to make her diagnosis.

My tears disappeared, not with relief, but terror, I had never come across this word before.

Ma was pointing to something on her chest. "Breasts – what grow here." And I saw the protuberances I had always overlooked before, sheathed in a blouse, safety-pinned with a grim finality.

It was an embarrassing sight; I dragged my eyes away. All I could think of and said was, "So big . . . "

Ma took it kindly and willingly elaborated. "You will also have them . . . all girls do. But be careful, don't keep touching it, so they grow alarmingly big. And don't let boys touch it. . . ."

"Why should boys want to touch it?"

"Boys do bad things – they like touching such things."

There were a lot of things boys did that I would have given anything to do. But I was fast learning that boys did other things I didn't know much about. And my parents for lack of any explanation were only issuing timely warnings. Remain on the safe side, and avoid trouble at all costs. Look out for boys because they make it unsafe for girls to move around freely in places. It was always possible that if they didn't like you, they could simply throw acid all over you and spoil your life forever. While nothing much would ever happen to them.

The one person who had an explanation for everything turned up later that evening. Mehta Uncle dropped in on us as he took his post-prandial constitutional. Right till the end before he lost both his legs in the accident, he kept himself fit and athletic. Father did not do so much exercise. In his spare time, he rearranged the old photos in his albums; sometimes he did the furniture too.

Bones is here, Father announced. Mehta Uncle roved around the room, stopping by every chair, refusing to sit on any one. It was his way of drawing us, one by one, into the front room. He moved on to his next act only when Ma too had appeared, last of all. He unrolled the sheet of paper he had been carrying around like a baton, under his armpit.

"The evening Oriya paper is full of it," he announced, "It's to do with the Naxalites. Their revenge on the victim's grandfather."

Father took the chair farthest from Mehta Uncle. If precedents were anything to go by, any conversation between them would soon develop into an argument. From there, it would progress into a shouting match, so by now they had learnt to keep the distance between themselves. Ma's eyes moved quickly from one face to the other, her face unchanging in expression. Mehta Uncle pushed across the paper and I peered over Father's shoulder to see. There was a photo of a girl, and an article obviously about her took up the entire front page. I couldn't read it because it was in Oriya, the second language I was now forced to learn in my new school, but I had a careful look at the girl anyway. It had to be her, before she was eaten away by the acid.

I had to commit her to memory as well, to inform Paul about her.

The photo was badly smudged, speckled black and white. And the girl wore spectacles – thick-lensed, black-framed grandfather-like ones – that ate up most of her eyes and the top half of her face. She had a perfectly round face, a mouth like a cricket bat, beginning with a thin line, before shaping itself into the broader contours of a bat. And she must have had long hair for two plaits drooped snakelike downwards from behind her ears.

Dear Paul

There has been lot of excitement in Cuttack, unlike in Delhi. Mehta Uncle came to meet us yesterday. He looked very serious because of yesterday's events. Someone threw acid on a girl just as she passed by our house. Very likely it was a boy she knew, but we are still to establish the exact facts.

The story was in the Oriya papers but Mehta Uncle asked me to give him my report of the incident. I had pushed my way in through the crowd because for a long while no one seemed to know what to do. I could hear her crying because it must hurt – all that acid burning into her, making her skin fall off like a sari being unwrapped, peel after peel from her body.

Everyone was moving forward, pushing me away. Then I saw a man standing in a corner. He wasn't trying to move closer, only just standing there. As if he was playing statue with someone. But something made me look at him. He was thin and tall and there was a cycle next to him. He wore a check shirt and brown pair of flare pants. And one of his pockets bulged funnily. I think he had hidden away the acid bottle there.

I conveyed my suspicions and gave a full description of the man to Mehta Uncle. He said it would be passed onto all the police stations. I would have caught the man on my own but he got a bit warned by my stares or maybe he had friends around who told him I was around.

Because he suddenly sprang on his bike and raced madly away. Mehta uncle was really impressed. He clapped me on the back, and said he would tell everyone, my principal and teachers about it.

Mehta Uncle believes it is those same men he was fighting against in Bengal – Naxalites. They are young men who are fighting against the rich, evil men in the villages. Mehta Uncle said that the girl was killed because old differences among them had to be sorted out. It scared mother for she said it only means that the Naxalites are now moving into other areas to create trouble.

Father got angry as usual. He said putting up silly reasons to explain a crime was just a way of glossing over police failures. Then he gave a whole lot of statistics. Of dacoities and thefts and the way women also were affected. He said law and order in the town was gone, finished, ekdum khatam – because no one was letting the police do its work. Uncle listened to him and then he also got very angry and they began their usual fighting-shieting . . .

When they fought, it only confused me more. They blamed the police, the landlords, the unemployed graduates and students, the refugees, the deprived farmers, everyone they could think of. Because when Father said something, Uncle had to say the opposite.

I will keep you up-to-date. Father and Mehta Uncle are not on talking terms but I heard Ma asking him to dinner. You write soon or else I too shall fight with you.

With my best regards,
A Chatterji

I was pleased with the letter. And I had also managed to provide as objective an account of events as possible by not taking either Father's side or Mehta Uncle's. Other details I could not put in because inland letters cost 35-paise each and besides offered only three small sides of blue paper to write on.

WET PAINT

In the English papers, the late edition that arrived towards late afternoon from Calcutta, sometime after my return from school, I saw the same news that Mehta uncle's Oriya paper had front-paged in detail. Only it was hidden in one of the inside pages, mixed with news of other states and there was no photograph.

January 21, Cuttack

19-year old Samarpita Mishra who was grievously injured by unscrupulous persons still lies battling for life in a city hospital. Police have launched a massive manhunt for the attacker, but it is still not clear whether there was only one person involved or if it was a larger conspiracy.

Mishra is a student of the prestigious Ravenshaw College in Cuttack and the granddaughter of the well-known Oriya novelist, Sacchidananda Mishra, who under the penname "Bhaktawar" wrote several novels glorifying the heroes of the Naxalite movement. He had also been in prison for some years in Nadia. The police are not ruling anything out. What looks like a love story gone tragic may have deeper angles and implications, D M Mehta, DIG, Crime Investigation told reporters. According to him, the police also suspect it could be political vendetta.

I read it twice over. It was the first time anyone in my acquaintance had had his name in the papers. But I had to hide the paper away because father would be in a foul mood once he discovered that Mehta Uncle had made it to the papers. But Father, not finding the paper even an hour after its scheduled delivery, co-opted everyone into the hunt for the missing paper. It appeared another hour later, from behind the bathroom mirror, damp and folded the wrong way. My intervention, all with the noblest of intentions, ended up having the opposite effect. Most parts of the Circuit House wore a devastated, disbelieving look following its ignominious subjection to a full-scale search and Father came into an even blacker mood.

Father's mind on the matter was more than made up. He made no secret about what he felt should be the desired course of action. Police forces, and preferably small teams of plainclothes men had to be deployed in the Ravenshaw college campus to probe the love story angle. It could be a jealous rival or even one spurned suitor who had taken revenge on Samarpita. "The papers . . . ," I heard him say to someone on the telephone, "They are all trying to play detective, trying to play the guessing game. Don't they realize that they should let the police do its job? Also such kind of reporting causes immense distress to the family."

Mehta Uncle had a different point of view – he gave full vent to his opinions later that evening. "Chatterji, I need more men . . . my unit is short-staffed. I need them to sniff out the Naxalites. Besides we are expecting more attacks."

Father said Mehta was being paranoid and jumping to conclusions. Besides, he couldn't spare any men because his unit too was over-stretched. He needed them to maintain law and order in the city. "For one crime, we cannot just forget everything else . . . the law and order situation is very bad. And getting worse by the day . . . I have also had to increase the number of guards outside the hospital because she is still to be questioned. And anything – ANYTHING – can happen yet. Who knows? I am sorry, Mehta you just have to do with what you have."

Mehta Uncle was incensed. The newspaper that had given Mehta Uncle so much publicity now became an instrument of threat, he held it close to father's nose and swung it there. "I will have to talk to the home minister."

Father laughed, and a few water drops jerked off his nose and sprayed the paper. Mehta Uncle withdrew it hastily. "You will have to wait until he gets back from Delhi, Bones. He might lose his own seat by the time he gets back."

The hospital where the girl had been rushed after the incident was an unprepossessing white building. Blank-faced windows lined its walls at regular intervals, some had curtains missing, others were closed over and barred giving it that sleepy, tousled look that most overloaded with work, government office buildings have. It stood on the road I took to school every day, a road that never really saw much action. But it underwent a total image make-over, a day after the Calcutta newspapers reported the incident.

Mohanty, riding alongside my rickshaw, drew my attention to the change. It was part of his continual attempts to ease things between us. I had made clear my resentment of him ever since I had known that Mohanty had been deputed by my parents to escort me to school, as times were "unsafe". All my objections had been stonewalled by my parents' silence. "Bhai goes alone. . . . He walks to school. Why can't I walk too?"

The silence was obviously a pre-arranged ploy on my parents' part to ensure I soon tired. But my satyagraha, comprising equal doses of a stiff silence and a formal demeanour, was designed to affront Mohanty, so he had very little chance of announcing to the general public his reasons for accompanying me. I sat in the rickshaw with my head turned firmly away from Mohanty, foreclosing any attempts at familiarity on his part.

But that morning his speedy actions took me by surprise. Our entourage had already run the entire length of the impressively-sized commissioner's bungalow, it had negotiated with ease the other bungalows that came after it, miniature versions of the main one, and we were soon passing the thin stretch of road that contained the hospital. The serenity of routine does lull the senses and so I had only myself to blame. By the time the faint crick that sounded as something in the distance lifted to a distinct creak, then onto a furious whirr, it was too late to chart out a course of action. The bicycle, then Mohanty on it, took shape under my eyes, and I heard and saw him deliver the pronouncement, the various other sounds had only been a prelude to – "See, there the police . . . " I looked to where his finger pointed and saw the road awash with action.

Scores of policemen were spilling out of vans, joining those already outside the hospital. They congregated in short circles like a gaggle of houseflies, dispersing sometimes, returning again after a short while. "An entire contingent of the Orissa Military Police. I know because my policeman friend is there." There was a congratulatory note in Mohanty's voice; he was pleased he had got through to me.

He got off his bike and the rickshawala, under strict instructions never to stray far away from Mr. Mohanty, halted too. Mohanty walked his cycle over to a policeman standing by himself at the gate. I could only see the back of Mohanty's head as he advanced purposefully towards the policeman but from the other man's unctuous smile, it was clear they had more than a nodding acquaintance. Next, Mohanty pushed his hands into his pocket and pulled out his silver-coloured betel leaf box. This he extended towards his policeman friend, while I settled back on my seat as best as I could, knowing the wait could be indefinite. Besides, I grudgingly conceded, it might bring in some more information. So far, I had only Father's and Mehta Uncle's versions of the incident to go by.

But Mohanty had other ideas. As soon as the policeman had popped a paan into his mouth, Mohanty looked back and pointed a finger straight at me. Instantly, everything in me shrivelled, then tightened up, as the policeman subjected me to a thorough stare. His eyes lingered on parts of me I hated.

"DIG's daughter there. We saw the entire business. Sad, very sad."

The policeman mulled over Mohanty's words and pronounced his verdict too, "Sad, yes, sad . . . "

The men chewed together in newfound bonding, then Mohanty leaned forward confidentially, to ask, "Any arrests. There was one cyclist."

The other man looked around, clubbed his hands together and rubbed them as if rubbing a precious secret into an ever-greater shine. He placed his baton between his knees, pulled his trousers over his protesting paunch and said, "No one knows. One may have done it, but there was a conspiracy, a big conshpeeracy . . . they wanted revenge on the girls' family, old family quarrel, I am told."

"Hmm . . . hmm . . . ," Mohanty picked his nose for more questions, then bent forward once again. "It is getting very dangerous this town. Very unsafe for girls. That is why Saar said, go with her."

For the second time in the course of that conversation, Mohanty's finger again pointed towards me. The policeman too turned to look, this time his assessment was more extended. His eyes bulging out of his face bore a greedy resemblance to his paunch. For some seconds I managed to stare back defiantly. But he might as well have been staring at something insubstantial, someone whose stare was not worth responding to. He continued masticating as his gaze dropped below my face to my pinafore stretched carefully over my breasts. I pushed my arms forward, hoping to hide them in some way. But his eyes had moved lower and this time I held in my breath, hoping to look slim. Then he looked away as if further descent was a matter not worth pursuing. He yawned as he answered Mohanty and the words broke his yawn up as they emerged from his thick betel-stained lips, "Haan ... very unsafe. They should not ... be-be-be allowed to go out anywhere ... very dangerous, this town."

Somewhere, in one of the hospital windows, a pair of curtains billowed out like a gaily-welcoming flag. The wind caught in its folds flapped for attention. The wind carried the policeman's next words clearly to me, though he had bent low to speak only to Mohanty, "You know, the matter is more serious. I stand guard outside her door every night."

He paused and looked around to see if he was being overheard, but I was studiously looking away, and far away the curtain still waved, trying its best to disengage itself from the breeze.

"I can tell you this, confidential information ... one by one everything about her is dying. Falling off, just like that."

He patted himself with relief on the stomach, happy now that it no longer had to store this confidential information.

"One eye has gone." He said again, "It simply fell away, when the nurse came to clean in the morning."

He must have seen the disbelief too on Mohanty's face for he insisted, "It was a real eye, not a stone or a glass eye, I tell you. We could still see the veins dangling loosely where it had pulled itself away from her face."

"Tomorrow, you will see, something else will have gone – her liver or her heart." He shook his head as the inevitability of the end proposed itself, "Sad case, very sad . . . doctors have little hope."

He paused and began again, only to repeat an earlier pronouncement, "She's gone blind now . . . see one eye gone."

Of course he was lying, I knew then he was. She had one eye still left, so she couldn't be blind. But he wasn't finished yet.

"I tell you, I am telling you . . . tomorrow, you come here. And I will tell you this. . . ." Red betel stains jerked out as punctuation marks and landed on the road, not far away from Mohanty, "I tell you this – her kidney will fail, bladder-wladder too, everything . . . like her heart . . . "

The policeman looked set to take us through every part of the human anatomy. Maybe like some parents, he taught his children biology in his off-duty hours. But it was getting late. I stamped hard on the thin aluminum floor of the rickshaw, and the sharp pain rode up in a straight line, from the heels to my knees. I shouted at Mohanty through sudden tears, "Mohanty, it's getting late."

The policeman and Mohanty looked at each other. I knew the unspoken message that passed between them. Big men's daughters. Throwing their weight around.

Refreshed by the unexpected halt, the rickshawala took to his pedals with alacrity. In the briefest of moments, our cavalcade – me in my rickshaw-carriage, feeling much like a godmotherless bloated up Cinderella and Mohanty bringing up the rear, exchanging a farewell nod with his policeman friend – had passed the road. The other policemen were still bumbling around, trying to stamp their presence into everything in sight. Just when we had reached the very end of the road, I craned my neck backwards, trying to pack into one glance as much of the hospital as was possible. She must be on a bed somewhere on the second floor – the Acid and Burns Ward. Lost in the white world of antiseptic and high security, unseeing, unaware of everything going around her, of the stream of VIP visitors who filtered in and out expressing sympathy, announcing special concessions for her, trying to outdo each other in largesse. Most windows already had their blinds lowered in sympathy. Only in a few places curtains still waved, putting on a deceptive calm. The falseness was everywhere – in the washing that dozed in the morning sun, the sweepers who worked away, hiding their resignation well. They built up a cloud of dust, chased it down the street and watched it collect in a dump, not minding the wind as it rushed up to scatter their collected efforts.

In school, the bell for assembly had not sounded yet, for everyone was still gathered around the stairs or the corridor outside the science lab. Bags were lumped against walls or columns as their owners chatted, ran a quick glance over the forbidden magazines usually passed around at this time, sometimes, even posters of Amitabh Bachchan and Kumar Gaurav. I found myself a place between two conversation circles, much in the manner of a plainclothes policeman, so I could pick up conversation threads emanating from both circles. My bag was some distraction though. It was heavy and I had to keep shifting it from one shoulder to the other. In between, I also had to be careful my socks didn't slip, that the rubber bands holding them in place had not snapped. I kept a pen in one of my socks pretending it was a pistol.

"One of your socks is longer than the other."

It was Appu, a girl in my class I had recently been introduced to. She was smiling at me, shaking her head too. Appu knew if she smiled this way, the tight curls framing her face bounced in a winsome, eye-catching manner. I looked down at my socks in haste but Appu's eyes were not on them. Instead she came straight to the point.

"Jesus, they are all saying that Mrs. Muller will give a test. Have you studied?"

I didn't get a chance to respond because Appu had moved on. "Yesterday I had too many guests at home. I didn't do the sentence construction exercise she gave us. Did you?"

And she held out her hand for my notebook. I obliged, watching her take my copy, whistling in a manner that impressed me. If the sisters were on the prowl, there was every good chance of her being hauled up for indiscipline. But evidently Appu didn't care.

As we walked to class, to dispose off our bags before attending assembly, she ran a cursory eye over my notebook, estimating a time frame by which she could transfer information from my notebook into hers. Once in class, Appu got to work; with enviable concentration, she copied everything from my notebook, not leaving out even the commas, even drawing the last line to indicate where she had finished, using just as I had done, a red pencil and ruler.

"What about assembly," I meekly ventured, when it was all done and my notebook had been duly returned to its usual place in my bag. She yawned in exaggerated boredom.

"BO-rring," she said, "the same prayers, march-past. I am staying here."

She could be right. Assemblies in most schools, and I had been to quite a few already, followed the same pattern. The others filed past, looking at her in an awestruck way, only a few left behind grim warnings, "One day, you will get into trouble."

The scrunch of feet on tiled corridors marching steadfastly towards the assembly room tapered away in no time, leaving the two of us absolutely alone. Appu had an impish grin on her face that confused me.

"Relax, no one will know."

If Appu thought so, I decided to believe her. I sat myself on a desk, arranged my skirt in a decorous girlish manner, swung my legs in the mischievous, attention getting way girls had, and asked, "Will Mrs. Muller really give a test?"

"Depends on her mood. And if we let her forget?"

"How?"

"Ask doubts, or if someone gets into trouble."

Our discussions were interrupted. The principal, Sister Michael's voice made a passage for itself, after much throat-clearing and coughing, through the public address system. Finally it broke through in a stern, no-nonsense manner. "Girls, please close your eyes in prayer. We must pray for the recovery and good health of one of us, a former student, who is in hospital. She has been injured in an accident – Samarpita . . ."

I jumped down from the desk. At last, I had something of significance to announce, "I saw it happen. In a rickshaw, and then someone threw acid at her. My uncle says it was a Naxalwadi."

A frown appeared on Appu's forehead, it changed soon into determined denial, "What's that – naxal what . . . my father says she was a bad girl, who had too many friends."

Appu looked around for any eavesdroppers, but the picture of Mother Mary on the wall was too high up to disapprove and in the assembly, the two-minute silence still held. Thus satisfied, she whispered to me more confidential information, "She had too many boyfriends. One boy hit her . . . and she got burnt . . ."

The question left my lips before I could put brakes on it, "How can you burn if someone hits you?"

Appu's lips settled into a stubborn thin line. "No, she was a bad girl. It happens when you have too many boyfriends. They get angry at you, and then take revenge. The boy was very angry with her, and his anger burnt her up. My father told me."

As if that explanation was decisive enough to settle the matter, Appu leaned back and together we heard the head prefect recite in a singsong voice, the morning pledge, "India is my country. All Indians are my brothers and sisters. I love my country. . . ." Hundreds of sonorous voices, still not roused from their morning sleep followed hers in a disorderly, frantic to-get-a-seat-in-the-bus manner. Indiaismycountry . . . allindiansaremybrodersandseesters . . .

We laughed before Appu decided to move the conversation onto a different track.

"Do you have a boyfriend?"

There was hope in her eyes, a plea behind her question. I nodded, hoping my insistent nods would cover up the lie. The hope in her eyes budded into instant excitement, "You do, what do you do?"

"Nothing, why?" Playing cricket surely didn't count as anything special. I played cricket with many boys, though Paul was special. All of them could not be my boyfriends. Then Appu would be well and truly shocked.

The excitement faded palpably from Appu's face. "You don't go out with him, like Archie does with Veronica? Does he take you for rides on his bike like Rishi Kapoor in *Bobby*?"

I agreed to all her propositions, "Yes, we had gone out for a ride on his bicycle once."

It was getting difficult to sustain the story. I stumbled over words simply because they refused to fit the incongruous image I knew I made riding on the front rod of anyone's bike. Even if I shifted myself to the back seat, I would still have been too heavy. Why, even the rickshawalas complained about it when they haggled with Mohanty over the price.

"Did he kiss you? Ever? This way?"

Appu pursed up her lips and produced a kind of cheeping noise, the sound made by hands rubbing over a balloon, or when someone was just learning to whistle. I turned my head away, hoping Appu would understand I was embarrassed, "No, never. We don't do things like that."

With dread I waited for her next question; I could almost hear the curiosity sizzle inside her like tiny molecules of electricity chasing each other enthusiastically down wires. But the next moment, the corridors, then the stairs resounded with the relief of several hundred feet, as the girls swept back into the classrooms, signalling an end to assembly.

There was no test. Mrs. Muller herself did not want it. Instead, she was in a surprisingly chatty mood. It was evident in the generous smile she tossed around the whole class. And when someone raised a hand to ask a question on the pressing matter of the day, she was only too happy to oblige.

"Miss, that girl in the accident. What happened?"

The smile vanished, Mrs Muller played with the duster, then with the chalk that crumbled into powdery dust in her hands, leaving them ghostly white. She pulled out a delicately laced handkerchief from inside her blouse, and dismissed the question with an easy answer, but the chalk marks proved more resilient.

"She studied here, even I taught her."

The questioner persisted. I was new to the class and I could not yet put a name to a face. "Was she a good student?"

"We-llllll," the chalk powder had faded somewhat, leaving Mrs. Muller's fingers a spectral gray, "She was and she was not."

Encouraged by her response so far, more hands began to assert themselves, the shuffling of feet grew in tempo as one by one the girls jumped to their feet, ready with their own questions. It added to my increasing storehouse of knowledge on Samarpita Mishra.

"She was a topper in college, Miss. I know, because my sister studied with her. And she was also a very good girl."

Mrs. Muller nodded absently. "She was, she was the head girl. Her grandfather or someone I think, was also a very important man."

Here at last was a fact I was aware of, I even knew his name. I was halfway in the act of raising my hand to announce this when someone beat me to it.

"What really happened, Miss?"

Mrs. Muller took her time. She drew something with chalk on her bulky teacher's desk, erased it with her fingers, began again, used the duster to rub things out this time, inspected her desk, its edges and ink-stains before the answer dawned on her, "You really want to know. Sister didn't tell you much in assembly but it happened because she got into bad company. B-A-D Company. Associated herself with the wrong people, with boys who just wanted to have fun. She made them angry and they took revenge – you know, badla. That was why they threw acid."

"But, Miss, it wasn't they, it was one." Appu had finally spoken, raising her voice from her seat in one far corner of the classroom. And because she must have thought it boring, she did the unthinkable – she remained seated, instead of springing to her feet, as everyone else had done.

"Miss . . . you know so much about it, why don't you tell us?" Mrs. Muller's voice was soft like a knife cutting into soft bread, watching it fall into flaky, crumbly pieces, dismembering Appu's resistance and she got to her feet with reluctance. "My father told me . . . he said the police were looking for a man, who everyone saw doing it . . . he threw it from a bottle at her and she burnt up, even though it was some watery liquid." And she stretched her arms out and threw, as if she were practicing a javelin throw.

A great white cloud of dust arose as Mrs. Muller thumped the duster hard on the table, giving her the look of an evil genie who had opened the bottle of knowledge and bad temper, "Ah yes, you are the inspector's daughter. You know everything. . . ."

Appu turned towards me. Her index finger rose to point straight at me, in almost the same manner that Mohanty's finger had pointed at me less than an hour ago. I was beginning to feel like a marked person. Appu's next words drew everyone's attention, chiefly Mrs. Muller's, towards me, "Miss, really, Miss. That was what happened. Ask her."

Fear and embarrassment spread over me, like the first taste of especially bitter medicine. Mrs. Muller's black eyes and chalk-whitened face pounced on me with relish, "Ah, the new girl . . . and what can she tell us?"

I got to my feet but it was difficult to meet all the eyes all at once – strange, not friendly and very curious. The teacher ran a cold glance over me, and I saw her lips twitch in amusement or sarcasm. "So new girl . . . you have a name?" she demanded.

"Aditi Chatterji." I mumbled my name, my head bowed, waiting for her next question.

"So Miss Chaatterjee, sorry Chutterji, what do you know?"

Appu's eyes were still on me – they held a look full of plea and yet I read traces of contempt too. She had made me her friend and that friend was letting her down. I couldn't let that happen. And I plunged into my rescue act, "Yes, Miss, I saw it happen . . . outside the circuit house . . . a man on a bike who threw acid on her . . . and she burnt up . . . till nothing was left."

There was silence. The girls looked at me, not sure of what to do. By all rights, I deserved their admiration. I had seen it happen; it was an unsolved crime; the police could call me on as a prosecution witness. Besides, I had also saved a friend in times of deepest distress. Instead I heard the duster call for attention, a series of loud angry thuds that dismissed every word of my explanation.

"You girls believe such silly stories . . . listening to gossip and what not, then poison each other's ears with it." But I persisted, holding on to my desk for support, louder than before.

"Miss, I saw it. And then even the newspaper said that. My uncle said. . . ."

The duster flashed into view again, high like a trident. She stared at me, for a long while, debating the treatment my kind of impertinence deserved.

"Aditi . . . Aditi, that's your name right? Do you ever look at yourself in the mirror?"

Everyone turned to look at me again, to verify Mrs. Muller's statements for themselves. I saw myself in their eyes. I did know how the mirror would look if I stood in front of it. Simmer in distaste at the unwelcome apparition that stained its shiny, glass front.

I shook my head. Mrs. Muller subjected me to an all-encompassing glance, just as the policeman had done a few hours before. An amused look appeared on her face, it grew in proportion to the time she spent looking at me. But while the policeman hadn't said a thing, Mrs. Muller made up for it and more.

"Look at her. She should have been called Oddity, not Aditi. Hair not combed. Ribbon is brown, not white. Clothes looking like she has slept in them. See the rest of her also. Socks brown like her ribbons. But she thinks it's all right . . . she does not need to see a mirror. She knows she can come to school like this."

"Look at the others. Do they come looking like you?" She stopped and could go on no more. I presented so horrible a sight that Mrs. Muller had been robbed of her gift of speech.

I stood at my desk till the period ended. I stood with my stomach drawn in, unable to do anything, even raise my hands to my ears, to dig away from their depths Mrs. Muller's acid words. I heard the flip of pages, the scrape of chairs as the girls settled into their lesson. My eyes fixed themselves on the desk, committing to memory every little detail. The cartoons drawn by someone in black ink, a woman's face in profile, with a nose like a balloon. It puffed slowly up but just stopped towards a series of inkblots – three perfect circle-shaped dots, in one straight line. Whoever had sat there before me must have jerked her fountain-pen angrily to make those appear. Towards the desk's edges, the wood had chipped away, leaving fairer skin. From a small hole drilled into its hinges, a cockroach appeared, twirled its antennae in my direction, but withdrew; even it had no sympathy to offer me.

Till the end of the day, I did not, could not, raise my eyes to meet anyone else's. My skin felt rough and bruised like old floor mats, on which people rubbed the dust off their shoe soles. Nor did I move from my seat for the next three hours, till school ended. Everything about me – my skin, bones, whatever made me *me* – was no longer how I had remembered it. Paul's face appeared briefly and withered away, like autumn leaves. I sat, bloating up with every minute, as Mrs. Muller's words branded themselves on me, leaving their mark like several coats of paint. Should anyone have cared to speak to me, I could have held up a placard – "Wet Paint – Careful."

M a kept herself busy the better part of one day making up a bouquet. The Circuit House gardeners had spent most of the morning collecting the flowers Ma thought appropriate for a sad occasion bouquet. In Ma's flower arrangement, the purple and pale yellow dahlia flowers took pride of place, the marigolds and zinnias stood around in attendance, the cypress leaves were shaped into a kind of Victorian collar, they made up a pleasing backdrop to the flowers. The final touch Ma provided with a red satiny ribbon. It had once formed part of several farewell presents given to her before she left Delhi.

Until Father came by from work, and informed Ma of the sudden change in plans, I would never have known it was meant for the acid victim in hospital. Father, who was a stickler for such things, insisted the sympathy call to the hospital would constitute a break with protocol. "The director-general's wife has not visited her yet. It might not look too good if you go there before her. After all, she is head of the police ladies club."

I was forced to stand in for Mother. I could tell it didn't please her. Not just not being able to go, but because I really made such a poor substitute. Even though I wore my one good dress that was set aside for important occasions like this, it did little to enhance my image. It was otherwise a nice yellow dress, with frills but on me, it took on all the proportions of a terribly swollen dahlia. The frills rose towards the end like froth in a milkshake. Also, because it had suddenly aged in the last year, the first button refused to stay closed. It clicked open each time I drew in a deep breath. "Leave it open," Ma said in last despair. A safety-pin would spoil the dress irrevocably. "Maybe you could take a stitch or two out. That way it could fit her," Father suggested. Everyone was looking at the dress; it had their full sympathy.

We reached the hospital much before the official visiting hour time. No one of course said anything to Father as we entered. Instead, as Father took his first steps into the lobby, everyone in the reception jumped to attention or paused respectfully in the midst of their actions. I followed, trying to keep in step, holding on to the flowers gamely for the marigold stems had already begun to sweat profusely through the red satin ribbon, leaving gray smudges on my fingers.

We were to take the stairs to the third floor as the lift attendant was on an extended lunch break. Father's sighs of irritation took on a progressive heaviness as we negotiated the stairs. And then in very unexpected a manner, a man's head took shape slowly beneath us, through the gaps in the staircase. The same head tilted backwards to watch us pass, and I knew from where he stood, he could easily see through the gaps in my frilly, frothy dress, and see his fill of my balloon-shaped knickers held together by tight elastic. He smiled, noting my discomfort, making clear his intentions of standing there until I had moved on. I took two steps, frantic in my desire to catch up with Father. He turned and frowned in disapproval, "Don't run. Behave. This is a hospital."

At the landing, there was a chart. A curly haired baby, blush applied to its cheeks, held a puffy finger up and the words . . . sh . . . sh . . . sh . . . spiralled out from her lips. They grew in size like smoke from a dated steam engine.

Look for Room 302, instructed Father once the stair climbing had been done. That was one department in which I could make myself useful. Because Father wore specs, he had to really squint his way past every door. But Room 302 was easy enough to find. Two policemen were stationed at its door and they appeared engaged in deep conversation. Possibly about the sad state of the nation's affairs. Or maybe they were exchanging notes on which parts of the girl had gone missing the night before.

"Good morning, Saar . . . ," a harassed look appeared on their faces, when we came up. "Good afternoon," said Father pointedly. They darted more harassed glances towards their watches, agreed that Father was right and then shifted their attention towards me. They smiled, for now they had found a reason to divert Father's sarcasm.

"Oh your little girl is here, and what lovely flowers."

I tightened my grip on the flowers. The marigold flowers jerked forward to deliver a stinging wet slap on my cheek. I brushed the dampness away, ignoring the now sardonic smiles on the policemen's faces; they too had noted how poorly the dress sat on me.

Father's voice intervened, through a gap in the door. "Mr . . . Mishra . . . Mishraji," a pause, and then again, "Aditi . . . ," the volume rose, issuing a stern summons. It was the moment for the flower handover ceremony and the handover person was nowhere in the picture.

"Coming . . . coming." And taking a deep breath, afraid of what I might possibly see, I walked through the door. What if Mohanty's policeman friend was right? Maybe her other eye had gone, probably lying on its side in a petri-dish, waiting for the nurse's cleaning pan. I raised the flowers higher, hoping they would help block my vision in case something scary did roll into sight. Then I saw Father's check shirt, and my eyes fixed themselves on his back in relief.

Elsewhere, the room was an impression of green and white. A white table and chair near Father, a green curtain behind that, swelling and ebbing as the wind rushed in through the door, overtaking me in its haste. Through a gap, I could see white again. A bed dressed up in white, standing on white legs. On one side of the curtains, I saw a white shelf holding medicine bottles, gauze strips and a clipboard holding on tight to several charts and lists. It could be her medicines, or it could be a list of all the things the policeman was talking about.

"My daughter, and my Mrs. arranged a bouquet for her . . . "

Father turned towards me and I saw the man he was talking to. An old man was bent over his stick and that made him only as high as Father's chest. The stick thuk-thukked as it took in every detail of Father's explanation, "You see, the shops were closed . . . now . . . but she sent flowers to cheer her up . . . it's home-made."

Father was frowning as he neared the end of his announcement; I knew it was meant for me. The chair screeched as I rushed forward. It was time for the much-delayed flower handover ceremony. I bowed, smiled at the man still smiling and held up the flowers. He didn't take them. He didn't even bend forward to sniff in pretended appreciation. Instead, he blinked, crinkled his nose and continued smiling; I looked at Father, flummoxed.

"My daughter ... flowers ...," Father attempted an explanation again. I felt the pressure of his hand on my back. Move forward, the hand was saying. He can't see properly.

I shuffled a step ahead. The man mimicked me; he shuffled a step or two backward looking alarmed. The vague old age outline around him now shaped itself into a more distinct pattern. I could see his eyes – one was larger than the other, unmoving and staring straight ahead as if it had been set in stone. The other remained in rapid blinking motion. I could hear the eyelids clash against the thick lenses of his spectacles, like a fan-blade at furious work. Lines asserted themselves all over him. Three parallel lines on his forehead, while others networked around his face in half-circles before converging towards the thin, white slash of his mouth. His mouth was in constant motion, it turned itself down, raised itself like a cup's broken half but no words poured out. And Father embarrassed by the silence, the wilting flowers that I still held on tightly to, tried to move things forward again.

"Mr Sachichananda Mishra ...," he introduced, looking at me for the first time with a trace of apology.

This time the lines around the old man's lips stretched towards his ears, eating up other lines on the way, even reducing his eyes to narrow slits. He was smiling for his name had been mentioned. The flowers shook in my hands. The flowers were probably nervous, they had got used to sitting cosily, cushioned in my sweaty palms. But the man still didn't take them; he bent forward to whisper some instructions.

"Why don't you put them in a glass?"

The glass he was pointing to sat forlorn on the medicine shelf, looking out of place among the medicine strips and other half-full bottles. He saw me looking at the glass and now his ears pinked in approval, "Smart girl . . ."

As I busied myself in arranging the flowers, Father endeavoured to make some conversation with the man the newspapers had called Bhaktawar.

"Who did it?"

Father had asked the question innocuously enough, his voice lowered almost as if he were asking someone politely on the street, "What is the time?"

Bhaktawar's walking stick checked the floor around him for answers. The curtain ends brushed the floor gently and finally Bhaktawar was prompted to speak. The cobwebs in his mind had been swept away by the swishing noise.

"You read my book?"

His walking stick rose in a right angle and poked the still-moving curtains with it. "She liked it a lot?"

The curtains bit gently into the walking stick, and the white of the hospital bed flashed into view. That was where the she, his sentence referred to, lay swathed in white.

A profound quiet settled down after this statement. It flushed in from everywhere, under the bed, the gaps in the cane chairs, the slits in the ventilators near the ceiling, even the old fan blades whipped it up so that it lay over us, embarrassed and curdled over like too-thick soup. The silence thinned when Father coughed, trying to reverse the conversation back to its starting point.

"How is she?"

The walking stick got into work again, preceding Bhaktawar's every word. "I am waiting for her uncles. Then I have to go also . . . work, you see."

There was a petulant note in his voice, like a child bored with a set routine. The flowers were done, in as best a manner as I could muster up at short notice. I had been strictly instructed only to hand over the flowers. There had also been a few sentences of comfort I had forced myself to memorize, but now I would have to store them away for a future occasion. The flower arrangement too had not been listed as part of my agenda and standing back assessing my efforts in fitting in as many flowers as I could into an ordinary-sized glass, I concluded that I did deserve some commendation.

But no one was looking at me. Bhaktawar was looking at his stick, which was in turn looking in misery at the floor around Father's feet and Father was looking at him, a frown of suspicion stamped on his face. He thought Bhaktawar was evading his questions. The stick moved around the black and white speckled floor, making uncertain movements of a geometric kind – half circles, a bit of a square and then an isosceles triangle. Suddenly it jerked and Bhaktawar raised his head to face Father squarely. His stick stood thin and quivering, making him look like a water diviner who has at last found luck.

"That book . . . even she. . . ."

Another silence settled in, during which I heard many things – the drip-drip of water falling insistently somewhere, a soft padding as someone went by, then a scratching sound very near like an old gramophone record refusing to move ahead before I realized it was his voice trying to give shape to lost memories.

"She . . . even you knew her husband, no? She had . . . borrowed my books?"

Suspicion gave right of way to startled surprise on Father's face. You could tell all this had inserted a very unexpected turn in the proceedings.

"I shall never forget her . . . nice woman . . . god knows what really happened."

His stick hung in the air for long moments, Father's eyes looked everywhere in search of new ideas to re-ignite a sputtering conversation. I held onto my frock uncertainly, without the flowers my hands now felt embarrassed at having nothing to do, but Father's face took on a pleased look, when his eyes settled on me.

"Good . . . the flowers are all done."

I looked back to my flower arrangement display and almost cried in dismay. Ma's carefully configured arrangement, dahlias in the centre, the lesser flowers in attendance, looked dishevelled and worn out with the effort to look cheerful. The marigolds had fallen forward in a bid to get the viewer's attention, the dahlias looked crushed like flattened pillows after sleep, and the cypress leaves lay neglected on the table. But Father's pleased look didn't fall off, "Good . . . Good . . . "

Bhaktawar's head moved to Father's unflagging compliments. I held my breath – after flower handover, flower arrangement, now it was time for the showdown – flower inspection.

The noise of the door opening with great force interrupted the show. A nurse, looking harried and bad- tempered, pushed herself and a medicine trolley in through the door. When she saw Father, she made a great effort to exchange her harried look for a look meant to indicate oh-sir-good-afternoon-nice-to-see-you-sir, but it soon slipped off. Hers was a face that needed Cellotape in large supplies so it could hold onto a nice, friendly expression.

The trolley squealed and protested over the floor as she pushed it forward. The gauze strips sat squat and heavy, holding on to their balance and the medicine bottles wobbled in alarm. She looked at Bhaktawar because it was easier to show a bad-tempered look to an old man who probably had forgotten how to rebuke people. It was Bhaktawar's walking stick that interpreted her look. It stilled and then moved sideways, out of the trolley's way.

"We'll continue our conversation outside." The authority had returned to Father's voice. I was forced to remain behind with the nurse, watching the door close behind Father. Maybe Bhaktawar would be more forthcoming outside with the nurse not listening in. I hoped Father would not subject Bhaktawar to special police methods; it could make him forget even the little that he remembered.

The nurse drew the curtains aside, the sun butted in through the windows. It flashed on the speckled floor, holding up bars of black, the brown powder of dust dancing in abandon. Each time the light moved with the wind, or when the nurse made a noise, as bad-tempered as the rest of her, the brown dust in their circles moved too. They neared, bounced against each other and just as quickly snickered away, to the sound of her trolley wheels being coaxed unwillingly towards the bed, the jingle of the curtains being pushed away again. Then someone in the bed moaned, a low, long held-back sound that meant she had held on to her pain for a while.

"There, there . . . I will put the medicine, change the drip and you can sleep."

Her gentle voice came as a surprise, even the dancing dots moved in a quieter rhythm. It was as if the presence in the bed had lent its voice to her. The policeman's words made a comeback. Maybe after the loss of her eyes, it was the turn of Samarpita's voice to go.

"Is she dying?" I put the question to the nurse. After all, I had to verify for myself the policeman's version of events. Instead, I heard the groan again, as if I had asked a particularly stupid question.

"Sh . . . child don't say such things. She is going to get well, soon. Then she will go home. Soon, she will get married and fly away like a bird, won't you Samarpita?"

She wasn't answering me. Her words were soft, as if she were crooning a lullaby, rubbing away the pain, putting the girl to sleep. She had her back to me as she worked, allowing me to take a quick peek at the girl. The curtains stood against the walls, where they had been pulled aside by the nurse, even the sheets around the bed had been rolled down but the room still lay in half-shadow, the air of tragedy was pinned tight to the walls. I found myself looking at a person with a face all pink but the rest of her visible over the sheets was a terrible black, the black left behind on the underside of kettles and overused kitchen stuff. Thick plastic tubes ran into her arm, her wrists, another into her nose, holding her down in place. They moved each time she breathed in or groaned, as she was doing now. I watched, hearing the policeman's voice again, his voice hoarse and coated with phlegm, warning of the dire fate that lay in store for the girl. Even from the briefest of glances I had of her, I could tell the deterioration in her condition had proceeded at a pace faster than even he had anticipated.

The other day, he had talked of an eye missing; there were his other predictions for the days to come – too sordid to even think through. I tried hard to rein in such thoughts. But everyone, without exception, had been wrong – Appu, Mrs Muller; while I myself had been utterly, comprehensibly, wrongest. I had worked out my own theory about acid victims, but the reality was different. Even if the girl did ever recover, she was no longer who she was nor could she ever return to her old self. A series of images flashed into my mind, some acquired a greater clarity amidst a rising panic. The monkeys in Delhi zoo, sleek gray coats, and startlingly pink faces. Quickly, I tried to erase the image, to replace it by thinking of all the possible beautiful things that the mind could hold in one given moment, but the harm had been done.

I should have heeded Thamma's advice. Thamma had once warned that thinking bad thoughts about a person, wishing her evil, even unintentionally, could set off other bad events, it could harm even the bad wish thinker.

The panic passed away to the sound of plastic as the nurse replaced the saline water packet on the stand. I must have had a dream standing up. I saw the nurse adjust the drip, rearrange the sheet, then she bent down one last time to whisper something, "You are going to get well, aren't you, my dear?"

The tube over her head shook its assent. The nurse looked pleased and watched Samarpita for a few seconds. She looked up to find me watching her and pulled back the curtains with great haste, leaving me looking at green once again. She needed some time unobserved to fit into her bad self. I heard the impatient rustle of her uniform as it caught against the trolley, the squelch of her rubber soles, the wheels creaking to life. I squeezed myself against the wall, hoping I could stay unnoticed until her passage.

But the nurse stopped very near. She was checking the medicines on the shelf, narrowing her eyes as she made a fresh set of recordings on the chart. Finally she put the flowers and the glass in which they were contained, into the trolley. "Don't use this glass as a vase." She turned towards me to issue her final reprimand, the roughness lacing her voice like car wheels dislocating the gravel in the driveway. "Glasses are for drinking."

The flowers looked unhappy at being meted out such brusque treatment. They drooped my way in a mournful farewell as the nurse wheeled away. I watched them go. The door opened, and other sounds from the hospital floated in. More trolleys in motion, running steps, a child crying, a man yelling, "Sister . . . Sister, he has done it again . . ."

The door closed behind the nurse, cutting off the man's frantic appeals. But the stretch of floor between the door and the first chair was no longer empty. A sheet of paper lay full length, taking up the entire square of a tile. One of its ends was jagged, torn off a writing pad. It had evidently fallen off the trolley and the nurse had not noticed.

I picked it up. A few lines in blue ink, words that were badly smudged. Probably water from the glass had spilled over or it was the flowers shaking in frustration. I began reading it aloud, hoping the sound of my own voice would help make the meaning of the note apparent.

Suggested titles for book – A Critique of Lenin

What is to be Done – A Critical Analysis

What is to be Done? Can it ever get Done?

A Critique into What is to be Done.✓

What is to be Done? The real and unasked questions.

What is to be done never gets done.✓

My recitation was interrupted by the door opening. Father was escorting Bhaktawar back inside, looking much happier. He smiled at me and I pushed the paper into the pocket of my much-hated dress. Bhaktawar too was smiling but in relief as he shook Father's hand, "Nice to meet you. I will make sure that you get a copy of my latest book. A critique of Lenin's much overrated work."

Father held on to his smile but I could tell he was none too pleased at the prospect. People were always presenting him books but apart from his files and the Calcutta newspaper, he had little time to read anything else. The note in my pocket suddenly seemed heavier. It was now ensconced far too comfortably for me to bring it out, and any revelation might bring forth a censorious remark from Father, Bhaktawar and even the nurse. The guilt seeped through my clothes, leaving the paper damp and crumpled.

Father still had his smile on when we rode homewards in the Ambassador. Maybe he had secured vital leads from Bhaktawar. The cross-examination had gone as per plan. Now it was my turn and I hoped I would be as lucky. "Baba, who did he mean when he kept talking of a she . . . she?"

Father thought, his fingers moved against the dashboard, tapped on his other hand, at last he took refuge in his standard course of action. He said I could not have heard right. "No. I did. He said that you knew her . . . and her husband? Were you best friends with him?"

A frown had been added to Father's finger tapping, "Did he now? I don't think so. Anyway you should not be thinking such things. Think of the poor girl and how happy your flowers made her."

For the next few minutes after that, we sat in a glasshouse silence. His thoughts and mine swirled in the narrow space between us, striking against the invisible glass wall that divided us, returning only to bang into other new thoughts. The banging, the collision of one thought into another, the jerking of the car each time driver Sahu changed gears or pressed hard on his brakes in turn brought up a fresh set of new ideas.

PHOTOS AND THEIR STORIES

Sometimes, when the past came back with its nagging questions, Father's photo albums would provide some answers. Some of his earliest photo albums – the spiral bound ones, had *Sweet Memories* etched over the front cover, the letters swirling high like a garland. These old albums came with black pages; the photo was placed within four paper labels to help hold it in place. These labels were sold along with the album. The newer albums were easier to handle. The photo was simply slipped into a plastic covering, which allowed another photo to be placed on the other side; besides, the photos were arranged in layers so you merely had to keep lifting one after the other to look at each one.

Father at one time had been an avid photographer. He subscribed to *Photography* and followed to the letter every instruction given in *How to Take Good Photos*, a book he had ordered from the Reader's Digest Book Club. In one particular experimental phase, he had tried to get people to look natural rather than posed and dolled up. He wanted to make it appear that people had simply turned up by accident in his photos or that they just happened to be there. They had not posed, or arranged their saris carefully, had not even pasted cheese-smiles on their faces, as they waited for the cameraman's "Ready?" And after the photos came back from the studio in a neat brown envelope, with a photo album for free, Father would ready it for pasting. But first, he would make a note at the back of every photo, mentioning the date and time the photo had been taken.

That was how he had written the name Ratri behind a photo pasted on page three of one of Father's oldest album. The photo I had been looking for. The photo of Father's friend's wife. I knew Ratri was that "she" – the one whom Bhaktawar had called "nice" and who had once liked his books. In his short, clipped policeman's style, Father had written: Ratri and Madam, 1972 July 16, 5.30 p.m. Madam referred to Ma – in public, this was the mode of address Father adopted towards Ma.

As far as I remember, no one had ever said anything nice about that photo. For one thing, it was a product of Father's experimentation in natural light photography. Ratri sat in shadow, and the curtains accentuated the dark clouds that ringed her eyes, as if someone had used a compass on her eyes, and drawn deep dark circles around them. She was smiling and that only made the clouds spread, spilling the darkness into the rest of her face. When people looked at the photo and the dark circles, they said it was because she was not a happy person. The sadness in her, the bad dreams she had at night, leaked out of her eyes, and gave her those dark circles. Even Ma, sitting next to Ratri in the photo, had a stiff smile, her lips stretched like a thin elastic band, looked set to snap back in place once the click sounded and Father looked up with a pleased smile to say, "That's done."

That was the only photo of Ratri I ever saw. But the empty spaces on other pages, in other albums, their labels left behind like forlorn frames, told me of photos that had been quickly pulled out in an effort to completely wipe out some memories. Especially memories of Ratri and the manner in which she had suddenly disappeared from everyone's lives, days or weeks after that first photo Father had taken of her. Father could not remove that photo because it had Ma in it and Ma would never have allowed one of her photos to be removed so unceremoniously. In other ways too, Ratri refused to move away, she remained fixed in people's conversations, because people could not stop talking about her.

Only, like Bhaktawar in the hospital, everyone else also referred to her as 'she'. It was as if everyone believed that addressing Ratri by name would bring her back and with her would return the scandal everyone, especially Father and Mehta Uncle, had different opinions about.

Mehta Uncle believed that Ratri had eloped with her boyfriend. They had been meeting in secret, even during the time Father was putting her into a photo, turning her into a face with too much black in his album. Ratri had planned it all out, and one day she had simply taken the train out to Calcutta. Similar incidents, Mehta Uncle insisted, were then happening everywhere in Cuttack. It was around the time the film *Bobby* played to packed capacities for months on end in the city's premier theatre – Chitra

Talkies. The theatre did roaring business with its three daily shows of *Bobby* and people came back time and again to watch Rishi Kapoor woo Bobby quoting poetry, crooning songs to her in all the diverse places they hid away in – a fishing hamlet, a highway, a jungle and even Kashmir. Everyone clapped in encouragement, the ladies wept and the frontbenchers threw their small change.

Narayan Chand, a police officer of some standing and whose family Ratri had married into, put in all efforts to institute a formal enquiry into Ratri's disappearance. A special police team was constituted under Mehta Uncle, but even this could do little more than confirm the connection that by now everyone suspected. That Ratri's disappearance was indeed like all the others. All the elopements that grew in spate as irate, anxious fathers crowded around police stations, muttering threats if the police didn't rescue their missing daughters and weepy, hysterical mothers waited at home, making endless phone calls to police stations. And Mehta Uncle told of the reports he had pored over, of poor boys running away with rich men's daughters, rich men, much older, waddling away with younger, poorer women; husbands making out with other men's wives and goondas putting in their bit as well. Kidnapping impressionable nymphets at gunpoint and then taking the late night train to Calcutta.

Mehta Uncle believed he even knew when Ratri had left. It happened on a night when the rain fell heavily and unrelentingly. *Ratri had stolen out from the back gate, so that not even the servant Bahadur could have stopped her. She had walked with quick, light footsteps down the streets, with no last backward glance of farewell. She held on to the bag that swung by her shoulders, that became heavier by the minute as the rain poured down over her, streaming past her hair, her face, slinking into her clothes, slapping against her shoes.*

Sometimes the lightning flashed and trapped her in a purple streak. A pale, shimmering shadow, black clouds stretched over her luminous eyes – widened in fear and something else – an excitement, the thrill of being free, and the sheer exultation of being in love. That was how she had taken the train – the last one that ran that week to Calcutta.

Mehta Uncle would take a big gulp, set his drink down, swipe his moustache with his hand and then tell us how he knew about this. "Puran Singh was there to get my consignment and he says he saw her. At the station with a younger man."

"Ah, so you have only Puran Singh's word for it," Father said, each time the story was told.

"Why would he make it up? He had nothing to gain?"

"He couldn't be sure, could he? It really could be anyone? How often had he seen her?" Father countered.

But I could tell what had happened: *It was always dark in the station, even during the day. Its low asbestos roof hung grimly over redbrick walls, holding on to its pent-up grief, for the station had watched over so many departures and farewells. A lone tubelight put-puttered in abandon; empty wooden benches waited to be sat on.*

Puran Singh had been sent to retrieve from the station godown the heavy crate of mangoes sent all the way from Mehta Uncle's village home. He sat on his haunches on the cold station floor, taking his time arranging the cloth band on his head, chatting encouragingly with the coolie who had offered to help lift the heavy crate onto Puran Singh's head. The men grunted and groaned, the crate baulked and wobbled, making a fuss before it was put heavily down in place – on the cloth band on Puran Singh's head. Puran Singh got to his feet in slow motion; his eyes lifted over the spittle-stained floor tiles, passed the penguin dustbins gaping at him, their mouths full of uncollected rubbish. His eyes took in the platform columns with their inscribed love messages, and finally stopped to stare in a prolonged manner at one bench that had without any notice, suddenly filled up. It was she, Puran Singh later informed. He was dead sure it was she, that memsaheb with the dark circles, who was sitting on that bench, waiting for the train. Talking to someone who sat near. A man, probably a young man.

How could Puran Singh have been sure? There he was, tottering under the weight of several hundred mangoes. Dreaming of the succulent

promise in each of them, sitting yellow-ripe in their bed of hay and
knowing too that at the most, if Sahib was generous, he would be lucky
if just the over-ripe, too yellow ones were tossed his way. His eyes
blinked away the perspiration and his wayward thoughts. It could
have been her and it could not. But Puran Singh had given a good
account of it all – that memsahib, it could only be her, waiting at the
station, with a big suitcase and with a man, not her husband.

"She was mad. Everyone agreed about that. She had read all those books
and became madder. So she ran away." That was how Father saw it. "She
didn't have to run away with anyone."

Ma too had an opinion on the matter, one where she dared disagree with
Father. "There had to be someone else, a man. Otherwise why would she
neglect her own child. She was always on the phone, or writing secret
love-letters. Ask the orderlies who went to post them. Then she saw that
movie and it turned her head."

And Mehta Uncle would take another swig and air his pet theory once
again, "Woh Naxalwadi thi. Actually she was one of the Naxalites, those
militants hell bent on subverting law and order. Even those educated
women were in on it. Mad . . . I tell you," he made a circle with his finger
around his forehead and let it stay there to make his point, "for them . . .
no family, no concern for children-wildren, kid-wid . . . fight with guns,
kill, go bang-bang and all for nothing . . . . She ran off with one of them . . .
I am sure.'

"Stop harping on the Naxalites, Bones. They were never a threat, then and
even now in this acid case. I am sure even Narayan Chand never believed
this of his bahurani," Father would snap. He had a point, because Ratri's
case had been closed, with no definite conclusion. And Narayan Chand
took to declaring, in every public gathering he was part of, that his daughter
-in-law was dead as far as they were concerned. She had gone but life had
to go on. When everyone's memories reached this point, Ma would become
very sad. She would pull at her sari and make her last reference to the
matter that would never have a satisfactory resolution. "That child of hers
. . . so neglected. And now people say he will always remain like that . . ."

For Ma, that aspect of Ratri's behaviour – that she had left behind a child who was not quite all right – was what was most condemnable. But Ratri's unexpected exit upset everyone because no one had been consulted nor had she left a forwarding address – the practice people adopted in such situations. The subject of Ratri remained forever a permanent fixture on the gossip list because of so many variations it offered. One could always refer to Ratri to boost a sagging conversation. She was also held up as an example when one wished to make a point about women getting spoilt by too much attention, too much luxury and too much education. Because everyone was free to make up all kinds of things about her.

As I always suspected, Father's indifference to my question in the car had been a put-on. Later that evening, I heard him repeat Bhaktawar's statement to Mehta Uncle, with some interpolations on his own part. They sat in the Circuit House verandah, watching the moths commit harakiri against the lampposts and the fireflies light up the bushes in celebration. "Mehta . . . your Naxal theory about . . . that woman's disappearance does appear exaggerated," Father began with much throat clearing so that everyone knew who he was alluding to. "I have heard something interesting from Bhaktawar. Apparently, she did disappear but she took away some of Bhaktawar's books . . . you know the banned ones, the ones you thought had been secreted underground. "

Mehta Uncle shifted his baton from one hand to the other, crossed his legs as if he were choosing one answer over another and replied mildly enough, "I know. But that lends more credence to the story. Bhaktawar was very upset about his books. He had lodged a complaint. He said they were important . . . you can guess why. But he is now old and senile."

"Come on, Bones, books cannot be so dangerous. They really don't fit into anything – into the disappearance and your current theory about Naxalites and the depth of their infiltration into Orissa."

"Chatterji . . . I tell you, they were an obsession with him."

"You are upset, Bones. Just because you can still never explain satisfactorily that that one disappearance that had really no connection to other events you were investigating. No connection whatsoever."

And so it went on, Mehta Uncle muttered darkly, "That's because I was not allowed to question Bhaktawar. But he was then very important. He had also been elected to the assembly." Father on his part tried to squelch Mehta Uncle's arguments. "If you had wanted, Bones, you could have. He too was involved. After all, why did he resign from the assembly after being elected? No one really wanted to pursue the case."

This trading of charges and counter-charges would go on, like a furious game of ping-pong, only gathering pace to spill over into other areas. They would move on to arguing about the merits of a particular case each had handled, the fallacy in each other's method of investigation, and all this while, their voices would rise in rapid degrees, making Ma very unhappy. She would murmur something about seeing to the dinner and make a discreet disappearance into the kitchen. Next it would be time for me to dig fingers into my ears for later I didn't want to work out who said what. Was it Father who raged and blustered, or was it Mehta Uncle, who with every tap of his baton, released words that could forever leave an imprint on the skin. I found it difficult to understand why they just had to argue.

The year when *Bobby* was a huge hit all over India Bhaktawar moped alone at home because he was upset at the loss of his books. While fathers redialled the number to the police station, to report on their missing daughters, Bhaktawar made over a dozen trips to the thana, in his old 1954 model Fiat, with front doors that opened the wrong way, to plead with the police to make some progress about his missing books.

When Bhaktawar finally realized the futility of his frequent missions of persuasion, he aired his grievances in every public forum. In letters to the editor columns he ranted at police callousness about the plight of ordinary people. At the Mahanadi Club, he waged a ferocious campaign against weaknesses in the criminal justice system that allowed petty crimes to go unpunished. Despite this, Bhaktawar's outcry evoked little response from the police. Senior police officer Narayan Chand even had him brushed off the premises on one occasion simply because they were probing other sensitive "disappearances" in the city. This made Bhaktawar rage even more. This country, he said, was being killed by the bourgeois spirit. Only money was respected. People paid and got the police to look into their case. For people like him, honest men, leaders of stature, no one had time.

Bomkesh, his servant, in the course of his daily confabulations with the other servants at the Buxi Bazaar vegetable market, revealed the true nature of his master's disgruntlement. "That woman used to be a frequent visitor to his house. She would come to borrow books. Which books you are asking? Arre, all the strange books that Saheb reads, filling up all the walls in the house. I have such a tough time cleaning them. And Saheb inspects them too so I can't even fumble for excuses. He catches me out and deducts five whole rupees from my salary."

"All right, all right, don't get upset. But did she come only to borrow books?"

"What do you think? That I don't have work, that I only watch them like a thief. All that they were doing? Aree, she was there for four-five hours, at least two-three days a week. When her husband was away, she would be there even longer, leaving the baby with an ayah. They would sit there, listen to songs . . . but I tell you, I didn't go around spying-shying. I have a lot of work, shopping, cooking, cleaning . . . "

"Saheb must be lonely . . . "

"He is . . . he is . . . but he is angry. Aree that Ratri Madam, it's all right if you had to go . . . but at least she should have returned Saheb's books. Saheb looks at the empty spaces in his shelf and weeps. He does not have the heart to do anything else. Saheb says you can't get the books anywhere now because they have all been banned."

He looked around and his voice dropped to a whisper. "Some books he had written when he was hiding from the police in a jungle. They cannot be published because his books, Saheb says, are full of fire. They can make even the quietest person rebel against the injustice of his fate."

The other servants soaked in this piece of information. They remembered the shopping they had to do, the chores still left undone, and one by one stood up to go. But there were some who lingered, hoping for something more. But Bomkesh would not say any more. He knew where to draw the line. After all, he had eaten his master's salt and in those days, loyalty still counted as an essential virtue for servants.

After dinner, Mehta Uncle laughed heartily as the story once again did a rerun. All that running away for a few books. But now Father had changed his mind. For him, the subject of Bhaktawar and his missing books was dropped from his list of after-dinner jokes.

"The books . . . there's something unfinished there, Bones," Father said. "Why does he still keep on about them?"

Father called Mehta Uncle Bones because he turned up in most of his albums. His was one of the first faces to appear in Father's albums, soon after Father took up photography as a hobby. Some of these early photographs were taken in Sambalpur, in one of the first houses Father and Ma had stayed in. I hadn't been around then; as I had been told, I was then just a restless spirit soaring in the sky. By looking at the photos, you knew at once what kind of a place Sambalpur was. A place suffused with rain, one that dressed everything up in varying shades of green. The dampness made the tall grass tickle bare feet. The green of the shrubs wiped themselves on hands that brushed roughly by, leaving behind that strange, secret smell. In places where the grass had been weeded away, the feet sank into the earth, as if the earth had pulled you in by the toe. Sometimes in the photos, you could see the peepul, its old leaves looking a dry white, but from behind, new leaves too showed themselves, giving the tree a funny young-old look.

There were several photos of Ma – on the portico steps, standing against the column, sitting on the ledge, or just on the floor, trying to admire the peepul. Sometimes, Father would be there, but the camera always contrived to slice off some or other part of his anatomy – either an arm that happened to be on the wrong side of the camera, or more often, top of his head.

That was because it was Bahadur who had taken the snaps. And he made a mess of it, despite Father's patient explanations. Each time they asked him to take the photo, one hand would be at work elsewhere, holding onto his knee-length, regimental khaki shorts, or keeping his hair in order against the wind. \

In one photo, Mehta Uncle stood between Father and Ma. It was the day he had turned up from Koraput where he was serving as the assistant superintendent of police. My parents were giving him a tour of the house and Bahadur followed them, recording every moment of it with Father's camera. This photo had been taken somewhere at the back of the house, near the back gate. Instead of the peepul tree, a bougainvillea creeper had determinedly sidled into view. It had arranged itself carefully over the gate, thrusting its head forward in places to smile into the camera. The creeper was the only one who looked ready to pose for Bahadur. Mehta Uncle's smile looked uncertain, caught between a wry twist and a lopsided grin. He must have taken a long time, arranging himself into an elegant long line against the gate. Ma's sari had wound itself like a silly curtain around Mehta Uncle's baton. She was smiling up at him, not really caring that most of Father remained outside the photo, only his hand swung in a somewhat disembodied manner, as he issued instructions to Bahadur. I knew Father was there because he had written at the back.

All of us, Sambalpur, 1968, September 29. Father had omitted to mention the time. In these very early photos, Father somehow never mentioned the time. I learnt later that Father had not even owned a watch at that time. Whatever little he saved for himself, he spent on his hobby.

Father looked at the photo for a long time before turning it over to Ma. Father was sometimes in the habit of rearranging the photos but it was this photo he rearranged the most. It was as if he didn't quite know what to do with it. "Look at Bones," he only said that time and I knew then why Father had accorded Mehta Uncle that special name. Bones because he was in the middle – bone in a cutlet, *kabab mein haddi*. According to Ma, however, it was in this photo that Mehta uncle most strongly resembled Biswajit, a film star she particularly admired.

After this photo, Mehta Uncle disappeared from the albums and even from Koraput. He moved through the forgotten villages and small towns of West Bengal. His mission – to stem the epidemic of Naxalism, to foil the attempts of the misguided young men and women who, since the late 1960s, had begun to fan out all over the jungles and villages of Bengal, determined to overthrow by means, violent and bloody, the bourgeois, capitalist, exploitative order. Mehta Uncle was determined to thwart them by all means possible. Even then, he had been sure that if Naxalism was not controlled, it would spread to Orissa.

And now, following the attack on Samarpita, granddaughter of the very same Bhaktawar, who once had drawn his inspiration from the Naxalite movement, it did look, as Mehta Uncle was beginning to brag, that his warnings had come home to roost.

Soon after Ma's aborted hospital visit, she had to contend with another disappointment. Father and she were invited by Durgamadbab for his niece's wedding to an engineer boy from Toronto. By all indications, he proposed to vacate the bungalow after that, to take up a new assignment in Bhubaneshwar. Father was already tense, because an entire contingent of the Orissa Military Police had been reassigned from special duties following the acid attack and put on traffic direction and guest management. Ma, however, was keen to attend, to confirm Durgamadhab's intentions of leaving, and to assess for herself the renovations that were required before moving in happened.

Ma provided us more details on her return. It would take at least a fortnight after the whitewashing, the cleaning, and the renovation was done the way she wanted it. "I won't have marigold garlands put up on every door . . . the gardeners can do other things to keep themselves busy," and the inconvenient slits on the steps had to be cemented over in case Thamma stumbled or let her feet slide into them. Also the terrible flowerbeds in the middle would have to go. Ma wanted a nice, green lawn. She wanted to put up an umbrella and some garden chairs in the middle, so she and Father could have their morning tea there, away from the daily cacophony of the house.

But the phone call that came later that night unsettled some plans. The phone came to life long after we had all retired for the night, ringing with a shrill urgency, begging to be answered. The noise struck sharply against my eyes, forcing them open and I knew it had to be one of my uncles from the States who always got the time zones wrong. Gladly I let my eyelids fall back into place, morning and school were still a long time away. But Father's excuses were not forthcoming, instead his voice, after his first grumbled hello, rose and my eyelids lifted up too. "She said that. . . ."

Ma too had lifted herself with the phone. She sat impassive and straight, like the four wooden posts on the bed's corners holding up the mosquito net. The call had something to do with everything that was presently happening in the city and so I listened with Ma to Father talking of a she who said this and that, all in the dead of the night.

"She gave a statement . . . recorded . . . ?"

"Who was the man on hospital duty – Shreedhar Misra? Good? Acha?"

Questions followed each other in a hurry, Father must be eager to resume sleep. But the last statement he made, before he put the receiver back with a sad clunk, clearly indicated that he would not sleep much anymore.

"Put more guards . . . I will see the statement . . . one hour."

Before Father turned over to retrieve his lost sleep, he gave clear instructions to Ma to wake him at four – he had to go to the thana. I stayed awake for some more minutes. The call was a definitive indicator that the policeman, Mohanty's friend, was a compulsive liar. If the girl could speak, if she had made a statement, that meant she was not dying.

A lull set in after that late-night-early-morning phone call, but when the morning proper came, soon after Father left, the storm broke, the phone-calls came in a spate, one after the other, insistent and cantankerous, like a baby's cries refusing to be assuaged. Ma dragged a chair to sit by the phone, but her nearness afforded the phone little comfort, it trilled and shrieked and Ma pieced together the news as it flowed from one phone-conversation into another.

It all began from that first phone call to Father. The girl had given a statement as to the possible identity of her attacker. The police had rushed to the college hostel, thrown a cordon around it, and then marched in to arrest the suspect. He had been taken to the Buxi Bazaar thana where, apparently in the wee hours of the morning, all hell had broken loose. And it was from this point onwards that the phone calls got more confused, each one presenting its own separate version of events so that Ma in turn had to make her own phone calls to sort things out.

The students were protesting against the high-handed and arbitrary manner of the police, who had simply marched into their hostel, picked up anyone they found loitering around, even if that person was doing something as harmless as attending to nature's summons. Since a prominent student union leader had apparently been named, the matter now looked in danger of getting politicized. Some political leaders had also issued statements but it was clear they wanted to use the affair, and student power, to discredit the police and settle their own political scores in the bargain. A heavy police cordon was thrown around Buxi Bazaar thana and the police had to resort to firing in the air to drive the students away.

The students sat down on the streets outside the thana. They climbed trees, and onto people's houses, raising slogans against the police and the government. Trucks bringing the morning milk supply to the city were diverted, bread vans were stopped and looted because their night long vigil had left the students with hoarse throats and a ravenous appetite. It left some people upset, not merely the local bakery owner but even ladies who had to send over-fussy children to school. There were other people who were delighted at this unexpected sit-down in the city centre. Rickshaws were halted and kindly turned away and as most transportation pulled itself off the roads, schools were thus either unofficially closed or saw very little attendance.

Mohanty turned up over two hours late, and he had two separate explanations for every hour of his delay.

"There is a jam – lot of people outside the Buxi Bazaar thana. That is why I am late." He began, his words muffled as he wiped himself thoroughly with his already soggy towel. He also tried to wipe away his disappointment for no one asked him to elaborate. Ma had by now pieced together most of the accounts. Besides, jams were not things to be made a big deal about. In Delhi, jams had been an everyday affair, for there were too many important people, and not all the roads could hold them at once.

Mohanty, undaunted by the unenthusiasm, moved ahead with his story. "Big crowd outside the thana – everyone crowding around to see that girl. She has escaped from hospital and people saw her flying out of the hospital, over the city. She was flying to the police station, seeking revenge on the boy who had made attempts on her life."

We looked at him in disbelief, I realized he was trying to scare me, just as the policeman, his friend, had done a few days back. Since Ma wasn't saying anything yet, it was left to me to put Mohanty in his place, "You are lying because you are late. How can she move from the hospital – she is injured, under 24-hour observation?"

"No Didiji," he looked mildly at me. Whenever either of my parents was around, he treated me with great respect, "now she has more powers, you will see. Many people have already seen her, floating past their windows, jumping from one roof to the other, and some even saw her on the thana roof. The newspaper people were trying to take photos. Even they had to believe. Such, such women, who are not dead, or are about to die, suddenly get strange powers. Now her anger has filled her with power and she will take her revenge, you see. With such women, it happens."

Mohanty finished wiping himself, he rolled up his sleeves and explained further that despite the problem, he had turned around and tried taking the longer route to report for duty. "But even on other roads there is a big jam. The crowds are headed towards the temple, and so they are blocking up all roads to the Chandi Mandir. The devi has special shakti to offset such evil. Everyone wants a special puja because who knows with that kind of evil flying around, anything can happen. A flood, a cyclone, even an earthquake . . . "

I knew a bit about Orissa's long history. There had been savage wars, intemperate cyclones, rains that fell in a berserk, never-ending manner, there had even been dry, heat-ravaged years but never an earthquake. Maybe that was why Mohanty put it last in his list of dangers. Because he feared, like the others now hurtling madly temple-wards, there was a distinct possibility that one could strike Orissa now. Strange events were unfolding all over the city. It was only logical that worse things would follow.

Mohanty's face had lost its usual smug look. Fear was making him wring his hands as if he were already in a temple, propitiating the gods, seeking their intervention. Ma let him off one hour earlier to join the queues outside the temple.

Ma received one final phone call after Mohanty's version of events. Mehta Uncle called to inform her about the special puja organized at ten. It was arranged specifically for very important people, with separate queues and no entrance fees. Mehta Uncle would pick her up half-an-hour before ceremonies officially commenced.

Others not so fortunate had to form the queue from late morning onwards. They dispersed from other crowds formed elsewhere in the city to discuss the day's events and moved to join the queue outside the temple, where they continued their discussions with the smallest of interruptions.

The Chandi Mandir, dating from British times, was a squat, oblong structure, gray-coated with age. It stood next to the old fort, and its plain looks usually attracted little attention. However, the main deity it housed, Chandi Ma, was credited with earth-shaking powers. As the town's guardian deity, she stood all day in her dingy cubbyhole, a black-faced, slender figure sheathed in a gold-threaded chadar, uncomplainingly receiving obeisance from worshippers who trooped in daily from everywhere across the town, hoping to transfer their troubles to her.

On ordinary days, the temple bells would chime in cogitated order – once in the morning and then again towards evening. But the queue Mohanty referred to, descriptions of which were also updated with every phone call Ma received, was the kind of queue the Chandi Mandir had never seen in the last one hundred years of its existence. Its bells chimed in unabated disbelief, taking in the four lines that converged towards the temple from every direction. Like a game of dominoes, each queue added to its length rapidly, as men, women in twos and whole families joined in. Particularly devout queuees came armed with a spanking clean stainless steel thali, lolling over with fruit, a coconut, a few grass strands, a pinch of vermillion, hoping to win divine grace with such open bribery.

At nine-thirty, Mehta Uncle came to pick Ma up. Father was in office and could not keep his promise of accompanying them.

I heard Mehta Uncle tramping up the stairs, taking them one by one, instead of his usual rush up them. It was as if he had readied himself for a long wait, knowing women invariably took a long time dressing up, arranging the puja plate and doing the other things women did to delay everyone. I heard the creak his bottom made as he sat the rest of him down on the big lounge chair in the verandah. Sometimes, Father too was in the habit of sitting there after dinner, watching the city go to sleep.

The curtains had already been drawn, the verandah lights had not been switched on to keep the night insects away. Mehta Uncle sat in darkness, two fingers to his nose in a thinking gesture, his eyes half-closed, lost in an igloo of silence so he didn't hear me creep up on him until I was almost there. Two things happened at once. I remember leaning forward to whoosh loudly in his ears hoping to scare him but his eyes flew open and he caught me just as I was swinging myself over the armrest.

His eyes opened without the usual preliminaries. No blinking at the faint light that still lingered, no unwilling screwing up of the eyes, or even a yawn. His eyes looked as if they had always been wide-open and that his eyelids had only closed themselves briefly. I wondered if Mehta Uncle, like some people, had see-through eyes.

"Hey, I didn't see you come . . . ," and stretching out his big hairy arms, he pulled me over the armrest and I found myself sprawled all over him. My nose was stuck in the space between two buttons of his shirt, and I was worried about my hair, that it had tossed itself all over Mehta Uncle's face, making it difficult for him to see. Other ways I was a bit uncomfortable too. My hips were jammed against the buckle of his belt and my knees, pushed into a rough triangle when I fell, were now trapped in the space between his legs.

"You are heavy . . . ," and laughing, he rearranged me, so now I was spread over him neatly, the two of us formed two neat parallel lines. The lounge chair at first protested at the added weight but soon quieted itself with a gentle squeak. In a movie I had seen parts of, a sailor and the damsel he had rescued had sailed together for days on end in a canoe just like the chair.

Mehta Uncle smelt of him. The smell of office, closed corridors and heavy, dusty files rose from the dark pools of sweat under his armpits, but his chin and neck smelt nice, as if he had quickly managed to spray himself with something gentle and very comforting just after a bath.

"Did you have to say something to me? Or were you trying to scare me?"

I shook my head and this time a flick of hair cut across his cheek but he didn't wince. I was trying to think up something to say when I saw Mehta Uncle's eyes. There were strange streaks of red in them and the darkness had leaked from his eyebrows to paint the space around his eyes. He smiled and I knew I couldn't be seeing correctly.

"You are thinking of something now?"

"Of course not . . . ," I tossed my hair again. Maybe he liked me doing that. He didn't seem to mind my weight either. I smiled, hoping he would see the dimple that still made a faint groove in my right cheek. Whenever I had an extra moment in the bathroom, I would stretch my lips to their widest hoping this would make the dimple embed itself ever deeper into my cheek, like Ma's did, but so far mine had shown quite retarded growth.

"I just had an idea. Can't I help you with the case?"

He stared at me, thinking this over. His eyes were scouring my face, following the way I parted my hair at the side to where I pushed them back behind the ears. His eyes then went lower still, around the neck and my shirt that began in a v below that. I found my arms were trapped around his waist so I couldn't raise them to rearrange the shirt, to stop him seeing the swelling of my breasts.

"Which case?"

"The acid victim one. I can help you look for the Naxalites, who you think did it."

"How will you help me do that?" his eyeballs were dancing in laughter. He was actually laughing at me. I fidgeted, trying to get away, but his arms were tight around me, and it was suddenly getting warm where my skirt was.

"Stop fidgeting . . . can't you lie still?"

He wanted to discuss it over. I thought of all the possible things that could work as a recommendation for me. Okay, I was a good athlete, in case the Naxalites gave chase I knew I could always give them the slip. Besides the movies showed you how to hold a gun and fire and I was sure I could do it too. More importantly, unlike most girls, I was not afraid of going into the jungle to look for Naxalites. And if I told him that Paul too was helping me on the case, he would be fully convinced.

"You have grown so big . . . ," his eyes were deep pools of black, his chin gave off that nice smell again. I tried to get my face closer to breathe him in. "Have you put on some perfume?" I heard myself ask when in fact I had meant to tell him about Paul and his involvement in the acid victim case.

He pushed my face into the crook of his neck. It was damp and smelled musty, the smell of doors long barred, holding back secrets. I tried to shift my legs again, something felt uncomfortably warm between them.

"Stop fidgeting. Why are you so restless?" His voice was in my ear, the words tickled the hair there and I giggled. His hand was tight over my shoulder, binding me down and I could no longer move even if I wanted to.

I felt his other hand race over my back, my shoulder. He did not look at my face but at that V where my shirt began, where a button had already come loose. His fingers scrambled in, I watched his hand, dipping lower seeking my breast. The right one. His fingers over them were light and probing and then the next one. Inspecting them for size.

He raised his head and his moustache brushed over my forehead. "So big you have grown . . . You will soon become like your mother . . . "

He pulled my nose, his voice a whisper, like winter's early breeze tingly on the ears. It was a Mehta Uncle I did not know. I tried to shift again because now the throb between my legs was like a hard stone. I tried also to return to pending matters, "I can help you, really. I have been telling Paul about it."

What I said had no impact for Mehta Uncle's other hand was now running down the back of my legs. I couldn't feel my skirt anymore and the back of my legs felt open and exposed. Had it fallen away when I had jumped on him? On the other side, my thighs felt warm and heavy, the sweat was gathering in trickles. His hand ran over my bottom, feeling, testing the elastic band of my knickers. Then almost as if he were in a terrible hurry, his fingers finding a gap in the band, scurried in. Like a quick marching group of ants, his fingers raced low, still lower to that place which smelled terrible, even when I put my fingers there.

I wondered how long it would take. I wanted to see what his face looked like, but his other hand held my head firmly down so my nose remained caught in the hollow of his neck. I felt him pushing my head lower towards where his buckle gleamed silver, and knew it was getting very difficult to breathe. I shook my head wildly when without warning, his hand burst out of my knickers, closed itself over my hip and he pushed me away so hard that I was flung halfway across the armrest. A flick of hair caught in my mouth, and the scream that threatened to emerge remained forever sealed inside me.

Mehta Uncle was running a hurried hand over his shirt, the same hand that must now smell horrible because of where it had been moments back but he was only trying to uncrease the crumples away. Suddenly too, I could see more of him. A thin band of light had strayed from the inside room and thrust itself sword-like across the verandah.

Mehta Uncle pushed me off the chair and smiled at Thamma, who was looking at me – her eyes limpid pools of trapped darkness. Mehta Uncle must have heard her come in. Thamma never wore slippers, and her feet, light as the rest of her, barely whispered to the floor as she walked. Mehta Uncle was laughing now, uproariously. His shirt looked calm and composed, his eyes glittering like shiny buttons in the half-light, "Your granddaughter wants to help me in the case, Maji . . . I told her to help her father. You know he has interesting ideas too. He thinks . . . "

Thamma was nodding. Her lips were moving and though no one could hear a word, I knew she was nodding because she could hear herself speak. I found my feet and made them move the rest of me towards the door. I saw my feet take shape in the narrow sliver of light peering through the half-open door. Mehta Uncle was stretching himself into a huge yawn, "I was telling her what had happened in 1964. That time when there were attacks on Bengali refugees, that insecurity. You must remember the time, Maji? You were so anxious about Chatterji all the time when you were in Calcutta?"

Thamma was shaking her head. She might have managed an answer after long effort but I had already stepped through the door, the lights were on in the room and everything looked warm and comforting. Then the door closed and I didn't have to see Mehta Uncle any more.

Dear Paul

This is to bring you up to date on the facts of the case. There are so many theories now chasing each other that it looks unlikely the case will ever be solved. I frankly believe the police deliberately add complications, the easier for them to declare the case closed and never solvable.

There were some arrests but under pressure from the government, most of the arrested boys are now expected to be released soon. The police are now following up other leads. For one, they claim to have tracked down the source of the bottle and the chemist of the offending shop has been taken in for questioning.

The second lead the police are following is that of a family conspiracy. The victim's grandfather was once in the Naxal movement. He had withdrawn from the movement a long time back and was living in seclusion with his family. Some old enemy might have tracked him down and exacted a terrible revenge on the granddaughter. The sisters in school however have a totally different interpretation, a third reason for the crime. They believe it's one of similar crimes happening in the town against women, especially those who have been led into bad company.

Please remember to burn up my letters after they reach you because the information is confidential. They are a report of leaks in detailed discussions between my father, Shri Chatterji and Shri DM Mehta. After certain unforeseen developments, I have decided to solve the case on my own and will keep you updated.

Aditi Chatterji

PS – I have posted back to Bhaktawar the note I found in the hospital. I found the address in the directory and sent it to him with an anonymous cover letter. I think he will be glad to get it because he mustn't have memorized the names as he wrote them down. I only hope the letter is not traced back to me.

PS – 2, As per the records in the library, Samarpita is not the only victim of an acid attack. Last year in 1980, Bangladesh reported 25 incidents of acid attacks. Women were in most cases the victims of such attacks either because they had turned down a suitor or because they had somehow earned the ire of their husbands. Most of them are young and now have a lifetime of misery ahead. There is the compelling case of one Amina Hassan. She was 18, when her life was ruined forever. She was returning from college when Mohammad Ali, a neighbour, threw a bottle of sulphuric acid at her. Amina sustained 60 per cent burns, most of a first-degree nature. The only hope for her, doctors say, is cosmetic surgery, which, in Bangladesh, one of the poorest countries in the world, is beyond the reach of most victims of acid attacks. Mohammed Ali received only six years in prison. He is a tailor and has a large family to support. In his appeal, he said he was sorry but he had been upset with Amina because she had been regularly turning down his marriage proposal.

That night Ma returned very late, long after the temple bells had stopped tolling. Which meant the special puja was also over. Father returned home from work and was upset because Ma was not at home to serve him dinner. I think he noticed Ma only on these occasions. He waited up for her, sitting in the same lounge chair that I vowed I would never sit on again. When I did hear the jeep come up the driveway, all the lights were already off and I knew it was very late.

I heard Father's slippers on the stairs. Slow and measured and very angry. In the quiet, I heard them talk, the three of them. The usual polite conversation between grown-ups. Then Mehta Uncle laughed his great, hearty laugh, the same one he had used on Thamma and I knew he was trying to cover up something.

There was a second side effect. Our move to the new house, an auspicious date for which had been set by a highly recommended priest, was put off because Father did not have the time. He said he had to crack the acid attack case before anything else could get moving. I knew he was determined to get to the bottom of things before Mehta Uncle did.

I awoke the next day with the realisation that I had changed irrevocably. I was walking strangely. Very stiffly. The lower part of my body had been nailed to my upper half, and I had to drag it with me wherever I went. To reassure myself that my legs indeed belonged to me, I stretched them wide, walked with deliberation and with exaggerated steps, but all this only brought back the deep, throbbing pain I had experienced the night before.

Earlier precedents gave me little encouragement to raise the matter with Ma. What if she dismissed me the way she had done when I had that terrible pain in the chest? What would Ma say now if I told her about a similar pain again? After all, Ma had known Mehta Uncle a long time. I knew exactly the first time they met. Sometime in 1964, just before the time Father was awarded the president's medal for meritorious service.

One of the album photos recorded for posterity the precise moment in which the president of the country pinned a medal onto Father's chest. All the people who appeared in the photo, the front row occupiers were looking at Father; only Ma was not. That was because Ma's head was turned towards Mehta Uncle, listening to him laboriously explain something to her. Was Ma too breathing in the same smell I had – of cluttered offices, dusty files and that sudden whiff of some nice soap? But as Ma later explained to Father, she was only being polite. Mehta Uncle had been craving for some attention, but she had not missed a single word in the citation read out in Father's name.

The citation read out to the President as Father stood in respectful attention before him, informed that Chittoronjon Chatterji had shown bravery of the highest order in preserving inter-communal amity. Shri Chatterji had displayed admirable restraint and initiative in preventing troubles in Koraput from spiralling into events of a more destructive nature. By taking quick action, he was able to control a volatile crowd, seething with emotions. The courage displayed was even more admirable considering it was Shri Chittoronjon Chattejee's first posting as a young police officer. As the announcer reached the end of the citation, Father's name rang out one last time and there was a relieved burst of applause. But you could see, even though it was only a photo, that Mehta Uncle's claps were a bit forced.

The photo in fact marked the start of the long-standing grouse Mehta Uncle had against Father.

Even I knew, though all this happened a long time back, that Mehta Uncle began dropping hints, very discreetly, to anyone who mattered that he deserved a medal too, especially for his services to the nation in quelling the Naxal problem. "If Chatterji can get it," he had written once to Narayan Chand, "there is no reason why I should not get it too. After all Chatterji simply stood with his gun against some unarmed, helpless refugees, while I scoured villages and forests, with only two men, looking for Naxalites who could attack us anytime, that too armed with smuggled rifles from China." Narayan Chand gave these complaints a patient listen, filed away Mehta Uncle's letters in a folder called "Grievances" but he wasn't really inclined to drop a whisper into the right ears. And Mehta Uncle's disgruntlement against Father festered and only grew.

Before I could take up the matter with Ma, though, there were other factors I had to consider. I had behaved badly. I had gone up to him, in fact had flung myself on him, when he was in the middle of some serious introspection. Very likely, Mehta Uncle had been sorting his tension out; Father's suspicions about a love angle to the acid attack clearly held more promise while Mehta Uncle's insistence that the Naxalites had plotted the attack to avenge themselves on Samarpita's grandfather seemed a tad far-fetched. That was why last night he had also appeared a bit hard of hearing. I had been trying to bring Paul into the conversation while all the time he kept harping on Ma. Somehow, in some way, it all kept coming back to Ma.

In 1964, Ma arrived in Koraput, very much a new bride. The map of eastern India in the Oxford School Atlas edition of 1981 showed Koraput as an inconsequential dot, embedded in the bone-dry, parched red soils that stretched over central India and left its splotches in a corner of western Orissa. By car, Koraput was a good ten hours away from the bigger town of Cuttack where all the big government officers were posted. But Father, who was only a new recruit into the police service, had been promptly despatched to Koraput.

It was winter when Ma came but she was well prepared, with two sweaters, shawls to match her saris and a woollen scarf. In the end, they proved of little use. It was December and summer had overstayed. Most days, summer's white cauliflower clouds elbowed everything else out from the sky, the faintest of nips that even Calcutta wore during winter was missing. Every afternoon, the town folded up and went to sleep, unable to put up with the savage, low wind that blew everywhere, stamping everything a dry, dusty red. The few straggly trees offered little shade, even for the stray dogs who sat limp under them, too listless to run after the few trucks and official cars that sometimes appeared only to zoom past the town's main road that was also part of the National Highway circuit.

The town was so dead, the heat so intense that Ma spent her days wrapped in a cocoon of silence. It was the maid Maya who first appeared to offer Ma some chance of conversation, then there were the afternoons she spent at the club, and towards the fag end of their stay, it was Mehta Uncle.

Maya was engaged by the PA in Father's office to do everything – washing utensils, clothes, sweeping and mopping, dusting, even cooking if required. At first, Ma had been nervous. Ma could barely bring herself to speak to Maya, because it was the first time in her life that she had had anyone to supervise.

But things changed the day Maya made fish curry; the way she made it gave Maya away. Ma was thrilled to discover that the crushed salmon mash made with a liberal helping of stiffly ground mustard and onion, with red chillies awash in a sea of rich gravy was made in the typical Bangla way. The Ghotis, on their part, who lived west of the new border created in 1947, after Partition divided up a united Bengal into West

Bengal and East Pakistan, fried their onions; they never took the trouble to crush them into a fine, feathery paste.

But when Ma made an attempt to prise out essential details, Maya chose to be irritatingly taciturn. She gave her surname readily enough, "Das," but Das was quite a universal surname. Dases were in plentiful supply not just in Bengal but also in Orissa. One just couldn't make out anything from a Das.

All Maya knew was that she had indeed lived in Calcutta for a few months but before that, everywhere. Howrah, Midnapore . . . her father knew more about such things if Memsaheb was really interested, she said.

Father, when he returned home, did not quite take Ma's revelations in the expected manner. He took his time replying. He must have first raised his eyebrows, while his tongue licked away the last remnants of fish curry from his fingers, and only when he was done did he say, "A Bangla . . . I didn't know, problem . . . "

Ma did not, could not, press him for an explanation. She was just a new bride then, remember. But Father's opinion was seconded by several ladies at the Koraput ladies club, who discussed maids and other equally vital matters during their weekly afternoon meetings at the club.

"She is from the refugee camp," the old Montessori-trained dowager who ran the prestigious Little Flower primary school in Koraput, whispered to Ma one loquacious afternoon at the club, as other ladies stared at their cards and the silver spoons smiled at each other from across elegant teacups. "It's true", said someone else, "the refugees from East Pakistan . . . they are settled in the area behind the school."

Forthwith, Ma set about re-establishing some formality in her relations with Maya. She returned to her supervising ways, noting down in an imaginary scribbling pad all that Maya did, what she did not. The imaginary pad came complete with neatly drawn blue lines with a red line at the margin, where she made her special comments. Comments that she deigned worthy or gossipy enough to relate to her husband over dinner.

But while matters like the salt levels in the food or the unflinching stain that lingered on cutlery items, could be blamed fairly and squarely on Maya, with matters like the high vegetable prices, it was really not her fault. For the terrible times they lived in, Father had a ready explanation. "It's those black-marketers . . . hoarding up vegetables, food stocks to sell later at higher prices. You know they don't even allow rice and sugar, let alone kerosene to reach the fair price shops. They like creating shortages . . . I am worried."

His airing of his worries ended with a dire prediction. "How long will things keep calm? Fights can break out anytime. If shortages are prolonged, and prices suddenly rise, there will be trouble."

The trouble he spoke of broke out in a most unexpected manner. It happened the same day Maya made, with tears in her eyes, an unconventional request to Ma. "Please, boudi . . . ask Shaheb to do something . . . our neighbour has lost something precious, his harmonium. The policewalas at the thana are not even willing to listen to the whole story."

"What story, Maya? Harmonium? You think the police has nothing better to do than go looking for a harmonium?"

Two tears gathered and squeezed themselves out of Maya's eyes; they swelled into black dots of dirt on her cheeks.

"For heaven's sake, stop crying and tell me."

"Our neighbour. . ."

"Yes, you told me, your neighbour lost his harmonium . . . he must have misplaced it. Who in his right senses would ever steal a harmonium? There is no one who can even teach you to play here."

But the story poured out of Maya in a flood, "The banias, they are always cheating us. Selling us rice, sugar . . . at high prices. They know we are helpless and take advantage of it. And Mahesh . . . Maheshda . . . he played the harmonium . . . "

It was the way she stumbled over the words, the telltale reddening of her cheeks that should have, Ma later recalled, warned her.

"Maheshda saw through it all. He would fight with them in their shops, and he would make up his own songs and go all over the colony and in the streets, playing them on his harmonium. He sang so well that everyone listened and the banias got angry. At first, they warned him. Then they sent their goondas to threaten him with all sorts of things. But Maheshda would not listen . . . We kept telling him – sing your songs quietly, inside here, with us . . . But no, he kept doing it even more . . . singing and creating more trouble for himself. Now it has vanished. But we know they have taken it away. To silence his voice . . . "

Ma said she would see what to do though privately she thought Mahesh sounded just like a good-for-nothing Romeo who had little work to do. But she did try petitioning her husband on Maya's behalf. His reaction however was unusually vehement. "Find a harmonium? You are mad . . . I hope it is never found. I hope it is chopped up into little pieces and thrown into the river . . . troublemaking thing. I am glad he lost it."

Ma ventured one last time, "Lost it . . . Maya says it was stolen . . . "

Father's laughter began somewhere deep in his chest and died away by the time it reached Ma, and so the amusement remained unshared. "Maya . . . of course, Maya would say this. She too is one of those refugees. One of those women besotted with that harmoniumwala. One of these days, there will be a real war in this town. You think the banias will stay quiet if he goes around singing those songs against them – making fun of them, their women. Already, the police sympathy is against him and the refugees. They are all troublemakers – TROUBLEMAKERS, making merry out of creating trouble. Idiots . . . Fools . . . "

A string of expletives issued forth with no evident sign of a full stop and it fell to the phone's lot to restore order. In Koraput, things were so quiet that even telephones retired for the night. But now it announced its presence, ringing like an alarm clock set to a definite hour. And Father silenced it. "Hello."

He said no more for the next few minutes. The quiet once more filled the house. It spread itself so thick that Ma nearly missed Father's last few words before he hung up. "I will see you in ten minutes," he said only, and as they looked at each other in the mirror, Father explained at length, "I have to go. The police station."

She followed him back to the bedroom, watched him dress in haste, pulling up his trousers, tossing his pyjamas away in frustration, "First a harmonium, then a dead body – those refugees. . . ."

Ma did not see Father much over the next few days. He came late for dinner and left in the morning, soon after breakfast. Maya too stopped coming. She did not come one day, nor the day after and the day after after. One of the all-knowing ladies of the club, always on hand to provide help and necessary advice to a young bride, had the explanation this time as well. "It was the dead body found on the tracks. One of the refugees was murdered. They are furious, demanding police action. There is going to be trouble . . . real trouble."

Ma did not have time to ferret out more details; she had to take on Maya's chores herself. In the afternoons, after the chores were done, Ma read the books she borrowed from the Ladies Club library. One of these was very new and still in its plastic wrapping when she brought it home. It was by a writer who had received a lot of attention with his first book. People said that in Bhaktawar's *Why I Do What I Do*, the fire seemed to leap out, a raging flame on every page. But Ma was only halfway through the book, when Mehta Uncle turned up as a young officer on probation. Since Father was too busy and didn't let him do much, Mehta Uncle kept Ma company. He took Ma everywhere in a police jeep, escorted by two constables who between them and on Father's insistence, operated the camera. The old palace and temples in Jeypore, the abandoned Jain monastery and the many waterfalls that dotted the district. The long-stretching summer had dried most things up, but it was here their friendship grew.

Trouble too swelled in the unrelenting heat. It gathered pus like a boil till one day it burst. The sky fell apart after a particularly hot day and broke down with rain. It sobbed its heart out, poured down on the red gravelly soil that lay in wild abandon all over Koraput; it formed pools of rust-coloured water in the centre of the PWD-maintained roads.

It rained so heavily that the refugees lost their patience. They had borne the heavy summer, the thieving banias, but the rains offered an altogether different challenge. Maybe it reminded them of the heavy rains back in their native villages in East Pakistan, and they were filled with the desire to return, an unquenchable wish that the rains could not assuage. They lifted themselves out of their squalour, using the plastic covers of their shacks as flimsy raincoats, placed everything else on their heads and determinedly set out on the long return journey.

And to those who came to a puzzled stop seeing that wet, straggly, but thoroughly joyous group following the rail tracks back to the east, they had the same, simple explanation, delivered with a flash of a smile, a glimpse of vacant, rotting teeth, the simplicity of sudden happiness, "We are going home."

It did not take long for the authorities to arrive. One after another, red lights flashing, sirens wailing for attention, they drove right up to the very edge of the tracks. Constables in ill-fitting khaki shorts and frayed shirts fanned out and stood over the ridge, and the two sides looked at each other, expressionless and unblinking, waiting.

No one knew where the stone came from, or who it was intended for. No one even saw it at first. It fell in a sharp, quick curve and struck a waiting policeman sharp on the cheek. Everyone heard his muffled scream and his rifle that fell first to the ground with a clatter. They saw the rifle somersault over the loose grass and the outstretched pebbles, its black nozzle raised like a hand asking for help. It landed with a hollow grey thud, its breath whistling out in a red cloud of dust.

Before another stone could follow, the firing began. In the curtain of rain, men moved like hazy figures in a dream, directed by an unseen hand that held the strings to their movements. It was that hand that directed very slowly, the hushed, determined pull of the trigger; it followed the curve of a slow creaking back as someone bent down, picked up ballast, hurled it back. It drowned out the staccato sounds of bullets. No one knew when the firing ended, or how long it had taken, but it stopped once the rain too was finally spent, and they saw those who had fallen. Some were spread in an ungainly manner over the ridge, clutching the ground to stop themselves falling off, others lay desperate on the rail tracks holding on to their few belongings. The silence lasted for a few seconds. Then the refugees still left standing squatted down on the rail tracks. Hiding their heads in their hands, they broke into the wails that invite pity. The policemen maintained their stony silence.

The inquiry later established the following sequence of events. The policemen had intended to fire only a few warning shots, for the refugees had violated strict prohibitory orders. Instead, the police had been attacked first – the stone established that. Then one of the refugees had grabbed hold of a rifle and the policemen had to fire quickly to restore order. The next day, Father bravely led his men into the refugee quarters to round up the ringleaders. One of them, Mahesh Sanyal, had caused a lot of trouble lately with his provocative and tasteless songs.

Some of them were soon let off, but others too dangerous were taken to the central jail. The policemen formed a cordon around the jail when they were taken away. And that was the last time Maya saw Mahesh. She never returned to work. She was found several weeks later by the Bastar police, who fished her bloated, rubbery body out of the Indravati river. She had strangled herself – around her neck was a thin leather strap, the kind that held up harmoniums. The post-mortem report revealed the presence of a six-month foetus. Her family didn't even turn up to claim the body.

The case folded up, and the inspector in charge closed the file, writing "suicide" – in one neat diagonal flourish. Then he sat back satisfied, instructing the havildar at the thana to store away the file. Carefully. The havildar wrote the name and number of the case neatly on white paper, pasted it on the brown cover, tied it with white string and stowed it away, among the other files, each one looking no different from the other.

Only Ma felt it could not have been suicide. Maya was not a girl who would do something like that. But soon after, too many things happened, one after another, and Ma stopped talking about her feelings. Father was recommended for the president's medal for meritorious service and he moved to a higher position. Even the rains returned to Koraput, wiping a green brush over everything, filling up the earth's cracks, erasing forever all memories that remained of that aberrant, never-ending summer. It was Mehta Uncle who was left alone in Koraput. He must have returned to being unhappy, he must have missed Ma very much.

Ma never returned Bhaktawar's book to the library. It remained stacked away among Father's other books in his bookshelf. She never did ever read it completely either, though I did hear her tell Bhaktawar, when she met him at the station, the time they sent me away, how much she had liked it. Ma liked making everyone happy. But why did Mehta Uncle have to be at the very top of her list?

The truth behind that early morning phone call to Father, that in turn had set off events with such unprecedented consequences, appeared in the next day's papers. Splashed across an entire front page, the headlines clearly visible from a passer's-by hand, on my way to school:

BOY ARRESTED FOR ATTACK

STUDENTS PROTEST POLICE ACTION

Mohanty's friend had the newspaper in his hand, rolled up in the shape of Mehta Uncle's baton; he held it up, conveying a similar amount of menace. Elsewhere, people took in the news, first in a hurried glance, before curiosity gathered, forcing them to read in greater detail. They snatched it up from pavement vendors, borrowed it after casting pleading looks at fellow passers-by.

In the afternoon, a procession organized its way past school. It appeared in the long gap of 15 minutes that intervened between recess and the meandering geography class and everyone saw it from the windows looking over the boundary walls. A variety of young men rode by on bicycles or marched down the entire stretch of road, deliberately cleared for the procession. They held up banners that used words cut neatly from the newspaper headlines:

BOY BLAMED FOR ACID ATACK
POLICE SHAME SAME

Smaller banners and placards followed, in attendance on the bigger one.

CSU PROTEST POLICE ACTION

FALSE KASE

DOWN WITH POLISE

The banner raising was punctuated by a few shouts. *Down with Police. Hai Hai. Hai Hai.* The shouts grew abbreviated as fatigue set in. *Police Hai Hai, Police Hai Hai.*

Some girls decorously covered their mouths with their hands before they erupted into giggles, but from others came half-shrieks and screams, full of a fear not yet worked out. As the realisation that they were the focus of such concentrated attention sank in, the young men turned around at the end of the road to give a repeat performance. The shouts were more passionate than before, gestures more theatrical, protesting arms raised a notch higher after every sentence, hoping to leave a lasting impression behind. Till the principal was forced to send the head girl around ordering all windows to be closed, shutters to be fastened hard; classes were to proceed with no disturbance of any kind. Clouds of dust rose from closed windows as if the young men had been blown away by a puff of the principal's breath. The men raised their hands to cover their eyes, shook their heads in mock disappointment and vanished with the firm fall of window latches.

Later that afternoon, on my way home from school, the statements appeared again. Now wearing thick coats of black paint, marring every bungalow wall that lined the road to the Circuit House.

INOCENT ACCUSED OF CRIME
SHAME SAME

Nearer home, the signs reappeared, bringing in several new ones too. They stood out, unrelenting in their accusation, black fingers of allegation clearly pointing to Father's role in the whole affair.

OFCER GO BACK.

OFCER, ENEMY OF THE STUDENTS

GO BACK, HAI HAI

No one really stopped to read, the traffic moved on, lethargic in the afternoon heat. The statements blackening wall faces screamed for attention, begged to be corrected. But the town, having withstood severe excitement over the last few days, had tired and lost interest.

Another hour later, the words on the walls, the slogans of menace, put on voices and appeared outside the Circuit House windows.

It began with a stone that hurled itself with stinging accuracy at one french window. Like a giant fist, the stone unfurled itself out of empty air and smashed into the glass pane. The window's face broke into a bewildered frown, lines formed over its forehead, and as comprehension dawned, it gave a thin high girlish scream and broke into tears – the splinters fell in crystal flakes, some on the sill, some lost balance and drizzled into the verandah, others dropped unprotestingly on the floor towards our side.

The quiet held its breath. Probably, the stone-thrower and company were waiting, just a floor below, for someone to appear at the window. They had picked their moment well; in the afternoons, fathers were not expected to be in residence. And this common knowledge kept everyone quiet; on one side it was anticipation, on the window's broken side, we cowered in fear. The startled frown on the window's face turned into a blank gaze of helplessness as no one came up to inspect the damage.

A broken window is no longer a window. It no longer does what ordinary windows are supposed to do – erect a semblance of distance between the watcher and what she chooses to see. An unbroken window, on the other hand, has that illusion of power. Pressed close to the window, hands on its bars, the watcher can choose to see only what she wishes to. The nose flattened against the glass almost in a snobbish gesture of picking and selecting what it behooved the eye to see. But a broken window can no longer keep the world at a distance. Through its cracks and splits, the world enters, first like a stealthy intruder and then with bolder, more assured steps. The many sounds of the afternoon now surged into the room, like a burst municipal pipe, through the streaky lines left behind by a stone-thrower's accurate aim at the bedroom window. Shouts and slogans leapt through the window, sought out alert, frightened ears, and all of us snuggled deeper into the quilted comforts of the giant four poster bed.

"Police go back . . . go back . . . back away . . . "

If someone had come up to the window, shaken a fist at them or a gun or had even engaged them in verbal fisticuffs, the slogan shouters might have been encouraged. But no shadowy figure flitted past, the window didn't even bat the eyelid it otherwise would have had someone pushed out a head and hurriedly withdrawn it. The disappointment showed – the slogans dropped in decibel levels as enthusiasm fell away in drastic degrees. When a police van finally showed its face and lurched down the driveway, most heads turned willingly towards it. The merest bark of an order, a prod with a baton and despondent stone-throwers, ineffectual slogan-shouters agreed to be pushed into the van, into lock-up.

Only after the last van door had firmly shut itself did we clamber out of our hiding places, and tiptoe across the floor to inspect the damage. A few faces from the van looked back at us through netted windows, but it could have been the policemen doing a last-minute check to ensure no rabble-rouser had been left behind.

It was Ma's word to describe them. She turned us away from the window, looked us firmly in the eye and said, "It's nothing. They are only rabble-rousers. It happened before when the bucket factory closed down." Then she calmly dialled the number to Father's office to announce her decision.

She was not staying in this place anymore. First the accident, then the ghost rumours and now the stone-throwing rabble-rousers. They had to move. She was sure they, the rabble-rousers, would return.

Within a week of the students' siege of the Buxi Bazaar thana, the police had to capitulate. Most of the arrested student leaders, whom the police had picked up in a midnight sweep, were released – no charges could be pressed. The students celebrated in a procession that made its way down the Cantonment Road. As on the previous occasion, they stood for hours outside Buxi Bazar thana, raising slogans against police incompetence. *Down with police, Hai Hai. Down with police. Hai, Hai.*

The police held onto their patience as they explained their decision to journalists covering the matter. They could do little else because the students and their leaders had the backing of a very influential city politician. The police announced their intentions of questioning the girl, the victim of the acid attack, in greater detail. More details about her attacker were needed, otherwise how could they make the city streets safe for all mothers and sisters? They begged the public for cooperation. Any information on the crime, any hints about the attacker were most welcome. Identity of informer, they assured, would be kept top secret.

The only response appeared in a statement issued by Bhaktawar's family. Sambuddha Mishra, the girl's uncle, Bhaktawar's nephew, issued a press statement. Mishra, speaking on behalf of his terribly distressed family, accused the police of giving into political pressure, of mentally torturing his niece when even her doctors were worried about the rapid deterioration in her condition. At a time when the family needed everyone's prayers, the police, it seemed, had other ideas. Having done with raiding the family's chemical factory from where the incriminating bottle had allegedly been procured, they had now thought up a new way of troubling the family.

The last item at the end of that very dramatic week had only one solo presentation. We finally moved. The next auspicious date was a month away but Ma was desperate to set up her new house. In the wake of recent developments, however, the shifting was carried out in utmost secrecy and in half-darkness. The little furniture unpacked so far was moved out in small batches. The sofas and the dismantled bed parts crouched under the covers hastily draped over them. The lounge chair that I hated was left behind – it was part of the Circuit House furniture. I had to manage two bags of my own. One had my good clothes – three frocks, including the dahlia one, one skirt, two shirts and the other bag had my schoolbooks. In the car, Father insisted all windows had to be rolled up. The morning breeze had picked up the smell of cloying defecation and snatches of it had already begun timorously drifting up to us.

I looked back only once to see the first rays of the sun streaming through every blank, empty window of the Circuit House. Now empty of curtains, the windows stared back, their hollow eyes like a skeleton's empty sockets, dark and brooding. And as the car took its last turn away from the driveway, the same eyes flashed up in violent anger. A single stream of light razed through the vacant windows and pinpointed its fury, a red-yellow flash of unbridled anger at the departing car and me.

The road to the new house led through a different part of the town. Smaller houses on either side were just waking up, a few doors stretched wide, yawning away the early morning drowsiness. But the road itself looked as if it had had a disturbed sleep. It was strewn with mismatched slippers, torn newspapers and sorry-looking placards, their words missing, or jumbled up. Adding colour and variety, trying at the same time not to look out of place, were the buckets. They stood straight up, others lolled on their sides, and some rolled over onto the road straight into the Ambassador's path.

Sahu, the driver, pressed the brakes with a hearty relish letting off a series of kittenish yowls. But the buckets didn't oblige, instead Father shouted, "Drive on, drive on." His hand pressed hard down on Sahu's shoulder, as if the pressure would force Sahu to comply with orders.

The car spurted forth with regurgitated energy, its wheels metamorphosed into wings that lifted it off from the pothole ridden road, over the buckets, their hollow faces staring up in astonishment. Father tossed us an anxious glance at the back – hoping to stop us from seeing anything. Windows bruised and broken, a placard still intact, clearly enunciating threats similar to the one that had appeared under the french windows. Yellow-brown leaves strolled across the road, picking up menace with every skitter.

"Yesterday's problem, Saar," Sahu ventured confidentially.

"Nothing happened yesterday. Just troublemakers driving us mad and the town also."

"Reminds me of Mohanty's bucketware," Ma ventured as the car resumed its slow, gentle run, its horns warning away any bucket shaped jaywalkers.

I tried to catch Ma's eye but she was looking out of the other window, at a distance much beyond the houses. Somewhere beyond the city limits, when there was nothing to impede your vision, you could see the bucket factory that had shot to fame ten years ago. It stood on a hill, buckets and all, over the bus terminus. Everyone knew buckets were not made there any more but you could always see, more clearly towards afternoons, the towers of buckets, each of an equal height, that sprouted behind the walls at irregular intervals. But now, following Ma's eyes, I could see the wall, flat and gray like the horizon, whereas the towers of buckets looked distinctly out of line. Some looked as if they had been pruned off, with a pair of gardener's shears.

"Well, everything has been raided again, even that factory . . . by spirits and the devils from the college. . . ."

Father's explanation broke midway as the car lurched heavily on its front heels. For a moment, it must have stood half-suspended in air, its backside up like the ruffled tail feathers of a cocky white rooster.

". . . broke in and made hell with all the buckets stored on the terrace." Father had switched to English in an obvious effort to keep the news away from Sahu. After all, this was still very confidential, to be discussed and sorted out by senior police officers.

"Apparently it all began over that student arrested in connection with that acid victim."

"Samarpita . . . I know she was in our school," I intervened, delighted, hoping I could help.

". . . first they raid the police station, trying to get the boy out . . . created absolute mayhem. Oof – the crowds too, who believed that some ghost was there, running over the prison walls, spouting blood and what not . . . bad day . . . Sahu the inspector, had a tough time. He had to fire in the air several times."

I tried again, "Yes, his daughter is in my class . . . we have discussed."

Sahu the driver, suddenly changed gears, and the car growled at his abrupt gestures. But he was only trying to get the Ambassador away from the errant buckets, stray glass shrapnel, a tyre abandoned to its own devices right in the middle of the road. Father leaned over and whispered another set of instructions to him. The car plunged down an even narrower lane, where houses grew right on the roadside, open windows blinked and fanned away unwelcome vehicles while clotheslines stretched from one house to the other like welcome arches. Doors shut in our faces as the car strolled by, almost at a crippled pace, because the lane left little room to manoeuvre. Old people, who were already preparing themselves to sit out in the sun, flattened themselves against walls as the car honked by. They stood up shakily, waving an angry stick or a gnarled fist once the car had passed. An indignant rooster sat on a roof and called out to his wives and mistresses to watch something unusual – a humped white creature tumbling ungainly and self-consciously on *their* road, calling itself an Ambassador.

The car took its time, shaking away the potholes and the buckets, dodging the clotheslines that dipped alarmingly low with the wind. When we caught a glimpse of the main road between the last two rows of houses, Ma gave voice to the relief everyone felt, even the car that was heaving with its recent exertions. She wiped the sweat off her forehead, and said – "Thank god, its over . . . never again."

Someone was there to welcome us into the new house. We, that is Bhai and I, were asked to say our hellos to Bhairav Mohanty. We craned our heads backwards to do so. He was tall, six feet and more and measured an equal width sideways, so he appeared to me like a huge, square block of lumbering granite. Even stretching my arms to take in one side of him would be a near impossible feat.

Bhairav Mohanty stood with folded hands before Ma and Thamma and said he was making only a small welcome gift. When he shifted, a servant materialized into view. He stood holding on to his grimace, while a mini tower of multi-coloured buckets stacked carefully over one another, sat tight on his head. It was then I made the connection – this was that Bhairav Mohanty the police was so wary of. Owner of Mohanty's Specialty Wares, politician and bucket-maker, Bhairav Mohanty was a very rich and powerful man, and also the city's self-appointed godfather. From the tension I saw on Father's face, I knew he didn't at all interpret this as a friendly visit.

Bhairav Mohanty lingered long after the necessary courtesies had been dispensed with. The servant held on to the buckets, not handing them over. It was obvious Mohanty was looking for a chance to broach the more important matters that were weighing heavily on him. He frowned, his bushy eyebrows moved closer to the centre of his forehead, two beetles snuggling together in conspiracy.

An unspoken message passed between my parents. Ma led the way in, her back arched stiffly towards Mohanty in an expression of disapproval. She always had a word or two about people who carried their work around with them everywhere. According to her, Father headed the list in this category, for he missed his work when he was without it. Work sat on his back like the vampire that refused to let go of the king Vikram.

Inside the house, the work to be done was piled up in several 'to-do' lists. The furniture had to be arranged. Now it lay strewn in haphazard poses, the jute strings had come undone from most crates and trailed unhappily on the floor. The dining table lay flat on its back, the sofas sat on each other, spoon fashion and the beds stood up like attentive soldiers, their heads a finger's breadth away from the old chandeliers.

Ma's impatience wasn't an auspicious sign. Besides, Thamma was already showing signs of restlessness. She was moving back towards the verandah where Bhairav Mohanty had already begun making a point or two to Father. They stopped when they saw her. Thamma moved slowly, her eyes were trained on her feet because she knew in strange settings she was liable to fall and set off a chain of troubles for everyone. Her new slippers slapped to an even rhythm on the newly washed tiles.

Father looked at her in irritation, "Is there something you want, Ma?"

Thamma smiled. She opened her mouth to speak but every word she had prepared for ready use had somehow beaten a quick retreat. Thamma didn't appear distressed, she turned the conversation to more general issues, "Is this gentleman having lunch with us? Isn't it rather late?"

Bhairav Mohanty stepped back in alarm, interpreted the look that passed between son and mother, between husband and wife, stole a quick glance at his watch. Lunch was several hours away but Mohanty reached his own conclusions. He hinted it was time he left but he hoped Mr. Chatterji would think carefully over what he had to say.

Bhairav Mohanty lumbered out of the gates, like a ship leaving port, leaving the house much shrunken in appearance. Even the air breathed a sigh of relief, as it moved around more freely. The buckets, dressed up in various colours, were left bereft in the driveway.

"Why was he here?"

Father stood before the packed-up furniture, raking fingers through his hair, searching for an effective, time-saving solution to the problem of unpacking. The effort left his hair in a state of disarray similar to that of the furniture and incapable of offering any resistance to Ma's inquisition.

"He wanted to know why we were arresting the wrong people. The student leaders were innocent . . . because the guilty people are actually roaming free . . . it is only adding to the insecurity . . . "

He looked unhappily at the furniture. His trousers were beginning to sag, its pleats looking like droopy worry lines. "He was threatening protests at what he said was evident police bias and their atrocities towards innocents. Just because one of the boys we let off was . . . well you all know why he was released . . . "

The words poured out, like a flush being pulled. "These politicians have no other work. They put politics into everything." He made it sound as if politics were a special kind of garnish, dipped into or sprayed over events to give them an added volatility.

"He's trying to get back at the Mishra family?"

A clatter came in response to Ma's question. The utensils, standing in order on the kitchen benches, like helmeted soldiers in perfect line, had toppled over, unable to put up any resistance to Thamma's impatience at the already delayed lunch hour.

The animosity between Bhairav Mohanty of Mohanty's Specialty Wares and the family of Bhaktawar, aka Sachidananda Mishra, had broken the town up into neat, well-defined spheres of influence, separated by thick walls of bitter tension. The origins of the animosity could be dated almost exactly to the time Bhairav Mohanty stood for elections – the only time in his life he had ever done so. Thus far. Because among the other threats he left behind for Father to mull over, was his promise of making a political comeback. To ensure that the bad would never triumph over the good as it seemed to be doing at present.

Mohanty joined politics in 1972, at a time when his career was at its lowest ebb and in the aftermath of the violent riots that hit Cuttack earlier that year. The riots were by all accounts unforeseen because even the newspapers had little inkling as to how it all started.

The *Hindustan Standard*, a paper that came out of Calcutta, described it in this fashion.

Cuttack city witnessed riots and disruptions in several places today. While exact details still await the findings of a governmental enquiry, informal sources believe that the fracas originated in the inter-state bus terminus between two groups of passengers. It seems a group of ticketless passengers who were pulled up by authorities, went berserk and went on a rampage, venting their ire on buses and the buildings around.

Mohanty's Specialty Wares sustained severe damage, expected to run into several lakhs of rupees. The owner, Bhairav Mohanty hinted at the possibility of organized sabotage. Our other informal sources mention it could be business rivalries that sparked off the attack on the bucket factory.

Several other establishments sustained damage as well, in particular cloth establishments in Sutahat and workshops on the city's outskirts.

A few people were also beaten up in the more sensitive areas. The police force has heightened its patrolling in the disturbed areas and bus services have been terminated until further notice.

For the losses he sustained, the government awarded Bhairav Mohanty a handsome compensation, and his loans were also waived. Next to the waste his factory had been reduced to, Mohanty forthwith set about building a fancy bungalow, with fortress-like ramparts made of buckets salvaged from the riots, an elegant and bucket-lined driveway while the stools where the drivers waited were actually upturned buckets. As the bungalow took shape Mohanty declared his intentions were not to show off, he only wanted to build a bungalow finer than the one the Mishras were building around the same time, in their 15-acre square land in Rajabagicha. It was named after Bhaktawar's granddaughter, Samarpita.

Bhairav Mohanty joined politics almost as if this too were a game of catching-up. Soon after Bhaktawar announced his candidacy for the Cuttack south assembly seat, Mohanty suggested his name to the right people. The time was opportune, he was already fairly known – the halo of a martyr was now securely nailed to his head.

Bhaktawar, that is, Sachidananda Mishra his rival, came from a family that had lived in Cuttack for generations. One of Orissa's largest landowning families, they owned several houses in Tulsipur, large acres of land in Rajabagicha and of course, that chemical factory in Paradip. For years though, Bhaktawar had been engaged in social work in the villages of West Bengal. Those years, the time of the late 1960s, "doing social work" was an euphemism for several things other than what the words really meant. And despite his parents' efforts in keeping this secret, it was true that Sachidananda Mishra had joined the Naxalites. He was the same Bhaktawar who wrote pamphlets and whose novels made the state, the landlords, and the police see red. At one point in time, there was even a reward of Rs.10,000 on his head.

One day in 1970 however, Bhaktawar returned home, in as unannounced a manner as he had gone, and proclaimed his decision to his parents. He would marry, join politics, and work towards Orissa's development.

It was this man that Bhairav Mohanty chose to fight and even vowed to defeat after he announced his candidacy that year, 1972. It was no surprise that Mohanty's election statement was designed like a bucket (Bhaktawar's was simpler, a pamphlet in red print).

As election campaigns heated up that year, Mohanty put into circulation once again stories of his ruined bucket factory and his own selective analysis of events. For Mohanty, the bucket factory was a symbol of his rags to riches story. He had set it up by dint of hard work, after toiling for years in the sweaty, all-purpose restaurants that sprouted unexpectedly in Calcutta's obscure lanes.

But why a bucket factory exactly?

It was the question Mohanty was always asked. So that even before the elections, his answer was ready and practiced. "It was all God's iccha," he said. The fact is buckets were needed by the dozens, to survive in the catering business. In Calcutta, Bhairav Mohanty had once managed a catering service that serviced Bengali weddings, thread ceremonies, house-welcome functions and even government extravaganzas. Each time such orders came, an entire unit would be pressed into the task of bucket acquisition, buckets were borrowed from friends and acquaintances who would hand over the buckets they personally owned.

But Mohanty's bucket factory in Cuttack was only the first step in a series of grandiose plans. While buckets would serve the needs of the catering establishment he had in mind, later he had plans, if the government was amenable enough, for a hotel on the busy Konark-Puri highway.

The factory, called Mohanty's Specialty Wares, MSW, began existence as a rough, makeshift shed, in the area called the House of Almonds – Badam Badi. No one knew why it was called that for it was a mountain of piled up rubble right next to the inter-state bus terminus. A pall of black smoke always hung over the terminus, staring sullenly down at the rubble, where only ragged children played and stray dogs mated over and over again, howling in a frenzy of pleasure.

The first few men Mohanty engaged worked in that makeshift shed, under its hard asbestos roof that grimaced and perspired under a ferocious sun. As months passed and the men worked, the buckets they made rose ever higher in straight tall columns, multi-coloured spires in the midst of fine red rubble. It did not occur to Mohanty to market his products. To engage people to go from door to door offering buckets to housewives, cooks, cleaners, anyone who had use for a bucket. Because Mohanty expected his buyers to trudge up that mountain of rubble and haggle over his buckets he sat on an upturned bucket, heavy in sadness while his skin took on the similar toughness etched over his buckets. The unsold buckets watched sympathetically, took in Mohanty's increasing girth and sorrow, and spread themselves all around, their own growth unabated.

The riots began one morning after the tower of buckets that stood on the very edge of the rubble came tumbling down. It was high summer, constant delays and late arrivals had left passengers in the bus terminus irate, bored and looking for excuses to vent their anger. The towers of buckets looked on as tempers rose. They shook, trying to balance themselves on each other's shoulders, their handles nudging each other in the search for more space.

Things happened at such roller-coaster speed that Mohanty's workers could not even raise a warning shout. The buckets fell over and began their rollicking journey down the rubble heap. One tower inspired the others and they followed each other down the hill. Running in mad abandon behind each other, bumping riotously into one another, laughing their hollow, tinny laugh. The buses came to a screeching halt, conversations ceased as all eyes turned towards that slow, rising cloud of red smoke. The chowkidar at the bus terminus blew repeatedly on his whistle, and waved frantically with his baton, but the buckets were made of sterner stuff. They sped down at a pace faster than before, the rubbish filling up their hollows, drowning out their laughter.

Wherever he campaigned, at every public function and forum, Bhairav Mohanty reproduced this story ad nauseam. It did look as if he would win because the sympathy factor was on his side.

When Bhaktawar's nephews, who served as campaign managers for their uncle, saw the huge gatherings Bhairav Mohanty's meetings evoked, they put out pamphlets, circulated leaflets, refuting Bhairav Mohanty's story. The story was made up, as artificial as the fake jewellery that dishonours every bride's family. In their version, the "authentic one", the Mishra brothers even put in eye-witness accounts and quotes, all of which made Bhairav Mohanty appear not a victim, but instead very very foolish.

An errant bucket instead of moving downhill broke ranks. It toddled over the makeshift driveway and thudded with the pent-up excitement of a randy he-goat on Bhairav Mohanty's door. It butted on his door demanding immediate attention and Mohanty forced awake, answered the door with sleep tousled hair and red-rimmed eyes. Upon which the bucket promptly dashed against his bare stomach, and subsided into silence.

Mohanty, lost in the last haze of sleep that lingers for a while, even after consciousness has dawned, misjudged his next steps. He stepped over the rubble and lost his footing. The way had been cleared for him, and apart from a few ineffectual yells and some high-speed flapping of his arms, he could do little else to break his fall. He followed in the trail left by his buckets, sliding down to end among the other buckets, his bottom in a particularly oversized vat and his head deep in another. The image was immortalized in the cartoon inserted into the pamphlet that Bhaktawar's family brought out.

People laughed when they saw it. The battle now took on all the contours of a full-scale war. Bhairav Mohanty gave a statement to the papers, "We know there are certain elements here who are jealous of my success. They will do anything to stop me, even try all kinds of dirty tricks to defeat me." The statement elicited a counter-statement the very next day. Sambuddha Mishra, Bhaktawar's nephew put out a full-page advertisement talking of the contributions of the Mishra family to Orissa. He mentioned his uncle's commitment to the cause of the poor and the underprivileged.

Bhaktawar won by a landslide. The prolonged campaign notwith-standing, his reputation alone would have ensured him a victory. Bhairav

Mohanty was never one to take defeat lying down. It was that defeat or rather Bhaktawar's overwhelming victory that made the two men each other's bitterest enemies.

The war between the families took on bitter proportions after the elections, even after Bhaktawar announced his retirement after serving only half his term. He resigned in the wake of new rumours, linking him with a lady who had vanished in mysterious circumstances, Ratri. Over the years, the war had only added new dimensions; it swelled and cut the city up into neat sliced pieces. The disturbances that followed the attack on Samarpita injected the rivalry with a new lease of life. And now it had nosed in, tentacles dripping menace, to ensconce itself securely into our new house.

Bhairav Mohanty's visit left everything covered in deep gloom; his gravelly voice loaded with threats had scattered itself over the driveway. Even the tiles on the portico where he had stomped around developed fresh new lines looking like cracked feet in winter. His presence remained in the dark frown held tight between Father's brows and was manifested in the vehemence with which Ma arranged the table, now unpacked, for dinner. Thamma repeated, as if she had learned the words by heart, that it was all verry verry inauspicious. A possible explanation for the reasons behind Mohanty's sudden visit, the presents he left behind as a gesture of friendly persuasion, appeared in the next day's papers.

A sorrowful Bhairav Mohanty appeared on page one. While he commiserated with the Mishras, he was of the considered opinion that tragedy was no reason for them to let their goons loose on other people's property (this was a reference to recent events concerning MSW). They were as usual trying to obfuscate matters, because they wanted to hush up the embarrassment. Everyone in the city knew about the girl's relationship and that the family disapproved of the boy in question. Mohanty also reminded everyone that the bottle used in the attack came from the Mishras' own chemical factory in Paradip. And to divert attention, Mishra's goondas were on the rampage, making the city difficult to live in, destroying property and everyone's peace of mind. The police too were in collusion for they had nabbed hundreds of innocent students for no reason. He warned that the students would not take this lying down.

The Mishras shot back with a full-page advertisement, a prayer for Samarpita's quick recovery. On another page, another report appeared, where an associate of the Mishras' blamed rivals for taking competition to vicious levels, where even innocents were not spared.

Following Mohanty's ominous warnings, the police tightened security and kept a close watch on Bhairav Mohanty, hoping to pre-empt his every plan. But of course, Mohanty had his informers who updated him with every turn the police investigations took. That visit to Father was in the nature of delivering a warning and to cut a deal. While Bhairav Mohanty assured Father of his co-operation, that he would try to control the student unions, in return for his assurances he wanted the police to turn a blind eye to the vacant bit of land adjoining his property, towards which he had long cast covetous eyes.

Father described Bhairav Mohanty as a consummate politician, a conniving crook, a too-clever-by-half charlatan, out to curry favours with policemen and the administration. "He gives interviews all over, criticising the police, accusing it of dragging its feet on the matter, shielding those really behind these riots. But his own dealings are shady. I tell you, there has to be some truth to all those timber smuggling allegations. Now he is also turning to prawns, illegally catching them in fancy trawlers and sending them to Burma, Thailand, what not places. And he sheds Alsatian tears when Brajadulal's sweet shop is looted and robbed several times over."

Robbing a sweet shop was quite a nice idea, I remember thinking. But Father was probably right in his suspicions about Bhairav Mohanty – anyone in his right mind would share the same opinion.

A Second Bad Beginning

In the days after we moved in, I was inflicted with a strange recurring nightmare. It could have been a bad omen, but I could not be sure of this and so did not make it public knowledge. But I still have a vivid recollection of how I described the nightmare, without missing a single detail, to Paul.

I was on trial. The charges against me had not been specified, I was only told the trial was to commence shortly in the attic. It was very inconveniently located, at the very top of the house, and had not been swept for years. I made matters worse by considerably delaying my arrival. First, the ladder had to be negotiated with caution as long lines of age had eaten into the wood, ready to break at the first crack of an unwary step. Then the crawl across an entire stretch of the roof, where rough stones and careless twigs grazed my legs. Unexpected bird droppings dotted the route and then there were the rows of necking pigeons. I did not embarrass them, like the policemen did. Every evening they picked on romancing couples at the Gopabandhu Park, just to get some keep-mouth-shut money. The attic entrance was a half-window hidden behind thick madhumalati creepers. Their flowers gave off a heady fragrance this time of the year but I had little time to linger and appreciate.

The cobwebs sealing tight all ends of the window burst at the sudden appearance of sunlight. I heard the clap of my foot on the wooden floor, the rustle of a surprised pigeon and I breathed in that smell that old things had - mothballs and dust, of false teeth and precious wood, and of damp cloth and of pigeon droppings.

"Sit down, slow coach."

Even Paul's voice rang hollow there, as if it had emerged from a coffin, then been washed and laundered before it was fitted into Paul. He sat at the very head of the table with rows of people I couldn't see yet on either side of him. They were draped in white cloth sheets, like unused furniture. Dust streaks ran down their hidden heads, like the last remaining strands of hair on old people's heads. As I looked on, bits of hair detached themselves and slithered down like hungry earthworms.

Paul raised his mallet into the air and banged lightly on the table. It made a tinny, disapproving sound and I saw that it wasn't a mallet at all but the small bottle-opener that was always kept on their fridge. It was one of those small things that always disappeared when Ma most needed it and now it was with Paul. Of course, everyone would now think I had given it to him and I would have to go through another trial, as farcical as this one looked set to be.

But the law said I was innocent until pronounced guilty, so I managed to muster up somehow both a straight pose and a reply, "There is no place to sit . . . and I don't have a handkerchief."

My voice was muffled, as if I had gorged myself on sand and grime. Apart from Paul, no one turned to look at me. But then they expected me to say all this. I moved on to settle more pressing and urgent matters.

"Why haven't you replied to my letters?"

No sooner had the question left my lips than it picked itself up, ran across the room, banged its head hard against the walls, the sloping high ceiling, and turned into an echo that played itself over and over, nearly a dozen times.

Reply to my letters? My letters? Letters? Letters?

Someone who had been sitting on Paul's right, rose and walked towards me. The mummy-like figure shrouded in white marched up to me, pushed me roughly against the door and announced in a tone that pushed me into the deepest dungeons of despair, "Since you are late and you don't have a place to sit, you can stand there."

If Mrs. Muller had somehow managed to find her way up to the attic, it meant nothing would go in my favour now, especially as she seemed to be working in close association with Paul.

"You are late." It was Paul again. I didn't have a chance to reply because another voice from the table followed this up with, "You can't stand straight."

"You are disobedient and spread false stories you are untidy you are bad in Maths, doesn't help if you do well in the races you are this and you are that. . . ."

The statements followed one after the other, in a rush and so much in a hurry that they left the commas and the full-stops far behind and emerged, breathless, and heaped-up like clothes, washed, spun and rinsed in a washing machine. All that was left for me to do was pick them up, sort them out, arrange them on the clothesline. Only then would I be able to answer them.

The small pause that followed was a hyphen. Just to help the echoes catch up with each other. And for Mrs. Muller to finish it all – make the last accusatory statement, like a grand finale. Sealing my fate once and for all. "She spreads stories about me. Calls me by a nickname."

That's not true, I stamped my protest hard on the floor.

A cloud of ash and dust and something powdery, like snow rose from the floor, it danced around my knees for a long while before slowly moving upwards like a curtain falling the wrong way up. It narrowed to a thin strand of hair, white and flimsy and made for where Mrs. Muller's head ought to have been. The smoky trail paused, then pushed itself in with unexpected force into Mrs. Muller's nose, making her sneeze. The mountain of her head heaved, the cloth around it twitched, a hollow opened up where the mouth might have been and the sneeze burst like a smalltime Diwali cracker in the room. It blew the covers off everyone, even Paul.

Hello Paul, I smiled delighted. Finally. But he didn't respond. He was staring at me, like everyone else. Gray and sodden figures but people I clearly recognized or knew about one way or another.

I recognized the optician Das, Mohanty, his friend the policeman, a lady who was crying and still not able to erase the black shadows of night from her eyes. There was also a man trying to repair a broken harmonium. He was crying bitterly for someone called Maya even as he struggled to hold on to his place on a bucket. The leather strap he was trying hard to fix back onto the harmonium fell off his hands onto the floor and snaked towards another person playing with his baton. When he looked up and our eyes met, he looked away first. Since that day, Mehta Uncle had not even deigned to look my way. It was as if he knew too, that there was no hope for me in the trial. But as I looked on at him, his gaze returned to me. He was massaging his left arm hard with the baton, making it grow longer and longer, till it stretched towards me. He was once more groping for my breast.

It is at this point that I sit up in bed and scream and scream.

Even a week and more after moving in, the house remained one that did not allow for quick impressions. It was a very old house; we were only the latest in a very long line of other families the house had held between its walls. The house was clamouring over with these other presences, its walls brimmed with a thousand secrets, the air outside it, trapped within high boundary walls sometimes felt stale and heavy with invisible voices demanding to be heard. Ma though was very happy; she was already planning a house-warming ceremony.

The boundary walls seemed even higher because of the creepers that lay over it. The driveway that went all the way around to the back of the house, I found of some use. It was smaller than the jogging track in school but at least I could practice on it for the sports day. A thick jungle of banana saplings appeared to the left of the driveway, just where it began. The banana trees grew scarily high in places; sometimes they hovered around the head like giant umbrellas leaving one blinded in green. You could hear then the sound of the forests in your ears – an unchanging, buzzing noise – halfway between a whirr and a wheeze that came from everywhere. Where the banana grove ended, came the old mango trees, every feature of old age etched on their gnarled trunks – eyes sunken in age, wrinkles cutting up the face and the branches loose, like tired flesh. One tree overlooked the boundary wall into the YMCA building next door. The other tree was smaller, its branches lost themselves against the domed roofs of the car hangars that came next.

According to Mohanty, the house's only confirmed resident ghost was housed in the old well at the back of the house. It was a deep well for the sky appeared a long way away at the bottom. Because of the ghost, the well was no longer in use; it was simply a landmark to be pointed out to guests, visitors, and children who needed scaring. The well's ropes were badly frayed, the lone bucket was all rusted. Mohanty did not tell us anything more than that the ghost had once been a woman before she jumped into the well. Ma stopped him before he could elucidate further because Bhai was already looking scared. That was another thing I had to find out. It appeared an important matter to settle because the ghost population in the town, if the acid victim too decided to join their ranks, appeared set to rise.

There was a second gate, another banana forest and a smaller garden. The house sat in the middle of all this, seeming to have a bit too much of everything. Two kitchens, four bathrooms, and two rooms for which we did not have furniture. There was only one room that was completely furnished. It was located to the left of the front veranda and Father intended to use it as an office room on days when he didn't want to go to office. I always wished a similar arrangement could be worked out for me. The room had a big office desk covered with a glass pane and cupboards that bulged over with old files and with photos of the police officers who were my father's predecessors. Not just Durgamadhab who had delayed moving just so his niece could get married in style, but others before him too. All old, stern-looking men, who looked censoriously down at me, but unable to do anything lest they spoilt the creases in their rigidly starched uniforms. Some names I could read easily. Lester Piggott-Smith (December 1942-March 1944), S M P K Das whose photo was just below his, in the next row, had served between November 1965-March 1967, but other photos were too high up and light from the open windows gave them a blurred look, whitening over things, even their names. Soon though, Father issued instructions that we were not to enter the room at any cost; he feared we would spoil the swivel chair by sitting in it too much.

The attic was just where the dream had indicated and needed a lot of cleaning up. I did this as best and as quietly as I could, hoping to make it more liveable. Only after I had done this, the old occupants of the attic chose to make their presence known.

I stumbled into them one bright early afternoon, when I found them crowded into the old "long John" almirah that stood at the attic's far end. The almirah had both a door and a leg missing, but the dolls didn't look the complaining type. Instead, they had that bored look that comes from doing the same thing for too long.

My affinity with them was immediate, maybe it was because I looked much like them – discarded and unhappy looking, complete with a dirt-streaked face. Most of them had either a limb or some other critical appendage missing, in most cases it was either an eye or a nose – easily repairable. Their clothes ended in jagged shreds as if they had been deliberately scissorred off. To my initial assessment, it did appear that they had at some point or another been victims of a vicious attack (it was too early to tell whether it had anything to do with acids). All of them, without exception, looked in need of attention. A bald headed doll in a knee-length sari had been singled out for especially harsh treatment. Only a few clumps of hair that could not be pulled off remained; her fingers, some chopped, were half hidden away within sari folds but nothing could hide that terribly hurt look in her eyes.

I made them comfortable, arranged some around the same judgement table where days before the jury had pronounced judgement on me, and others on the leaking sofa that took up an entire stretch of the attic wall. A couple found a place on the woebegone armchairs with seats missing. A few sat on the footstools and on the ledge, and a couple of soldiers with an arm missing on different sides, stood guard at the half-door behind the sofa that must once have served as the attic's entrance.

A smaller table sat just where the room sloped downwards over another corner of the house. This was where I wrote my letters, made notes and compiled facts detailing my own progression on various matters, including the acid victim's case. I shared that table with several cockroaches and a spider who lived among the drawers and in the gaps in the wood. Sometimes the roaches read over what I had written. They bumbled over clean white sheets, leaving behind tiny blue or black ink dots making it seem as if I had decided to fill pages up with nothing but full-stops. I had already wasted several sheets of paper because of the cockroaches. In the old cane basket that served as a dustbin, the waste had begun to swell alarmingly like a persistent pimple. One day before long it would burst in my face, leaving it plastered with dirt. The spider was more circumspect; she traipsed elegantly out from some lost corner, twirling a sharp, single web thread behind her like a gymnast's exercise rope.

If it hadn't been for the dolls, I would never have recorded the first instance of Mehta Uncle kissing Ma, nor would I have been apprised of the latest developments in the acid attack case. For some days, I had been occupied, in school and even on my return home with gathering stuff like old bits of cloth, paper, other essential accoutrements like gum, buttons, needles, threads and anything else that would help restore the doll accident victims to some normalcy. In some cases, I was happy to report some recovery. The buxom lady with the yellow sari, one arm extended to cover her bulbous stomach now displayed a shy smile though a veil still covered half her face. I had washed away the decade-old dirt on her by soaking her in a mug, soapy with Ma's preferred shampoo. I redrew the moustache on the face of the Chinese soldier, though only after considerable deliberation because he was from the same country that had inflicted 1962 on us. But the doll that bravely held on to its torn skirt, its lace long ripped away, the sequins missing in most places presented by far a more serious challenge.

Sewing on new sequins was difficult because the skirt in question was frayed and brittle like old paper. In spite of my best efforts, the skirt fell away in fine flakes and the sequins followed, scattering themselves over the floor, laughing at my efforts. Some could be salvaged, but most still managed to elude my fingers, slipping through the thin gap in the wooden floor.

A white, dust-streaked blade flashed into view, followed by another and another, as if someone invisible was feinting with a sword. Beyond the passing blades of the slow-moving fan, the drawing room appeared. A patch of baldness on a man's head smiled up at me, on its shiny dome I could see the three fan blades passing by one after the other, also the small bulbs twinkling in the chandelier, even the swing of the drawing room door as someone entered. When he stood up I pieced the rest of him together as Mehta Uncle.

Ma was in the drawing room. I saw the top of Ma's head, her hair neatly coiled, the narrow middle parting in her head marked in deep red. Mehta Uncle reached for the glass in Ma's hand but he did not take it from her. Instead his head bent towards her and I saw myself looking down at the red parting on mother's hair flowing into a straight line right into his bald spot. His hand lay over her hand on the glass and remained there until the three of us heard the door open again. The heads spliced quickly apart and it was Father's head with its shock of hair, black giving way to white in some places, that now made its appearance under the fan blades.

"We have to get going again," he announced. The words floating up to me sounded extra-terrestrial, coming from a long way off. I leaned closer to hear better and my knees scraped against the floor. The next moment I was looking down at the three of them, looking up at me, assessing the ceiling. Mehta Uncle wiped something off his head; possibly a sequin or two had crash-landed into a particularly hairy thicket and he had salvaged a bit of the wreckage.

Father provided the first explanation. "It's the rats . . . must do something about it."

Mehta Uncle shook this statement off, with a giant guffaw. From where I sat, pressed against the floor, knees bunched against chest, I saw his chest heave with laughter. His laughter clambered up, threw itself against the fan blades, making them whir faster in a frenzy of excitement.

"It's her . . . it has to be her."

After he said that, the silence from outside came in. It threw itself over the drawing room, like a fisherman's net cast wide to envelop almost everything. Mehta Uncle put his glass back on the table and the blades too slowed down, each one moving ponderously across the bald patch on his head. Ma raised a hand to adjust her hair and I heard the soft clink of her bangles, as they slipped back to her elbows.

"You know the story, don't you? She ran away . . . but who knows what really happened?" he asked Ma.

"Mehta, stop this nonsense. You are starting something up again," admonished Father. "It's over. Finished." But Ma interrupted, "I didn't know this other angle . . . that she really . . . "

They raised their heads towards where I sat and just as quickly dropped them. Everything held its breath waiting to hear Mehta Uncle's response.

"There has to be some truth to the story," began Mehta Uncle.

My ear was touching the floor in desperation now. I could hear the hurried retreat of the cockroaches as they ended the day's chores. The leaves ran over the roof, first in a slow rush then in a hurried dash. They fell over the glass pane in a curtain of rust and burnished red. And my hair stirred as someone breathed in deeply. I looked around but the furniture looked innocently back, their cloth covers shifting in the thin breeze. And from the window, the shadow of the mango tree crept in. A bird's beak was magnified into a ferocious pair of pincers. Closer still, the last remains of the light threw itself on the floor, and I saw clearly the red stains. Bloodstains.

"We have heard, haven't we, that the well has a problem . . . " Mehta Uncle sounded apologetic as if he didn't really wish to frighten her.

But he didn't know anything more. His one-line explanation was hardly a story. I knew the other bits lay hidden in the bloodstains I had just seen but first I wished he would hurry up with his story. Come on, I thumped impatiently on the floor with my fist and then cursed myself as three pairs of heads once again lifted themselves to look at me. I stared back, defiant, not even allowing myself a blink. Things were always that much louder in the attic. And now a thin trickle of dust woke up from near the old sofa and made for where I was, making a faint scratching noise.

"We do hear funny noises, actually . . . cries and sounds of bangles . . . " Father too was beginning to believe there was something in the story. Ghosts have that power. A whiff of a rumour can breathe them into existence. And Father was scared, I could see his fear-struck eyes fixed right on me.

"How could she do it . . . such a young girl, with such a young child . . . "

The men shrugged their answers, their eyes on the ceiling.

"Who knows what did happen that night – the son was always away. There were just the three of them. Narayan Chand, the children and . . . and . . . her."

"No orderlies?" asked Ma again.

"Who knows . . . ," then Mehta Uncle said, in as low a voice as before, "who knows . . . besides, Narayan Chand was too powerful a man." And with that answer that was hardly an answer, the silence hushed things up again.

But while everyone was agreed that the case would never have a complete conclusion, this time Ma did want to get to the bottom of things. After all, if we were going to stay in the house, sooner or later, we would have to acquaint ourselves with all its inmates. "But what happened really?" she insisted again and this time Mehta Uncle changed the subject, "What happened to that boy?"

"Which one?" Father's voice too had gone all soft. I had to crane to hear him, and Mehta Uncle completed Father's sentence. ". . . the boyfriend . . . the Naxalite. . . ."

"We don't know if he was a Naxalite, Bones. He was just someone . . . Samarpita knew. You are giving credence to rumours all over again."

An argument seemed imminent. Mehta Uncle didn't appreciate being put down in front of an audience, especially if that audience solely comprised one member, my mother.

The dust rose from the bloodstains on the floor and burst into my face like a teargas shell, temporarily blinding me. When I looked again through half-open eyes, I saw figures moving hurriedly in the haze, like actors setting the stage, before the curtains parted. Someone near drew a sharp breath in, but it could well have been the last of the dust clouds, snaking away tamely, leaving a thin grey trail behind.

One floor below, the three of them were still looking up at me. "What was that noise now?' Only I could see the frightened expressions that flitted across Mehta Uncle's face, his eyeballs looked set to fall out from their sockets.

"Nothing," said Ma first. And it was Father and Mehta Uncle who repeated after her, as if her words were a mantra to drive away lurking evil spirits, "Nothing . . . nothing."

"Just the rats." Father toted out his original explanation, his eyes carefully scouring the ceiling. And this time Mehta Uncle did not contradict him. His guffaw did not the set the fan moving again in a fresh burst of enthusiasm. He twirled his baton in the air, slapped it gently against his wrist and returned to pending matters, "The boy too is denying it . . . the students have threatened to fight it out in the streets . . . "

The end of Ma's sari caught itself in her mouth. "How did things get so bad?"

The pause in the conversation stretched for so long that even the calendar shifted in impatience, its thin rod slapping the wall in a gesture of "Come on, hurry up, hurry up." Mehta Uncle spoke very softly, for once unsure of what to say, "Sometimes big fires start from small flares. And these college students are a volatile lot – things are pretty bad these days, no proper classes, no exams on time, fewer jobs to take up . . . "

The phone rang, the three of them turned their heads towards it but Father reached it first. It was one of the shortest calls he had ever received.

From where I was, I could tell the call had ended much before Father finally put the receiver down. It was obvious from the darkness that descended over his face. In the manner he rubbed his hand over his eyes trying to wipe an unpleasant image away. Father turned around very slowly, and I heard the words reluctantly fall from his lips, "He committed suicide. . . ."

No one spoke, the calendar flapped in the wind, the red of the holidays mixed and flowed into other dates like blood that spilled over everything, leaving behind ugly irremovable stains. They were upset because someone new was dead now. Mehta Uncle moved back, his bottom aiming straight for a sofa the way iron filings are pulled towards a magnet. The news had hit him hardest. All the leads he had set up, following countless arguments with Father, had now bunched up like fingers into a fist, to strike back at him with venom. Father and Ma were looking at each other, then Father's shoulders rose in a 'I give up' shrug. The soft bang of the door behind him brought a new cloud of dust into the room. It rose through the gaps in the ceiling and stopped me from seeing the things I wanted to.

Mehta Uncle looked broken but it was little use going up to him. Lately, he behaved as if I didn't exist any more. Possibly he suspected I was trying to break up his friendship with Ma. Several times I had tried to sort things out by barging into him each time he came around. Once I had pushed my face through the gap in the newspaper as he read it and he had simply rearranged the pages over me. I had sauntered into the portico when he had rolled in with his jeep but he sidestepped and stepped into the drawing room. I had stared at him through the veranda window as he sat in the drawing room, tossed my hair the way he had once liked and he had finally raised himself from his chair. I heard my own breathing, suddenly loud. A cold icy hand moved lower from my throat into my heart, then Mehta Uncle took a chair that faced away from the window, put a hand over his eyes, and pretended to be sleeping.

Following the city news in the papers that came from Calcutta was a futile exercise. It was always hidden away in the inside pages and the time taken to locate it was always more than what you spent in reading the whole thing through.

The front pages had the usual boring news – the visit to Delhi of the Nigerian president who preferred headgear in the shape of baskets, floods somewhere farther away and disturbances in the south because some people wanted to use someone else's well-water. In the inside pages I finally located a small two-para item – it appeared at the very bottom of a column in the fifth page. I would have missed it had it not been for the headline – Troubles following Acid Attack.

Cuttack, February 18 – Students of two colleges in the town – Ravenshaw Collegiate School and Christ College – went on the rampage after police invaded the hostel premises and arrested students suspected of being behind the acid attack on a twenty year old girl earlier this month. Students attacked the Buxi Bazaar police station, several shops on Manglabagh, stormed the inter-state bus terminus and some factories. Sources in the police allege that the students who have been arrested have Naxalite links and were running a smuggling racket from within the hostel premises. There is no confirmation of this.

Meanwhile, the unfortunate victim still fights for life in a city hospital. The attack on her was at first suspected to be an act of vindictiveness on the part of a spurned suitor, again a student from one of the two colleges mentioned but there are also rumours of a wider conspiracy. Cuttack last witnessed such disturbances in 1972. The police are saying they are doing all they can to bring the situation under control. Bhairav Mohanty, the industrialist turned politician, has called for central rule in the state as the state government seemed unable to maintain law and order. There is every indication that Mr. Mohanty will once more return to politics but as yet he has not made his plans known.

The Oriya papers were more detailed, though I still found them difficult to read. Sometimes I had to make up words, construct my own sentences to fit into places when reading became difficult.

Security has been tight – because of the protest rallies that are being scheduled today all over Cuttack against the – – – ways of the police. Some students arrested by the police – – – – – – riots were released because the police had no – – – proof of their guilt. In view of the protest marches, police patrolling has been intensi – – . They have been posted at various sensitive spots, which saw severe destruction and damage during the riots.

Meanwhile the police have not yet made a breakthrough in the series of strange incidents reported from the St Joseph's School for Women. Mr. Mehta, DIG Crime Investigation, has been ~~criticized~~ circumcised for the slow progress police is making. Since mid-February, several thefts have been reported from the St Joseph's Girls' High School. Some of the objects include a needlework box, a deodorant, left over cloth from the handwork room, lots of pencils, scented rubbers and a few kerchiefs. Police are still looking for the motive behind the thefts. A top-secret inquiry is on and its results would be made public when these were available, concluded Mr. Mehta, dismissing suggestions that the police were truly at their wit's end to explain the occurrences. Mr Mehta did grudgingly admit, though, that the police were up against a master-brain at work.

Meanwhile, the strange behaviour of Smt. Tarunbala Debi, mother of DIG Administration, C Chatterji, and the grandmother of the more famous, Aditi Chatterji, the fleet-footed athlete of St Joseph's School is causing concern. Aditi Chatterji has something of a reputation in breaking impossible records in the distance races, and she is expected to sweep the medals tally at the School Sports Day and in the New Delhi Asian Games next year.

My progress on the acid attack case was muted over the next few days. The sports day schedule had been announced and I wanted things to play according to plan. For instance, the weekly horoscope indicated west as the most favourable direction for my sign. To ensure every day began in a manner horoscopically favourable, I took to getting out of bed from the west side. That meant slithering out of the narrow space between bed and wall. The wall left scratch marks on me, and I felt like a bear that had somehow lumbered out of a deep earth cave. But bad things can happen despite every precaution, the veneer of benignity a day began with could all too soon fall away exposing the unmitigated disasters that lurked ahead. Bhai used those words first, after listening to the cricket score on radio. India's batting efforts to avoid the follow-on against Australia had been an unmitigated disaster. The team had collapsed like Mohanty's buckets right from the first ball.

Doubts set in within the very first hour of my awakening. With the shift to a new house, the road to school would shift likewise, and foolishly I had not taken into account the time it would now take me. If I urged the rickshaw to hurry up, go real fast, Mohanty and rickshawala would exchange looks and I would be left in little doubt as to their true opinion of me. Big Man's Daughter. Spoilt Brat.

My hopes of getting to school early were dashed quickly. It happened within minutes of our departure when the rickshaw turned into a pebble-strewn gully. It trembled at the sight of grinning potholes, and squealed into a brake each time scrawny, half-naked children teetered into its path. When this happened a third time, the rickshawala turned to me and smiled through teeth blackened in neglect, the embarrassed boils on his face pink in apology, "Only for a little while, baby," he said and I felt my heart do a funny twitch. No one ever called me baby. It felt nice even if he did not mean it.

But the rickshawala's actions were replayed the very next minute. He pressed hard on the two thin bars of his handle, the rickshaw's front-wheel again clamped down on the road, and I stopped my own head seconds before it made to strike sharp against the rickshaw's front bars. A sun-sized pothole rose from the earth; it wasn't half as deep as it was wide, and evil brown water lurked in its middle. A giant teardrop left by an unexpected shower.

By the time I raised my head, the man responsible for this latest upheaval, was up and running for his life. I had never seen anyone do that but this man, I knew, was doing precisely that. He stepped away from the pothole, warded the rickshaw away and ran on as if his life was ebbing away and he had to save it somehow. His shirt flapped loose by him as he ran. I could see it had been torn away by design because there wasn't a single tear, instead it had been deliberately ripped open in places; his trousers wore streaks of mud, dust and dots of red. He dragged behind himself half of a pair of slippers and a very scared expression was screwed tightly onto his face. The man ran on, without a backward glance at anything, not even the crowds that gathered like rapidly falling raindrops to watch him run for his life.

The man nearest my rickshaw explained to no one in particular, "It's the trouble in the recruitment office." A note of pride coated his every word and invited congratulation for being the first to break the news.

Mohanty came up to take up the role of questioner-cum-inquisitor. "What happened? You mean roy-iots?"

Another man shrugged in response, eliciting furious looks from the first speaker, "No one knows . . . "

"There was a line since morning – today's Tuesday. But there was more than the usual crowd today. The officer came late. . . ."

"No . . . that was not it. I was coming back from there and some trouble erupted over someone breaking the line . . . and someone else got angry and that. . . ."

"For such a simple reason . . . ," Mohanty asked, tongue in cheek. He was so much in the habit of having paan in his mouth that most times his tongue unconsciously found its way there.

"Do these boys need a reason to fight . . . look at what has been happening everywhere . . . Acid throwing, attacking places, factories . . . fighting for no reason . . . "

"What is the police doing . . . I ask you . . . they are just playing politics . . . "

"They are taking all effective steps," broke in Mohanty hurriedly. He was scared I would report him to Father for a) gossiping and b) not speaking up in defence of the police. "They are doing their best to bring back the situation under control. How much can the police do anywhere? They send a force somewhere else, and in this place, problem happens . . . they are also human beings, two arms, two legs like you all . . . I tell you, people expect too much from them . . . "

He stood there shaking his head. The man we had seen running for his life had probably managed to retreive it because he was no longer visible. He must have plunged down one dark lane out of many others, driven like nails between the old, rickety houses. Standing as they had been, for decades in the same position, adjusting to each other, in places leaning closer to rub cheeks against one another, the houses stood holding on to their secrets, impassive to everything unfolding outside.

Small circles formed around the first one, passing the conversation on, watching it move from circle to circle. Soon other straggly, half-complete circles came up – like kid goats struggling hard to stand on their own still uncertain legs. They talked of the bad situation, how sad it all was, how peaceful it had once been. What the boys had done. What else could they do . . . no jobs, no help, everywhere corruption and even the police . . .

The rickshawala played with a green check cloth. He was rubbing the handlebars energetically and soon his hands strayed towards the bell, setting off a short, self-conscious ring. The sound inserted itself into each circle, drawing the men apart, reminding them to resume their everyday lives. The rickshawala bit his lips, raising the cloth to his mouth in abject apology, but people had already begun to move away, as if their enforced camaraderie, the heartfelt exchange of secrets and fears now embarrassed them.

The rickshawala's clawed feet reluctantly pushed the pedal to life. The rickshaw hood now pulled over my head, jiggled with his every push, it mulled over recent events and watched the rickshaw take an unexpected turn to the right.

"See there . . . the police have blocked the way."

I turned to see the cylindrical vats placed in the middle of the road, one against the other like orderly schoolchildren doing their morning drill, behind them appeared the upper half of several policemen, waving us away with batons and furious hand gestures. They looked like bigger, bobbing extensions of the cylinders. Mohanty rode up to complete his explanation. His feet were ponderous with knowledge on his pedal; it creaked all the way up to his face.

"That is the road to her hospital. You didn't recognize it, no?"

I could have kicked myself hard. After all, I had passed the hospital on so many other occasions. Mohanty, enjoying my discomfort, sidled up to the rickshaw, put his hand on the hood, and clarified the matter. "That's because we are on the other end of the road."

I swallowed my pride to ask. "She's still there?"

At once, Mohanty's voice dropped to a whisper, "No one is supposed to know . . . she was taken away some days back for secret questioning . . . "

He might have been speaking the truth. News, in all its variant versions, was now so freely available that anyone could set himself up as an independent transmitting and broadcasting authority, picking up information, resuscitating it for further speculation. "She is still under heavy guard because she is giving secret information to the police."

It was the rickshawala who shuddered at Mohanty's explanation. He led his rickshaw away from the sight with a sudden, inspired burst of pedalling. My hair escaped from the ribbons originally imposed to confine it. It tore away, first in tearaway strands, then in heavy locks that lashed my face. I narrowed my eyes, so my vision could creep through the narrow gap between my eyelids but the wind blew unseen dust specks into my face, and my eyes in turn smarted and burnt.

I was forced to lift my hands to beat away the assault on my hair, but one hand refused to oblige, it lay trapped under my school bag. I usually managed my bag light, but now my hand tingled, with the added weight of something sitting on it. It was someone with a heavy behind, who finding my hand trapped in a wrong place, repositioned herself on the bag with relish, leaving behind a gnawing numbness. It took me some time to disengage my much-in-demand limb. Next I felt an odd constriction in my right side, as that someone now dug her elbow into me, demanding more space. My feet in their black-buckled shoes were impaled under the weight of someone's firmly stomped foot over mine, and even the air I inhaled had taken on the added smell of something else – of coconut hair oil and a gentle rose perfume.

Every elapsing minute registered a rise in my discomfort levels. My stomach hurt from sitting in a cramped position and the plastic covers of the seat were damp from the sweat trickling between my thighs. I had already been pushed from the middle to the left half of the seat and the rickshaw had tilted alarmingly on to one side, as the other person shifted and shuffled next to me.

The rickshawala was much too nice to turn around and ask me how I had managed to put on so much weight so soon. But the bones on his back stood out with the effort of pulling something heavy. His ribs bared in a grin, were white and sharp like the fine workings on the cane chairs at home.

He was also nice enough to attempt a conversation with Mohanty. After all, they had been tagging each other for time enough to establish a conversational bonding. When Mohanty clapped his hand on his forehead and spoke up just to make himself heard, "My god, such trouble in this city. I have never seen anything like this before," the rickshaw slowed to commiserate with him. "Yes, I have been here for ten years and nothing . . . no, nothing like this . . . "

But Mohanty did not respond. It was beneath his dignity to strike up a conversation with a small-time rickshawala. He was in government service and he would only talk to people at the same level. He moved several paces ahead, and maintained a respectable distance even after my entourage had turned the gate to my school. First Mohanty, flapping his left hand to indicate his intentions to people behind and the rickshawala following, a wheel or so later, his bell tinkling in a subdued manner. It could be the fatigue of a long journey but I knew otherwise. Only when the rickshaw halted and its wheels turned aside in some relief, I could tell for sure. That whoever it was that had travelled so long with me had made up her mind. Enough was enough and she had slipped away, leaving just the three of us to lurch into the school compound.

I could do little else but shrug off the matter. If I did report it, hinting about the presence of someone unauthorized, hitching a free ride in my rickshaw, I would be accused of – *"believing in malicious gossip, and for spreading rumours with malafide intentions"* – words and phrases I had sometimes seen underlined in red in Father's heavy files.

I was late but the school building did not appear foreboding, nor had the compound been emptied of rickshaws. Though the first bell calling for silence must have already tonged, the girls, some, my classmates, were deep in conference, pigtails bounced on shoulders, passing on secrets. I negotiated the maze of rickshaws, crossed the tight-wound circles of girls, but my further progression ahead, towards one of those heavyset columns near the stairs where I hid myself away every morning, was blocked by the presence of two police jeeps. They stood right near the stairs, their faces turned towards each other, keeping to themselves and everyone away.

Three-four policemen emerged in minutes from the principal's office, Sister Michael followed a few decorous steps behind. It was a very serious looking procession, and when they were a foot away from the jeep and could proceed no further, the policemen u-turned. They saluted Sister Michael by pressing their policemen's batons to their foreheads and Sister Michael acknowledged it by a gracious incline of her head. Then she scampered back to a safe distance as the jeep engines revved up, black smoke jetting out from an ample behind. A respectful silence watched the jeeps drive away, loud in their own importance.

The curfew on conversation was relaxed with the departure of the police jeeps. A group near me discussed the mobs that had featured in action around the Manglabagh police station. A girl insisted it was her rickshaw that had braved the rain of stones and sticks people were hurling at shops in Ranihat, forcing them to close down. Some people had been beaten up outside the Cuttack hotel. The factory on the hill was attacked too, once again. Only one person had some good news, one that made the day considerably brighter. "You know, the road outside Mrs. Muller's home has been blocked. There are many policemen there. Not even allowing anyone to leave or come in. She won't come today."

In the assembly, Sister Michael still had her serious face on, her expression as closed as the rest of her tightly starched self. The policemen had obviously left behind a lot of homework; she passed it on to us.

"Girls, you know what has been happening all over the city, don't you? How the atmosphere has been vitiated and the rising crime rates? The police were here and they conveyed their worry to me. What we were agreed on was this. . . ."

She looked around and smiled. We held our breaths. Would she declare a holiday? A picnic?

"It is all up to us. To make sure this doesn't happen. After all, as women, we form particularly vulnerable groups. Vulnerable means helpless, unable to defend," Sister Michael added on her own volition. She had caught the puzzled stares, the surreptitious prodding, the girls nudging each other to find out what that word meant.

"After assembly, the sisters will go to every class in turn and give you some special instructions. On how to conduct yourselves in public and prevent crime. Then we can break for the rehearsals. This year the sports day will be dedicated to Samarpita Mishra."

Everyone dispersed for class in silence, eyes downcast, feet following each other in martyred fashion. It was as if we were already mourning for Samarpita.

The instructions followed a strict protocol – beginning from the senior classes and moving progressively downward. From sentries posted at the gate and messages passed on from class to class, we were fed regular updates. Sister Geraldine carried a chart, which, folded up, was as tall as she was. She looked like a placard-bearing 'rabble-rouser'. Sister Rufina balanced an open register in her hands, which she kept ticking off each time a class was done.

Our turn came soon after recess. We returned to find Sister Rufina standing at the door to the class, ushering us in, her face set to a stony expression, fingers on her smoky gray lips morse-coding a message. Be quiet. Serious business ahead.

Sister Geraldine was standing against the chart, which, unfolded, hung from the two nails over the blackboard. Neither of them smiled at us as we came in single file, careful not to brush against each other. The tubelights that lounged on every wall and came into use only when the rains left everything dark and broody, were now on and gleamed dully back. The windows had been closed shut, the shutters pulled down and after the tallest girl, the last in the line entered, Sister Rufina pulled the door shut behind her. Suspense bubbled down every row, unseen and hidden. Backs suddenly straightened themselves, hands lay folded over each other on the desk and a sincere, pious expression appeared on every face, in perfect emulation of the sisters.

When all of us had taken our places, and had our rough copies and pens out in front just in case we were asked to take notes, Sister Geraldine shifted away from the chart and moved towards the teacher's desk. "Girls, take a look at this chart."

It covered the entire length of the blackboard and was done in very loud colours. At the top, there was a three-word explanation – Female Reproductive System.

A thick tube in pink lay coiled over most of the page, and there were lines of blue and red running through it. Sister Geraldine took action with her pointer; Sister Rufina positioned herself more firmly against the door, to catch any inattention, wandering minds, or to stop anyone from barging into the class.

"I am sure you know what this is about."

No one did. The reproductive system, even our biology teacher had explained, was for a more senior class when they were less giggly about such things. But no one dared raise a hand to explain it to Sister. She wasn't even expecting any, because she looked around and launched into the same explanation she must already have dinned into five hundred ears, spread over four classes, divided into sixteen sections. I was finding it difficult to work out how such long, terribly ugly things, could fold themselves up so easily to fit inside me.

"This is just to answer any doubts if you have. I am sure you heard about the kind of things happening to women . . ."

Sister Rufina nodded in approval and we nodded following her example.

"Things like rapes, acid throwing, eve-teasing incidents. Why does this happen?"

Sister Rufina answered, "We must be careful not to let it happen. After all, it is us women who have to bear it and we must not in turn, give provocation."

She pulled her wimple well over her forehead, brushing back hastily an errant provocative flick of hair. Sister Geraldine looked seriously at all of us, her eyes on every face.

"Sister is right. We women must behave decently, give no cause for Pro-vo-ca-tion."

She enunciated the word clearly, each syllable falling with a gentle slap as a mild breeze from the fan rustled her sternly starched habit. She moved back to the chart. "This is how the female body functions. Take a good look though I am sure you know parts of it by now. This will help you understand your urges, the way your hormones may function on certain days of the month."

We listened, careful not to miss a word. The charts slapped against the walls, the fans moved ponderously already bored and outside, some flat-footed girls ran by. Sister Rufina looked towards them in disapproval. "See," she pointed past the closed door, "that is no way for a woman to behave. No decorum or decency. As women, we must always give a good impression of ourselves. That way, no one can take advantage. Just because we feel certain urges, we must hold ourselves back."

It was Sister Geraldine's turn to nod encouragingly, running a hand down her habit, over the pleats. The sisters were always so wrapped up in their habits that every urge had long been locked away inside.

"All that is happening around the city. First Samarpita... someone threw acid on her. You know why?"

We had heard the explanation before but Sister Rufina insisted on telling us once again, "Because she was a bad girl. Got into bad company, was too free in her ways. Moved around with too many men. You should never make that mistake."

The all-encompassing first person plural had been dropped and along with it all pretension. The sisters were above all this, it was we girls, who were bad, because we gave in to urges, behaved with no decorum, did not bother to create a good impression about ourselves. A barrage of advice now torpedoed its way towards us.

"Wear decent clothes."
"Be alert."
"Don't talk to any man just like that."

I wished I could take notes but no one else was and I would look silly doing it. You only took notes for things you could cram before the exams. I mulled over my confusion until I felt something cold thrust itself against my arm. My heart began hammering heavy metal drumbeats against my chest. That someone from the rickshaw was back again. She had even crept into the classroom, determined to shadow me everywhere. The cold dug in deeper, forcing me to look down. A dictionary that had begun its circumnavigation around the classroom from somewhere in the back rows had now docked at my desk. I looked down at the word ticked with a red ballpoint pen.

rape, r~p,n. (obs.) rapine, plunder, seizure: carnal knowledge of a woman without her legal consent. – v.t. to seize and carry off : to commit rape upon : (obs.) to ravish or to transport as with delight. – n. r~per. – adj. r~ping, (her.) tearing prey : (obs.) ravishing, delighting. [Prob. L. rap~re, to snatch, confused with rap (2).
rape, r~p,n. a division of Sussex. [Origin obscure.]
rape, r~p,n. a plant (*Brassica Napus*)near akin to the turnip, cultivated for its herbage and oil-producing seeds : applied to various closely allied species or varieties. ns. rap-cake; refuse of rapeseed after the oil has been expressed ; rapé-oil ; rapé-seed. [L. r~pa, r~pum, a turnip.]
rape, r~p, n. refuse in wine-making. [Fr. rpe.]

The *Chambers's Twentieth Century Dictionary*, reprint edition for 1968, offered four meanings for rape. But that one word, tick-marked in blood red, only confirmed the suspicions I had of late been developing about men.

"If you have any questions, now?"

The sisters had finished, and were rubbing their hands hoping the friction would somehow bring forth answers.

But no questions emerged. The sisters looked at each other, shrugged and Sister Geraldine made her next offer, "If you have questions and are feeling shy to ask, write a note and drop into this bag." Sister Rufina withdrew a much folded market bag from her ample pocket. "Its all right if you do not write your name, just your class and section."

"We will reply when we have our next instruction class." Sister Rufina added and held open the market bag, moving from seat to seat, staring in a kindly fashion at all of us. But that was deceptive. I knew she was looking us all over, even under the seats for any breach of discipline. I really hoped the dictionary had made a discreet disappearance. I had two questions, and dropped them hastily into the bag, watching them mix with the other slips, hoping there was no way the handwriting could be traced to me.

Is lying with a man, who is not your father or your brother, on an armchair, rape?

If you write letters to a man, who is not your father or your brother, is that ~~Provocation~~ Provokation ?

The first question had taken me a lot of thought. I had not mentioned Mehta Uncle by name because he had his informers everywhere. Right at this very moment, they could be spying, looking on from over my shoulder, following my every word as I struggled to hold on to a very leaky pen.

The rehearsals for the sports day made up for everything else that day. Even though a few leery policemen stood alert by the high walls, baton tapping against thigh, their presence a warning to any rapist, any acid attacker, or eve-teasers who happened to be lurking near.

My name was down for the 1000m heats and I made three entire rounds of the jogging track easily enough. Most of my competitors gave up too early. Either they were too delicate or were already taking the sisters advice to heart. It was unladylike to pant and perspire through three rounds of the track, when all the time the wind tore at ribbons and threatened to pull up skirts.

I ran, trying to outrace the wind. It chased me from behind – trying to snatch at my hair, gleefully lifting my skirt, shoving it between the thighs. Soon it became a cold whistle in my ears; the sweat ran like welcome rivulets of water down my shirt, gathering in places like deep black cesspools, as if someone with an official seal had stamped dampness on parts of me. I saw the flash of trees standing mutely by, and dry leaves running up to the track and stopping as I neared. And the dust rose from under my feet and swelled into the kind of dust cloud that formed in movies, when hordes of marauding horsemen rode into a village.

They were all watching me, urging me on – Paul was on his feet, my parents were clapping and Mehta Uncle stood with his baton raised high in a salute, especially for me, even Mrs. Muller looked balefully on. She could do little to stop me running the race of my life. It was the fastest I had ever run. I knew now what it meant to fly, how that girl not really dead had flown at breakneck speed over half the city, scaring most people out of their wits, and into temples.

I ran on for a while longer even after the assistant PT master had blown on his whistle. I stopped only when the wind dropped and the silence spilled over from the audience and tripped into my ears. The clapping was reluctant and forced and I who had raised my arms to the skies in the way champions did, brought them hastily down to my sides. My name was down as a contestant for the 1000m, but I no longer wanted to whoop for joy.

Sahu's car, Father's official Ambassador came to fetch me from school that day. When the girls saw the sternly officious car, the switched-off red light sitting cushy on the bald roof, their gaits slowed, conversations stilled to shape curious glances towards the car. I walked to the car in slow countable steps. Ma's sandal first peeped from under the door, assessing the situation and then her voice stepped in, sharp and worried, clearly zipped up under the effect of unnamed fears.

"Hurry up, there is trouble . . . " she was moving away from the door so I could sit easily.

She followed this up with, "Why are you late . . . ?" but her head had turned towards Sahu telling him through the rear-view mirror he could move.

I wanted to tell her about the race but Ma was wiping away the silver dots of perspiration that winked on her forehead where the sun gently highlighted them. Ma instead told me of the troubles that had broken out in select places, rupturing like boils in a city already simmering with tension. At Ranihat, then in the college, in the recruitment office, then in the cinema theatres . . . everywhere . . .

"Why?" I asked when Ma paused in her narrative.

"It's the students. Upset with the police action. And the politicians are egging them on." Then she stopped, looking askance Sahu's way in case he was following every detail of the conversation.

"But Mehta Uncle says it is the Naxalites."

"That too . . . but who can tell . . . when trouble once starts, it sweeps everything away, coats everything the same evil colour. Who can tell then who is fighting against whom or for what?"

Ma was given to making such vague, philosophical statements when she couldn't bring herself to agree with either Mehta Uncle or Father. Or it could be because she was unable to decide what to believe in for fear of hurting either. I leaned against the foamy seats and breathed in deeply the stories, the scent of my mother, the freshener that lingered on the cushions, and yawned.

"What a day and it might get worse with the bandh that has been called tomorrow . . . just see," said Ma, catching me in the act.

I closed my eyes, thinking over something that had just occurred to me. In spite of everything, it had to be the most peaceful and the happiest day I had ever known.

I rolled the windows up to the point where the lever would rise no further and sat back, feeling the soft warmth of the foamy leathery seats under my bottom; I heard the pleasing hum and the slow turn of the wheels under my feet. In a rickshaw, you had to sit in a particular manner, holding tight either to the seat or to the rods beside you, otherwise the jostling, the rattling and the shuddering could get unmanageable. In the car, I breathed in freedom in deep gulps. The freedom this city had snatched away from me. The freedom I had lost because I could not go to school on my own, because I was a girl and could no longer do what I had always done, because of many becauses. I prayed the car moments would stretch as long as they possibly could, go farther than an elastic rubber band stretched tight between one's fingers. But happiness was like everything else and my bubble burst in the moments that lingered between the Ambassador's relieved halt before the gate and Mohanty's meditative lumber up from the portico to unlock it. It was that moment when Ma wiped her by now freely perspiring face with a perfumed kerchief and announced in deepest relief, "Thank god, we are home finally. I was worried whether we would get here in one piece."

You should never look at happiness, stare it in the face, or even ever acknowledge that you are happy. For that would be wasting time. You think you are happy but you don't allow yourself to be happy, to savour the moment itself. So that when it is gone in a whiff, you are left with everyday feelings. That day had been so complete – Mrs. Muller's absence, my success at the races, even though no one had bothered to cheer for me, then Ma turning up to fetch me home – that I knew it had to be the most perfect day in my life. I longed to lie back in cushiony comfort, keep listening to Ma, watch the world go by, and feel the happiness swell like a balloon in my heart. I had been watching it so hard, feeling happy that I was happy, that I never realized that it could go phut, all too soon.

Amrit Bazar Patrika, Calcutta

Bandh called in Orissa.

March 1, Cuttack. The opposition in Orissa today called for a bandh to protest against what it claims has been the government's high-handed manner of tackling the recent disturbances in Cuttack and a few other areas in Orissa. In the capital, Bhubaneshwar, student organisations have demonstrated against the continued raids and crackdown on their hostels and institutions.

Today, stray incidents of looting were reported from market areas of Cuttack but the situation has since been brought under control. The state government is carefully watching the situation. The CM has cancelled his visit to Delhi but has denied that his government has asked the central government for assistance in bringing the situation under control.

INTRUSIONS

The Oriya papers carried more news in greater detail but again I did have some problems in translation.

March 1, Cuttack – Police have intensified their investigations into the chain of thefts that has so unsettled the citizens of Cuttack. The thefts that began soon after the riots have left the police bumbling in search of answers. The Home Minister is actively following every turn of the investigations.

The DIG in charge of investigations, D M Mehta, is taking anyone looking remotely suspicious into custody, but he has admitted that so far there has been no progress. The chowkidar of the St. Joseph's School, where promising distance runner, Aditi Chatterji is at present a student, was also taken in on charges of suspicion but soon released for lack of evidence. Later some rickshawalas were detained for a few hours but released because the police could not press charges against them. The rickshawala union has protested at the high-handed manner of the police and have refused to transport students to the school any more.

Meanwhile the latest series of disappearances include a sketch pen set belonging to Monalisa Mohapatro, some comic books brought into the school illegally by Sharmilee Misra, snapshots and autographs of leading cine stars of Orissa, a cricket bat, a used chocolate box now used as a needlework set, a ruler, a fancy paperweight, a Chinese doll. The last few objects have so far had no claimants but callers who reported the thefts to the police station did not want their identity made public.

The city elsewhere continues to simmer with tension. The police say more than 300 persons have been taken into preventive custody. Official estimates as to the exact damage sustained during the riots that broke out over the city last February place the damage as anything between 50 lakhs to 2 crores.

The first victim of that day's bandh was Bhai. But Thamma also disappeared for a whole two hours and reports of the first intrusion into the attic came in.

Bhai had started the day in a manner markedly different from other usual days. By getting up early. He followed up this uncharacteristic act by getting ready early, then he announced to no one in particular that he was going for a cricket match.

"You can't go. It's a bandh."

"But it's a holiday."

"Its not...,"said Ma with finality in her voice. "It's dangerous to go out...no one will even step out of their houses...it's a bandh. You better stay inside." A bandh meant what it stood for – bandh – closed, a complete shut down.

Thamma disappeared barely an hour after I had moved to the attic. Since there was no school, there were several things on my agenda. I intended to give the dolls special instructions in the manner of Sisters Rufina and Geraldine; my brief was to ensure that my endeavours in this regard were less scary, more usefully instructive.

First on my agenda was to help them master the use of several weapons. The sword, a long scale from Father's office, and a knife from the kitchen served as demonstration equipment. I was telling them the right way to duck in case of an acid attack when the voice intruded.

Mohanty's voice, spindly like the rest of him, floated into the attic, through the half-open glass pane. I had left it ajar to give the attic a badly needed airing. I did not heed Mohanty at first. He was in the habit of singing to himself as he polished his bicycle. Most of these songs were of a devotional type that kept him company as he sat, reverential in a cross-legged manner, giving the bicycle a concentrated rubdown, using his checked towel folded several times over. But the song soon picked up both momentum and volume, begging to be appeased and Bhai, who had been sulking since his enforced confinement, too joined in. "Maji . . . Maji . . . Thamma Thamma . . . "

I had to go then. As I squeezed my way through the pane, I felt their petulant glances on me, "It's all right. I am on a mission to rescue Thamma."

Thamma had to be where no one would have even thought of looking. The office-room that was strictly off limits for just the three of us – Bhai, Thamma and of course, me. My name always appeared in such forbidden lists, where it gave no one any credit to appear. Except, of course the sports lists. Only Mohanty, because he cleaned it up in the morning, and Ma, because she was Ma, were allowed into the room.

I took the long way around the attic to throw everyone off (but considering the spate of intrusions that were to break out shortly, evidently such precautions hadn't helped). I went around the entire length of the house, down the banana grove, over the flowerbeds, and then that proud final dash across the verandah.

But there was already someone before me. Someone I had never seen, and whose face was lit up in the oddest possible way as the sun fixed its gaze obliquely on him. A blob of light pointed to the remains of lunch stuck fast to his gums. Yellow and pink in the light, his teeth needed a good brushing.

"So you are looking for your grandmother?" he asked, and his spectacles flared in understanding. A thin breeze pushed its way in, nudging the door open. Something shifted in the glass panes of the door as well. The man who had been about to subject me to a very serious questioning lifted his face and I saw him sitting inside a glass frame high on the walls in the room I was not supposed to enter. Chests twice as tall as me tottered under the weight of files, gloomy brown and unprotesting, pushed into every available shelf space.

The man and several others dressed in a similar manner stood far above the lowly files, smiling continually from within their glass-framed prisons. Sometimes when the light shifted, a stray yellow beam slashed across the glass, and a window appeared somewhere between eyebrows and upper lip. Someone's right cheek broke each time the breeze butted in through the window. The fan blades cut a rough swathe through each shiny forehead. But the man who had first addressed me smiled benignly from over the files. He looked very harmless at first glance, but by now I had learnt a lot about first impressions.

His smile turned white in pleasure as I stared, unable to look away. When he saw my knees begin to quiver, his smile broadened, turned a clearer white and a flash of silver streaked across the glass. It was Thamma's sari reflected on his glass frame.

Thamma sat undisturbed, absolutely at ease in my father's swivel chair, his spectacles, harsh and black rimmed covering half her cheeks, a file held upside down in her hands. She did not seem in the least put out with my exchange with the strange gentleman in the photo.

"Thamma," I called to her, in relief because I was not alone with that man. Thamma raised a thin, stick-like finger not wishing to be disturbed. I walked up to the table, put my hands on the shiny glass panel. My arms appeared like short tree stumps in the glass and I whispered close to her ears, "Thamma, Thamma. It's not safe here."

Thamma took a while raising her once deep brown, now dimly turning hazel, eyes. The light zipped into her eyes, then spread over her whole face, as if a golden carpet had stretched itself across an empty room. Then she smiled, a slow smile that pulled her lips and stretched the light wrinkles on her cheek.

The two porcelain fairies on the pen stand, holding aloft several pens in their conical golden yellow hats, shivered as the light and Thamma's attention fell on them. One of them jiggled in protest as a pen was plucked out, leaving behind a moon-sized crater. Thamma proceeded to write her name on the file that had fallen open obligingly on a page half-empty. I could see the green lines, like train tracks depicted in an atlas, race up from her hands to her elbows before losing themselves in the white blouses she always wore, fluffed sleeves, now brown and dirt-edged. Thamma held the pen tight between her fingers and it took her a very long time to write her name – Tarunbala Debi – in bold red, large, loping letters that resembled the dancing fishes and eccentric seahorses in my science book.

When she was done, the file closed on its own accord. Thamma fell back on the swivel chair, turned it around with a delicate stroke of her hand. I saw her twirling out of sight with a high-pitched giggle. Mud stuck to the lined grooves that grew deep on Thamma's feet. I looked up to see Thamma's head fall to one side of the chair and heard her soft snores.

The man in the photo still looked down at me, a smile playing around his moustache. In another minute, he would take a step back, raise a finger and run it across his moustache in a thinly veiled threat. "What do you think you will do now? I will be watching you anyway."

The fairies on the pen stand tripped in alarm. The paperweights, inside which lived some unusual creatures – a panda, a drummer boy, a man and a woman looking at each other, a reindeer trying to push its way out of the glass with its antlers – sat stodgily on the table looking for any piece of paper to hold down. I lifted the reindeer and raised it high. It slipped from my hand and dropped onto the table making a sad, hollow thunk. Nothing happened. I waited, as did the reindeer who remained where he was, though cracks had now appeared in the roof that was too high for his antlers to reach. A thin white scratch also appeared on the smooth glass face of Father's table. It stood out – a sore and derisively eye-catching scar on a once beautiful, unmarked face.

The other objects on the table, arranged as per Father's strict specifications, looked mutely on. Rubbers and blotting stands, notepads, and stick-pads, pencils pared down to a precise point, more pen stands, and more paper-weights. Confronted with such an embarrassment of riches, I thought of the table that stood by itself in the attic – forlorn and bare, crying to be dressed up. The reindeer in his toppled over cage looked on from his upside down position. The crack in his cage looked as if a giant snowflake had shattered itself against the glass ceiling. Father would be furious if he saw it. The reindeer paperweight had been a gift from someone in Finland. Sooner or later, I would have to mend it – paint it over with some colour – the blue or white of the sky or seal it with Cellotape.

The man in the glass frame spoke up again but this time, he was addressing Thamma, "Thamma, Thamma . . . Maji, Maji, Maajii, Maajeee." But the words came not from his throat where his Adam's apple bobbed with the effort but from somewhere outside the window. The search for Thamma was still on.

The next moment, Mohanty's nose poked its way into the room through the rose-pink window curtains. The silence entered first for Thamma's snores had broken away and she was staring at Mohanty, trying to place him. I really couldn't blame Thamma. His head between the curtains gave Mohanty the look of a trapped goat but he spoke in a high-pitched rooster's squawk, "Memsaheb, they are here . . . here in the office room."

The way he said it, the manner in which his eyes came to rest on me, anyone would think we had been caught with our hands in the cash till when all I had in my pockets was a paperweight that needed fixing.

The dolls were cheered up all the same. With the woebegone reindeer trapped like them, in his own world of glass. Following the same procedure as with the other things I had procured thus far, I informed them it was only for a short while, for all this had to be returned. Because everything had been brought up there without permission.

But an intrusuion had taken place in the attic in the few hours I was away. When I returned, a quick glance told me nothing was the way I had left it. The last remaining covers over the furniture had been blown away, while the attic had been subjected to a hurried search. The dolls had tried to put up some resistance, tried to put the instructions I had given them to some use, but they lay face down on the floor. The dustbin had fallen over, scattering rolled up bits of paper. Some had crackled open as the intruder had tried to decode my secret messages. The almirah had been broken into for its other still intact door was now swinging freely trying to catch my attention.

I was caught unprepared, with little clue as to the intruder's possible identity. The break-in could also have a very simple explanation. An exceptionally short, sharp dust storm had found its way through the open window and blown my cover. But that was the police's way of doing things. Looking for the shortest, simplest solution to a case that would help close another file. *File Closed. Investigations complete.* The DIG investigating would write in a flourish. After which it would be sealed in red, tied up with a loose, loping white string, then stored away in a cupboard. For future reference, to cite as a precedent when required.

Possible Suspects

It could be one of the two men (or both) who conversed with each other, standing at one of the YMCA windows, directly away from the attic window. They must have kept track of my every movement, knew also that I moved in and out at the oddest hours. It was very simple for them to make a break-in. They had only to jump onto their window ledge, follow it for a while before making another jump over the boundary walls into our bungalow. The mango tree nearest the wall now looked as if it had someone hidden away in its branches. On the other hand, just because the tree was there, it did not necessarily follow that there had to be a man in it. It simply looked too big, leafy and full-bellied with branches to be just occupied by a few birds and a few still-green mangoes.

The man in the photo downstairs could also be a suspect. He had appeared in the attic within minutes of my return. I caught his face grinning back at me in the open half-mirror of the almirah. I had been bending low, to check as I often did, if the faint dimple had embedded itself deeper in my cheek when I saw him. He still had the same grin on.

The man in the photo had pulled off a near-impossible feat. He had climbed out of his black photo frame in my father's office, walked to the very edge of the cupboard, and squatted on his heels before jumping several feet below to the floor. He must have walked past a sleeping Mohanty, who slept with his newspaper over his face, his mouth an unexpected hollow where it had sucked in a bit of paper. The photo man must have walked to the side of the house and climbed the mango tree in a trice.

He had shaken hands with the man already hidden in the mango tree and then jumped lightly from tree to roof. He had flicked the hair back over his forehead, rearranged his glasses on his face and walked along the parapet towards the half-open attic window. Next, he squeezed himself in – lifting the upper pane a bit and sliding through. Wincing and cursing, for he had grown a bit thick around the waist from all the time he had spent sitting comfortably in Father's office room. He brushed himself down and smiled his evil smile at the dolls, who, braver than me, stared right back, not even shifting in the sofa to make space for him. Finding himself unwelcome he had crawled right under the sofa, found the old brown photo frame, presently unoccupied but crumbling with age and neglect, and snuggled into it. From time to time, he would stretch out his neck to peer into the mirror, straighten his tie, and flick the hair back from his forehead once more.

He had been about to do that again when I had come in the way. He shifted this way and that, wriggled his waist over the frame and craned his neck, but the square of my back made it difficult. Finally he had stood on his toes, reached over to grip the rod that ran along the roof of the frame and glanced at himself over my shoulder. And that was how our eyes had met.

There was a third suspect. It could be a third suspect or it could be either of the first two, or both of them acting in unison. *Abetting and aiding each other in crime.* There was no complete description I had of the third suspect, but he was the only one of the suspects I had actually seen. I had caught sight of half his leg on a few occasions when he had walked past the glass pane. Maybe he didn't know of the attic yet, and was plotting an intrusion. Or maybe he was trying to scare me away, make me evacuate premises I had occupied first so that he could stake claim to it.

Two nights ago he had made his first appearance and I had not treated the matter seriously enough. *Gross Negligence, Criminal Apathy,* the police would have called it. Every night, when the breeze outside rose or a cloud flitted past the moon, the shadows the branches made on the glass took on a different pose. Either it was a dog's mouth hanging open or it could metamorphose into a club fitted with nails shaking itself with menace. That night, a stegosaurus had visited, huge leaf-like appendages attached all over its head and neck. Its head was turned towards the glass and in the breeze, its pointed mouth nudged softly against the pane. But the breeze soon grew heavier, and with it came the sound of a "crack". Not the sound of a window being pushed open but a foot falling on a dry leaf. The stegosaurus parted its mouth and we listened for the sound together, a second time. A dry leaf skittered against the glass, and with it followed the clear sharp straight outline of a trouser against the silvery lit up pane. It stayed there for the briefest of whiles before the canvas was swept clean once again, like blackboard etchings eased away by a duster. A last crackle of leaf, the sound fading away in moments and then my sigh of relief – it fell like a whoosh of air on the floor, blowing away the dust, like tiny carom pieces.

So far I had three possible suspects but there could be more. I had to keep them away at all costs. I had to arm myself – not with a knife, a stick or even Mehta Uncle's baton, but with Father's revolver.

Dear Paul

I hope you received my request for help and advice on the matter of repeated intrusions into the attic. This is needed as I have to leave town for a couple of days. We are taking my grandmother to Puri to see a holy man. They think she is possessed by the ghost but I of course have other ideas. She can see things we can't. I hope no further disturbances will be reported from the attic in my absence.

I shall resume my reports, keeping you notified of developments once I return. If for reasons of confidentiality, you are unable to write to me, I shall understand. But please do write. I have been here nearly two months, three days and so far, haven't heard anything from you. I miss playing football, cricket and all my friends, especially you. So please write.

With my best wishes,
A Chatterji

The sadhu baba had his ashram in Puri, a three-hour drive from Cuttack. Father thought it best to start early, for the sun could make things unbearable. It was so early that I did not remember brushing my teeth. I remembered standing before the basin, hearing the water gurgle down the pipe, watching it disappear into blackness, winking back dots of silver. The white foam of toothpaste stood last in line before it too was sucked in greedily, with the wheezing cough of an asthmatic patient. It was so early that Thamma was asleep when we started. She sat between Ma and me, her head on my shoulder.

Even the car was quiet, its horns muffled, as if afraid to wake the road up. Once on the highway, however, the car shook itself away from the city, like a braid of hair falling free from the confining grip of a ribbon. Trees on either side stood marked red and white and paddy fields dozed inside their carefully marked plots. Sometimes a squat, bulbous temple spire appeared, its saffron flag waving in sheer habit. Mud-brick houses peered shyly from under thatched roofs, trying to brush away stray tendrils of pumpkin that jumped from roof to roof. At some places, houses wheezed into several others to become one village. The monotonous brown patches of walls spilled over to form one square, splat block, and I had to blink often to make sure I wasn't asleep and that it wasn't the colour of my closed eyelids I was looking at.

The sadhu baba lived in a house that had no rooms but huge halls that led one to the other, with ceilings that appeared to have been hastily clamped down when the halls threatened to grow too high. The high ceilings were speckled by chandeliers and fans swung from slender black columns, a half-spun web of a giant spider. On the walls, square slabs were arranged neatly by each other like a perfect set of teeth, bearing information about donors and amounts they had donated. Many important people, especially those in the government, looked up to the sadhu; making donations was one way of conveying their appreciation of the help their careers had received because of his interventions.

The first hall was strewn with shoes, scattered on the floor like confetti. Taking the cue, we took off our shoes in a carefully chosen corner Father pointed out, so later they would prove easy to locate. The hall after this was full of the people who belonged to the shoes. They moved around, puppet figures pulled by the high chandeliers, matted locks dripped like seaweed on every shoulder, vague smiles creased every second chin. The door pushed into a corner of this hall led into another, far bigger than either of its predecessors. And here instead of moving around, everyone sat cross-legged on the floor, eyes tightly closed. All that could be heard was the combined sound of everyone breathing in and exhaling at once, as if a giant animal slumbered somewhere in the room. We made our way ahead, stepping over extended knees, outstretched hands, muttering our "excuse mes" to the backs of differently sized heads. We followed Father in an orderly queue as he led us to the divan at the very end of the hall.

Even from a distance the divan presented a bloated look. Heavy cushions preened in their bright colours, their tiny winking mirrors studied the audience in front giving nothing away. Ten rows of people away, I realized what gave the divan its flatulent appearance. A man lay spread-eagled over three cushions, his stomach heaving in unembarrassed content – as if he were on a plastic raft, luxuriously adrift in a swimming pool. On stools around the bed, vases overweight with exotic flowers pumped their scented fragrance into his nostrils and the aroma of sandal wafted towards him from incense sticks stretched out in the manner of guileful belly dancers.

The bed took on a more populous appearance as we neared. On its other side, several pairs of hands announced their presence. The hands lavished attention on the man on the cushions, their ministrations turning every visible part of his skin an apple red, before vanishing into different sized bodies, cut away in half by the intervening divan.

Father stopped and the procession behind him also halted. The man lying on the cushions opened his eyes very slowly as Father folded himself into a namaste, his torso bent a full right angle away from the rest of him. The baba smiled, his lips pressed tight together, the attendants stopped pressing flesh at the interruption. It was clear they did not approve of the sadhu baba shifting his attentions anywhere. His hand fluttered in the air looking for something to point at but Father deciphered his gesture well and bowed again in grateful acceptance. He whispered that Baba wanted us to sit down, right where we stood. And despite our considerably delayed arrival, that was how we got to occupy front row seats.

The sadhu baba held his smile as we took our places. His attendants resumed their exercises and the baba leaning back against the cushions, finally decided to speak. His words, slow and measured, rose in stages, like a bucket pulling itself out from a well.

"How is work with you, Baba?"

Father didn't reply. He did not even look for words to speak with. Father just sat there, chin drooping on to chest, the lines back on his forehead. But I could also see new lines, falling away like weak sun rays from his eyes, his lips shaped like an upside-down crescent. My father was getting old and still could not talk of the other things that worried him. All the other things besides work that worry you but fall into the category of unmentionable things.

"Work is not good." The sadhu baba answered for him and Father's head came up, briefly catching the baba's eyes before moving down again. Father was forcing himself to agree.

"Ah, Ah," the sadhu baba said leaning back, stretching one leg obligingly out for an attendant to pummel. The attendant's fingers moved up, down and around, she pressed with a studied concentration; her eyes were closed in prayer, her lips shaped into a beatific smile. She wanted nothing more from life than to sit by a bed like this, pressing and pumping flesh for eternity. But the sadhu baba had other ideas.

He fluttered with his fingers again, tossed his head briefly from Father then back to the attendant and at that silent order places were exchanged. Father rose, and with exquisitely gentle movements sat himself on the bed, at the baba's feet. He lifted the baba's feet, placed them on his lap and the pressing, pulling and pummelling recommenced.

"Ah-hhhhh," the baba sighed deeply, his eyes looked up at the ceiling and then he pronounced the one word Father had been waiting for. Father bent forward, reverence writ large on his face. "Ashanti. Ashanti everywhere."

Father looked profound, as the wisdom of that pronouncement slowly collected in him. Murmurs of confusion descended in parts of the hall, as members of the audience begged to be enlightened.

The sadhu baba went on, "There is no peace anywhere and I see it on your face. There is tension in your work. Because you are much too attached. Attachment, Baba, is the real cause of suffering. You seek too much reward in your work. But that is what makes you attached and causes misery. The work itself should be done, rewards and results are for others to think about."

Father agreed, his hands clasped together in front as he held firm the divine words of wisdom. Thamma was smiling sagely.

"I am happy you have brought Tarunbala Devi here. How is she?"

He took Thamma's thin, shrivelled wrist in his, the lines across her delicate, crinkled skin stood up in nervous anticipation. Thamma's hand shook in his baby-soft, well-massaged hands, looking for a way to release itself.

"She is still . . . ?"

This time both Father and Ma nodded. The seriousness pulled their chins downward with a gravity that had more to do with his presence than the actual state of Thamma's health. She had been fine all through the journey.

"So you are now at the house Narayan Chand was in?"

His eyes travelled inward into his forehead as he sifted through logically arranged shelves of divine wisdom for an answer. "Even that house has ashanti. Too much of it pouring through its walls, everywhere." He appeared to know all about the evil spirits who lurked in every dark corner of the house, who pumped ashanti in through the walls, using their powerful bellows.

He stroked his chin, ran fingers down his beard and over his fine, silky hair. After a long while, his lips opened again for wisdom to pour forth again. Heads lunged forward again, as if afraid to miss the slightest pause, or even a punctuation mark. "Many evil spirits that only a special prayer service . . . a yagna can drive away . . . that is what I suggest you must do."

His advice ended with a loud, prolonged wail. It came from a woman leading a boy in, her wails tom-tomming their progression from the door towards the sadhu baba, following the same route we had taken a short while ago. The weight of her pent-up sorrow had left her severely hunchbacked. The boy behind her, moved slowly like a man who had overeaten. He was exhaling hard, the pronounced snorts of an advancing rhinoceros. The people sitting in orderly rows, unsure of how to react, obligingly raised knees, lifted inconveniently placed elbows or other intrusive limbs out of the way and thus assisted, that incongruous pair meandered its way towards the bed.

The woman was dragging the boy by the hand, almost pulling him because he would pause, look down at everyone and grin. As the party of two advanced, it became easier to read his features. The head was in the shape of a small carton, grocers use to deliver stuff to households. His hair long and unkempt kept falling over his eyes like a beaded string curtain, his lips wobbled and shook but he couldn't cry, because all he could do was grin, showing twin rows of uneven, chipped teeth.

When the woman had finally located the baba's feet, she pressed them against her face, her wails dissolved into funny kissing noises that didn't seem to embarrass the sadhu baba at all. He waited till she was spent. Till the sounds she made squelched and dried up inside her.

"Everything will be all right, Maya Debi." He said, his eyes gliding over his soft, quivering belly before alighting on her tightly wound-up bun, her crumpled blouse and the thin, plain sari covering her.

"I cannot manage any more. I am old." She raised herself to say this; the bones in her back croaked like the old furniture in the attic.

"It's getting difficult." And she gestured towards the boy. The boy lunged forward, pulled at the woman's sari and whispered, "Thakurma, I want to go home."

The woman, his grandmother, turned despairing eyes towards the sadhu. "He doesn't learn?" the baba asked. He stared at the boy whose thumb moved deeper into his lips till his grandmother's hand darted out to slap him hard on the wrist. The sound broke like a whiplash in that room full of shanti. Once her hand darted back into place, her vocal chords were pressed into service. She let forth a string of hastily threaded together woes.

"He goes to the special school but shows no interest. If they ask him to draw, he draws funny, strange things. Otherwise he does not want to read anything or write. His teachers say he cannot even write his own name. He has been three years in the same class."

She paused to consult the lines she had committed to memory and then picked up the thread of the story again, "I have so much trouble – my knee, then the headaches I get. It doesn't let me sleep at night. Still, I have to get up every day at five. It takes at least an hour or two to get him ready. His school is also quite far. Now, it is difficult to get on to buses. My knee . . . "

Her voice died in a whisper. The sadhu baba's eyelids had closed and she peered, fluttering her eyelids as if the sound would penetrate the sadhu baba's extended bout of silence. "Ashanti, ashanti everywhere," he finally said as his fingers played their old tune through his beard.

Relieved, the woman resumed, "Nowadays, he does not listen to me. I do not have the strength to drag him around. Even to come here to seek your blessings, he gave me a lot of trouble. And last week," she fortified herself with deep breaths before delivering her last remaining scoop, ". . . and last week, he let the hens out and killed the chickens. He dropped them one by one into a bucket filled with water . . . "

And with that, she came to the end of her narrative, wiping her glasses with her sari, looking at the sadhu baba coyly from under her lashes. The boy grinned at his grandmother, and asked again, "Thakurma, can we go home now?"

The baba looked towards the boy and towards the ceiling. At last he knew what to do. He stretched his hand out towards the nearest attendant. The woman in turn stretched out her hand towards a bucket (there were rows of them behind the bed, probably another bulk gift from Bhairav Mohanty), picked up the first thing her hand rested on and placed an orange in the baba's extended hand. The baba smiled, sniffed at it and held it invitingly towards the boy.

The boy lunged forward, grabbed the orange and clasped it hard to his chest. The baba looked at him, anticipation in his eyes and the boy frowned, his black, bustling eyebrows meeting at a common point as he made his own assessment of the baba. When that was done, he craned his neck to look beyond the sadhu baba and demanded, "I want those too."

A new series of wails crackled forth from his grandmother like the vigilance office siren that sounded everyday at nine.

But it was a voice from behind the boy that spoke up. "No, be a good boy and just say thank you." It was a deep, gravelly voice, giving the right inflection to every word, leaving the right pause between them. I turned around, and found that the man had once again stepped out of his photo in Father's office and was now moving with determined strides towards the sadhu baba.

He was wearing the same pair of spectacles and even his smile was unchanged. One single quick twist of the lips, that he offered my parents, once he was done with the head bowing and feet touching. He squatted on the floor as everyone else did, but he took his time, arranging his kurta decorously over his thighs. It was evident his mind was set on a plan of action to handle the unfolding situation.

First he turned to the woman to say, "Take him away. You know he always wants all that he sees." Then it was the baba's turn to be addressed.

Spreading his hands out in a helpless gesture, he explained in tones, soft and cajoling, "He is getting to be more of a problem child. All the other children are doing well in boarding school. This one . . . I don't know what to do with him."

The boy was exploring the orange. He turned it over in his hands like a cricket ball and then pressed hard on it. A stream of liquid rocketed out; it struck me on the cheek, leaving a faint orange-ish whiff, it left a blob on Father's trousers, and a sheen of silver on the man's spectacles. His eyes blurred, making the black eyeballs appear even larger, cruel stones set in a harsh, expressionless face. Now he looked more than ever like the photograph. His raised hand hovered in the air uncertainly but the boy, who had by now decided that peeling an orange was a task beyond his abilities was shoving it inside his mouth. The man snatched the orange away from the boy, but he remembered to keep his smile on. The same swift twist of the lips as he said, "Now, now, don't be naughty."

The boy stared at the orange he had been so cruelly deprived of and burst into tears. His heavy head shook as if his body suddenly found its weight unbearable, he wailed with his stubby fingers, their hard brown knobs like old, uncracked walnuts, covering his face.

The man smiled at everyone again and shook the boy hard by the shoulders. The jerking stemmed the flow of tears. He looked apologetically at everyone and murmured, "I just don't know what to do with him. Such a problem child."

"Yes, I can understand," Ma spoke up. The overpowering silence in the hall had bestowed her voice with some assurance.

"Sometimes, it is a challenge. We have one too," And her eyes moved. They bypassed Thamma, whose disinterest in the proceedings was already evident from her tiny snores, moved past Bhai who still held on to his awe-struck cross-legged position before the baba, her eyes stopped at me, where I sat, bunched up over my knees.

"We don't know what to with her . . . she refuses to behave properly in school or with people . . . says and does strange things. The teachers have sent us notes about her already." The chandeliers quivered in agreement and the sadhu baba and the photo man turned to look at me, profound sincerity in their eyes. Yes, it was time they decided what to do with me.

I sat back, wondering how to counter such unsubstantiated charges. It must have been Mehta Uncle who had filled her ears. Instead I did the unthinkable. Like the lady and then the boy before me, I burst into loud sobs.

I must have cried for a while. The more I concentrated on the right howl, I could pretend that I did not see or hear any other thing. Ma trying to catch my eye, Father's embarrassed shuffling and Bhai, unsure still of whether to put on his superior "only girls cry" look or to giggle in shared amusement with anyone who looked his way. My back burnt with the combined assault of several curious stares from the back rows. The man who had stepped out of the photo must have stepped back in, slid the glass frame across himself, and leaned back to resume smiling.

A housefly buzzed overhead, surveying the scene. In my half-scrunched still crying position, I could follow the fly as it dived under the bed, scrounged among the mountains of fruits and flowers, buzzed away again in annoyance. It soon reappeared, its buzzing lifting a notch higher as it made straight for the sadhu baba. I heard the hurried swish of clothes, frantic flutters as several hands offered to swat away the fly. At the sadhu baba's tired, bored voice, "Open the windows, it will go," the buzzing picked up pace, sounding angry and irritable, like an old man interrupted mid-flow between his rambling reminiscences. A clatter of bolts, shudder of panes, thud of wood striking walls hard followed and then the warm sunshine trooped in. Bringing with it the smell of leaves falling outside, all yellow and crinkled, the smooth turning of car wheels in the portico and distant shouts. My tears stopped momentarily. The fly had cheerfully rushed out at the sight of all that light and airiness. I badly wanted to follow it, chase it down the neat rows of flowerpots, see if a butterfly had hidden there. Especially one I had seen long back – yellow, with black dots, all unevenly shaped.

In the car the quiet had erected an invisible barbed wire fence, it allowed no word, no discreet look to surreptitiously sneak past. Sometimes though when the car braked unexpectedly or lurched on the uneven road, gaps appeared in the fence and words long clogged up in throats pushed each other through the gap.

"It's hot inside, isn't it?" said Father looking back at us on the back seat. I felt his eyes on me, hoping I was done with all the crying.

Thamma raised her head from its usual place on her chest and replied, "Yes, he was sweating profusely when he came in. He must have just come in."

"Who?" The word bounced around the car with some force before being re-directed Thamma's way. Thamma smiled her vague smile, "Narayan Chand, but he hasn't changed."

The car jerked, my head banged against the rolled-up window, knocking a new thought into me. Narayan Chand, who had lived in the house before us long back. The man who had stepped out of the photograph in Father's office – Mehta Uncle's one-time mentor and confidante, Bhaktawar's bete-noire, Ratri's father-in-law.

Ma raised her hanky to her lips as if the name was particularly offensive, and her muffled reply poured through every thread of that fine-laced piece of cloth, "You are mixing up, that was the son, Suresh Chand."

Thamma laughed, a low wobbly laugh that jogged her lost memories, "Suresh . . . so big he has grown."

No one said anything. The quiet turned into a heavy summer cloud that refused to move away elsewhere. The car negotiated an octroi gate, a boy rushed past chasing a cricket ball, a dog cleaned its ears, its paw raised indecorously in mid-air. Half-open windows with curtains lying flaccid in summer stared back at us, shadowy outlines of things inside, furniture or beings, shimmered, tried to take shape before Ma spoke up again.

"Strange, no . . . what happened to the family after she . . . went away . . . "

I felt Thamma's eyes on the back of my head, her whisper ruffled my hair, "That Narayan Chand, he did something . . . he was terrible, a badmaish."

Once again everyone was looking at her, but Thamma was sorting matters out for herself. "They were alone, always . . . the children were small. Suresh was always away, as a doctor in Baripada, that was when . . . when he . . . "

Ma nodded, her eyes had a sudden shine in them. "Yes, yes. I have also heard that . . . it really could not have been just a rumour. Didn't Narayan Chand try and threaten Bhaktawar also . . . accusing him and Ratri . . . "

I saw Father's eyes drift towards Bhai and me in warning and Ma said no more. But the bubble of happiness had returned once again, sending shafts of lightning joy down my arms, and legs, to areas that the tears had left numb.

The visit to the baba had after all had some payoff. I had found an explanation to the bloodstains – one, logical and ready-to-fit. It was that villain, Narayan Chand who had killed the bahurani, the woman no one wanted to name – Ratri. Clear-cut images flashed through my mind like a golden blob of sunlight falling on cold, lonely tiles in the haze-filled attic room. It had once been a children's playroom. I should have guessed from the size of the furniture.

But how had he killed her? He was furious with her because she had refused to give him information, to betray Bhaktwar. But had he poisoned her tea, or just crept up on her from behind and slit her throat with a knife. After it was done, he decided to drag her to the well and dump her there. There would then be no awkward questions asked, no body would ever be found.

The boy had played with his orange and hadn't said a word. He had smiled when his grandfather took his mother away. Narayan Chand must have smiled the same smarmy smile he wore in his photo, "Be quiet like a good boy. I will just be back."

His grandfather and mother moved slowly down the stairs, the boy had followed the red stains they left behind. Every now and then, his grandfather stopped, his foot between stairs, his ears alert, hoping to pick up any noise, even the faintest squeak. Somewhere the boy made a slithering noise and his grandfather turned. And hurled something at him – something sharp and pointed, that left a scar on his left cheek. It was still there, though half-hidden by the ungainly locks of hair that fell forward at his every step. "Go away, you rascal."

He had not listened. In the darkness, he saw his mother was not walking at all, but was being dragged by the arms. Her feet slithered over the ground, making that noise that he would remember all his life – the menace-filled glide of a snake at a zoo. Then the splash as she dived into water, his grandfather smiling in encouragement.

He ran to peer into the well. But all he saw was the water, it threw up bubbles and then sat as still as glass. Ma. Ma, he called, the water only gurgled in response. Then angry fingers gripped him by the throat. His head hit the old columns of the well, twice, thrice, several times. Since then, he had been left this way. His grandfather seemed angry because he had not listened. So many times they had been warned not to come near the well.

He saw his grandfather looking down at him. And he knew that he wasn't his grandfather any more. He knew he just didn't want to remember anything anymore. The white clouds swirled over his eyes, choked up his mind, eating up like hungry termites all that remained of his memory.

Narayan Chand had dialled the number for the police station. His daughter-in-law had gone missing, he reported. He was sure she had been kidnapped – he even had a suspect in mind. Someone he believed the investigating team should question. And because he was such a powerful man, people queued up to sympathize, to offer helpful suggestions, asking questions over and over again. How had it happened? And such a shame too, to happen in such a well-known and respectable family. Narayan Chand stood next to his son, Suresh, and people commented also on their likeness, on the now onerous responsibilities before them. Narayan Chand nodded his head dolefully in acknowledgment, moving his hands helplessly. Suddenly he looked a very old man. "She is gone. What am I to do with this child?"

The search for Ratri foundered after a while. Every trail that looked promising petered out into a dead end. But everyone, even the police, continued to remain sympathetic. Hadn't the family already endured a lot of scandal? It was best to simply forget. Within a year, Suresh married again, and still no one said a word. After all, it was clear that Ratri had gone for ever.

When I awoke, Father still seemed shaken. "How could a man . . . and to his own bahu?" Father was staring straight through the front window, looking at nothing.

He was sorting things out, like he had to. "Then the grandson . . . left like that. The baba was right, that is why there is so much evil in the house, so much ashanti. I have felt it since I came here . . . the riots, the problems with the police and students."

"The Chandi Mandir purohit. Maybe we should consult him for an auspicious day," Ma suggested.

Father took a while answering. "Provided his anger has now cooled . . . he was upset at the police. The crowds that day of the puja had become unmanageable."

Then he hunched his shoulders as the decision was torn from him, "Okay, we will try and ask him."

The highway in front unfurled into a broad grey expanse that narrowed into thin straight lines. I craned my neck several times, trying to see over Sahu's shoulder, but the lines refused to meet, each time we neared. Frustrated with the unchanging scene around me, I turned my attention to my latest missive to Paul. The matter was urgent enough to merit a telegram.

Pleased to report success on one matter. Stop. Please search immediately for man called Narayan Chand. Stop. Chatterji. Cuttack.

Now if only I could issue a similar alert for Mehta Uncle.

"There is a room upstairs, no?" Ma's voice sliced in knife-like, crumbling up all my thoughts.

"It was boarded up, I was told," Father responded. "The Purohit should offer puja in every room. Otherwise what is the use?" whined Ma. She had taken so many pains over the house, and nothing seemed right.

"He will find it difficult. And they charge by the hour. The more rooms he has to do, and he will become unaffordable."

Ma looked out of the window. Father extended another alternative, "Look I will call the PWD guys. They will board it up once again. You don't think there are ghosts there."

Ma persisted, "I have heard a few scuffles. Some strange noises, as if someone was walking around." I could have kicked myself. I knew I could be a bit heavy-footed at times. Jumping and rushing around like a mad March hare.

"Its your imagination . . . chase it. . . . It's running away again."

"No, I am sure that place is haunted. Something happened there."

I agreed, I could tell how Narayan Chand had killed Ratri. But boarding up the room was no solution. And I could not think of anything to stop it. The only images that floated around were that of a man's half-leg swinging past the glass pane attic, plotting a murder, and a boy's mad all-knowing smile looking at everyone, wanting to say, "I know who did it."

Apart from me, was there anyone else who would believe him?

Two Different Solutions

As per Ma's bidding, Father contacted the purohit soon after and I found him at home one afternoon just after my return from school. I had done well in the rehearsals once again, though Mrs. Muller had again blown the whistle a fraction too early even before I had taken position. Of course, she wanted to spike my efforts and help her favourite, Cherry Flowers, win. In life, such things happened.

I tore in through the gates, my mind still on the race. The same happiness had made me jump down from the rickshaw much before it had taken the turn towards the gate. Two men on bicycles had leered, a motorcyclist glided past, his eyes raking me over but something light and fluffy bounced inside me, making my feet feel like rubber, with springs attached. All of this fizzed out like a spent tyre the moment I felt the purohit's critical glance on me.

I moved with dainty, decorous steps towards the car around which they stood, making the final arrangements.

"I will be here," he was saying, his eyes turned heavenwards seeking confirmation from the divinities residing in that part of the universe, "you will send your car for me."

It was a statement, not a question. Yet my parents confirmed. They would, they would.

"At ten, soon after the morning puja."

He looked around the garden. No appreciation lit his eyes, though at this time of the year, it was leaking colour as several flowers had bloomed at once, vying with each other. The cannas – red and gold, offset with white; the pale yellow chrysanthemums, the dahlias pompous with their own weight, and the tiny, mellow jasmines like pearls strung around the green lawns.

"We will need marigold garlands."

Marigolds – their fluffed orange heads bobbing on thick, smelly necks, pared to a diet-thin stem – were the only items missing from the garden. Removing them after Durgamadhab's exit had been Ma's way of asserting her authority.

"We will get them," she assured; Mohanty for his part, looked woebegone. That would mean an extra errand to run.

The purohit looked at me again, remembered to look disapproving, then his eyes moved and rested with welcome relief on the car's bonnet. "Just a minute. Let me see if I have got it all done."

He clicked open his fancy briefcase, took out a leather-encased diary, an expensive looking pen and a pair of gold-rimmed reading glasses, that sat half-way in front of his eyes.

He began checking off every item in the list. "Hmmm . . . hmm. Yes I think it's all there. Only, I must have an alarm clock handy. I have to be back to the temple at 12. Its lunch hour and the devi has to be fed at 12.30."

He patted his own stomach in appreciation, shut his briefcase, looked at his watch and announced once more, "So I will be off."

His scooter took its time. It groaned and retched before rumbling to reluctant life. Only to die away the very next moment. He looked apologetically at the departure committee that flanked him on all sides, "All the mechanics are big chors, they will fleece even the shirt off your back. And if you go to them for something, they will do some more damage, so that you keep coming back there again . . . real thieves."

"We can arrange for it at the Perfect Motors. That's where all our cars go." Father's voice was so soft it looked as if the wind had snatched away his words, then served them back, all garbled and squeezed out like a limp dishrag.

Purohit Moshai nodded, granting Father the favour of doing something for him.

"Did your special puja really scare away the acid attack girl?"

In the interests of the attic and its occupants, if for no other reason, I had to ask him this, to gauge for myself, the potency of his powers. Ma and Father concentrated on looking at the driveway. The force of their combined gaze on the neat square tiles drilled a hole just big enough to swallow me up. One big gulp, I would be gone, and the earth would sit back, pat its stomach like the purohit was just doing, and belch in a very satisfied manner.

But the purohit was rubbing his stomach for quite another reason. He was arranging his dhoti decorously over himself as he took position. He wore no shirt, but wore a sturdy dark-tinted helmet of the kind teen gangsters wore in movies and a gold plated wristwatch. He resumed his attempts to again coax life into the machine. Twice, thrice he pressed his starter and finally it burst into life, spewing out frothy smoke like an overheated kettle.

"No," he said. "No . . . " and he wasn't noing to my question. He was noing away a thought that had just descended in his mind, "No, too much evil, too much . . . but what can a small time priest like me do? No one is willing to spend much on a puja anymore."

And with that last accusation left behind like an unpleasant cake of dung on the pavement, and a toss of his helmeted head in farewell, he was off.

The attic's latest acquisition was a desk calendar. It had once occupied pride of place on Father's table, and some of its squares bore deep red ink marks where Father had checked special dates. One red mark commemorated the visit to Bhaktawar in the hospital, another the day when a spate of temple activity had thrown the entire police system into chaos. In the filing system of my own memories that was the day the evil spirit had entered Mehta Uncle as he sat by himself in the veranda. The calendar was lying face down on the table, when I had seen it, floored by a stack of newly arrived files. I walked in casually, whistling in case anyone stopped to ask me my intentions, then whistled my way out. Mohanty had been attending to the telephone.

The calendar would provide a distraction for the dolls – for on one side, there were a series of landscapes, enchanting scenes from the National Geographic magazine and it would help me as well, to count the days down to the sports day.

Five days away, there was a rehearsal again. For the 1000-metre, there were seven of us, which made running something of an overcrowded activity. From where I stood, I saw Mrs. Muller's frown, a quick shake of her head but it soon stabilized. I was afraid she would call me out any minute – "You, Chatterji, you can come off . . . " After the first half-lap though, three of us took clear leads. There was a mile long gap between the stragglers and us. We had the run of the track to ourselves.

Another impromptu rehearsal a day later, and another realisation dawned. That Cherry was too fast for anyone to even think of beating her. She ran on roller skates, while the rest of us lumbered behind, chasing her like heavy-duty earthmoving machinery reluctantly pressed into action.

The purohit came back again with a stopwatch. He moved from room to room, timing his every move and the time the mantras would take. We followed him as he moved, careful to keep a respectful distance, I however, had my own reasons. Would the attic be taken into consideration or not. But the purohit halted when he saw the stepladder leading up to the attic. He stood under it, rubbed his weasel chin, looked up at its rickety steps and categorically shook his head, "The diffusion effect will have to do." Bhai pulled at Father's shirt and demanded to know, "What's diffusion?" The purohit turned around, took his time in switching the stop-watch off and said, "They don't teach you physics well at all. That air drifts upward to fill up all available space so the blessed smoke will rise high to clear away evil and ashanti."

I could already see the sweet-smelling smoke drift up through the cracks in the ceiling, snivel through gaping holes in walls where nails had once been murderously driven in, squeeze past the split window pane. The tight, swirling clouds would swell in minutes to take on the shape of a thick mushroom cake and the dolls taken unawares would choke. But a high-pitched squeak rang out in the still air full-stopping my morbid thoughts. The purohit's eyes were round saucers of fright; his trembling finger was stalled in an upright position.

"What was there . . . ah . . . ," his relieved laughter gushed out like an unrestrained jet of shower water. . . . "Only an eagle . . . ," I thought . . .

The usual look of disapproval on his face made a comeback. Marked by the twin lines that ran on either side of his hooked nose, showing his perpetual disgruntlement at the state of things everywhere. Girls ran around, dressed badly, boys tried to be too clever and worst of all, people did no puja at all, leading to ashanti everywhere.

Ashanti – there was simply too much of it around. All of it couldn't be blamed on ghosts and evil spirits who had somehow lost their way. Sometimes I wondered why the municipality did not launch a disinfectant drive against ashanti the way it did with mosquitoes after the rains. The ashanti that hid in corners, or dug itself into tunnels or had sunk deep into a well, would then be forced to emerge. It would lie limp and flaccid, caught in the stranglehold of the disinfecting gas, everything about it shrinking as the air was sucked out in a painful gasp.

On the second last day before the big day, Mrs. Muller exacted her revenge. I should have been prepared for it. But the news burst over me like a thunderclap as I took my usual practice run around the jogging track during the hour-long lunch break. Cherry strolled by, a mocking smile gummed to her lips, well aware that the end of the race was a foregone conclusion. Her eyes ran pityingly past her competitors and stopped on seeing me. "Your name's not there." She said flatly, her arms akimbo like a wrestler's.

I didn't stop. Cherry had never talked to me before and the statement didn't make sense. But she said it louder the second time. Raising her almost invisible neck high, so that the words popped out of her lips like accurately aimed slingshots. Other heads in the vicinity reared up in curiosity like herons taking a break from insect-hunting in the weeds. "Your name's struck off, Chutter-whatever." There were a few giggles, open smiles. Cherry sauntered around, checking for non-existent blemishes in the well-washed jogging tracks, "Check it out."

I stopped but stood my ground, my chest felt bouncy after my recent exertions, and from the words that slammed into me. Everyone's stares on me felt like the strong headlights of a car trapping me, making me unable to move or feel anything. "Really," the word emerged like crackled parchment, the effort of just saying it brought tears to the eyes. I narrowed my eyes the way I had practiced, so that there was little danger of the tears falling out.

I had little need to consult the notice board. Muller had always intended to do just that – strike my name off because she knew damn well I had a good chance to come third or even second.

The only place to hide away was the sports shed. Muller was away for lunch and quite likely she would remain there for the next part of the hour.

Even the hockey sticks crossed their arms around each other telling me how unwelcome I was; the badminton rackets stared hollowly from their pegs on the wall. The cricket bats slumbered against the stumps, balls strolled aimlessly by and the nets had already stretched themselves out on the floor, in exhaustion.

The sports shed was much older than the rest of the school. For the first classes were held in the shed, when the rest of the school was just a bare skeletal framework of rods and bars holding fast to each other, of bricks rising like a tide from below waiting for the mason's slap of cement. The signs of age were everywhere. In the inerasable tear-stains the rain had left on some portions of the wall; cracks in the windows where the flimsy paper coverings had given way in places; the crippled door that put up a creaky protest against the wind. A lone bulb swung by itself from the tinned ceiling, it had stayed switched off for as long as anyone could remember. The cupboard was the only thing that stood firmly in place. Its doors shut by a heavy Godrej lock, its bulbous end resembling the paunch of a police constable.

The rough net strings tore into my face, the dust rushed in to clog my nostrils and I heard myself sneeze and cry at the same time.

"Ssshhh . . . Shhsssh"

It was the wind shushing me to stop crying. It had stepped daintily in through the window and now lay trapped inside Muller's big sports whistle. Sshh . . . Sshh. I had missed seeing the whistle before but now I saw it languid by the nets, its string stretched on the floor, moving sinuously in tune with the flirtatious wind.

Each time Mrs. Muller held the whistle tight to her lips, it was transformed into a bully. A single pull of it meant an order no one dared disregard. Even when it stood at ease against her chest, it held considerable menace. If its bulbous, shiny head was turned someone's way, it meant trouble. A long-drawn, piercing pull of the whistle meant the races were off. Every time Muller did this, the balloon of air around her stilled, as the whistle sucked everything in greedily and then released it with relish. The sound it made shattered the stillness, scattered the air bubbles and broadcast a whistling message to everyone – that as long as Muller and her whistle were inseparable, her power was undisputed.

WHAT WORKS ...

Cuttack, March 24

1 *Following the riots in the city of Cuttack and adjoining areas, the state government is expected to announce a series of high-level transfers of police officials in the city. The union home minister expressed his displeasure at the state of law and order in the city.*

2 *Moving into action, the state CID has submitted its investigations into the riots. Our sources reveal that the police have allotted blame in differing proportions to factors that include an estrangement, business rivalries and even student riots. The police also released several people arrested over the last few days in connection with these riots. Senior police officer D M Mehta has denied that the police are playing safe by blaming everyone. "The police have no ego-hassles about anything. The guilty never go unpunished."*

3 *Samarpita Mishra, the 19-year old graduate student who sustained severe burns after acid was thrown at her in a busy city junction died last night in a city hospital. The police admit that all available clues to the identity of her attacker have dried up and blame public apathy. Influential politician, Bhairav Mohanty, has called for the investigation to be handed over to the CBI as vested interests in the police, close to the Mishra family are trying to "hush up the case".*

4 *The 110-year old St Joseph's School, of which Mishra was an alumnus, is to celebrate its 70th sports day tomorrow. The daylong function that will be graced by dignitaries and high-level government officials will be dedicated to the memory of Samarpita Mishra.*

The sports day began on a delayed note, the delays then followed upon each other much like a relay race. The chief guest, the state's director general of police received a belated welcome. In fact, he had arrived ahead of schedule because the streets had been emptied in advance for his cavalcade to pass through. The watchmen in school had been taken by surprise. The only official intimation they had received till then was to keep the grounds clear of rickshaws and cattle. They had waited for a new set of instructions to arrive; instead the principal herself emerged, flustered and frantic with apology.

Her apologies were drowned by the school band, which taking its cue from the principal's arrival, struck up the welcome song. The chief guest allowed himself an expansive smile, as did his wife, the chief guestess. Escorted by a still considerably agitated principal, the guests trod their way along a red carpet, down the school corridor, flinching and smiling as girls posted at regular intervals showered them with rose petals or sprinkled rose water.

As the end of the corridor beckoned, a wave of thunder growled and rushed to meet them. The sound of furious, forced clapping. The claps went on and smiles stayed in place as the guests were ushered into red leathery sofas specially sent across from Mohanlal and Sons, Furniture Makers since 1965. The usual routine followed – garlanding, speech outlining the importance of the occasion, staff introduction, handover of the pamphlet with event sequence outlined. Local reporters, who were only too familiar with the rigmarole, turned towards the tray-bearing waiters, asking them in careful undertones – orange, cola? No, lime, they were brusquely answered, and perspiring hands gladly took whatever was on offer.

Another delay followed as Sambuddha Mishra, city industrialist and uncle of the unfortunate acid victim, began a speech that had a promising start but soon meandered. The reporters had followed him first with much anticipation. Their writing pads held open to an empty page, hoping he would let slip something sensational besides what they already knew. An advance copy of his speech had already arrived in several newspaper offices, where Mishra had announced a closure of his chemical factory and had turned the land over for the construction of a women's rehabilitation centre in memory of his niece, Samarpita.

Of course, everyone, not just the journalists, knew this move was an attempt to hush up the whole story for wasn't the offending bottle of acid (though the police were still very tight-lipped about this) a product of the same chemical factory. Moreover, the central government was on the verge of pushing through stronger regulatory measures and the factory seemed a likely victim. Nevertheless, the most stirring part of Sambuddha's speech received a lot of applause. "I hope the rehab centre will have all your blessings. It will be a place for refuge for similar victims like my young niece, whose life was nipped when just ripening."

Bhairav Mohanty's entry coincided with the last flurry of clapping. Mohanty's assistants must have timed his entry well, so that the two men did not share a dais. But the reporters held their breath as the two men neared each other. There was the briefest of pauses as the men took each other in. Probably, they were equally surprised for despite the venomous rivalry between them, the first and only time they had met face to face was in course of that vicious election campaign of 1972. As realisation dawned, faces were turned suddenly, too deliberately away – and the moment passed into history. The journalists were left bereft, and shrugged the matter off philosophically. Some days you could not pull off something spicy, you had to settle down to a long boring afternoon. Of course, there was Bhaktawar's much-awaited autobiography to look forward to, but already hints had been dropped as to its contents: that Bhaktawar was keen to avoid controversy, that he would provide some romantic details of his past, the matter over Ratri, his early retirement from politics and probably just the usual bits on the festering family quarrel – nothing remotely spicy. The reporters settled deeper into their chairs and proceeded to snatch a quick nap, even as another delay, one that was to be by far the longest, played itself out on the sports ground.

The delay had its origins in a theft reported by the school sports teacher. Mrs. Muller strode up the steps onto the dais, her fluster pulsating around her like a radioactive halo. She stepped past Bhairav Mohanty who sat on his seat as if it were a bucket, frowning in constipated displeasure. To soothe him, the mike sputtered out a thin explanation, "We apologize for the delay. The races will begin in a short while." Mrs. Muller bent down to make her excuses to the white-capped head of the principal.

Someone else took over the mike, regaled the audience with bits of trivia – that the school was once a sanatorium for sick soldiers, that it had its own celebrities to boast off. The lilting voice of the step-in entertainer took on a sombre note as the unfortunate acid attack victim was mentioned. It perked up when it spoke of the accretions the school had acquired over the years. The trophies it had won in the sports arena.

All eyes were on the shenanigans on the dais, the confusion that settled large among the staff, unravelled over the school grounds, stinging everyone waiting with similar symptoms – everyone fretted, fumed and fidgeted in nervousness.

At last, the drum DUMMED to life.

And the reason for the confusion, Muller's evident distress was clear. Her prized whistle had gone missing. The thief had struck again but while the school function was on, it couldn't be made public.

The drum sounded again – triumphant at having edged out the whistle from its stellar role.

The races had been scheduled in an interesting manner – the middle distance events interspersed with the speed events, with other field events thrown in for diversion.

Muller's face was hidden deep in her dark square glasses. She was bent over the drum; without the whistle, she looked shrunken, bereft of authority and power. The sun caught her hair and turned it into steely silver. Lines ran down both ends of her lips, making her look what she really was – a crotchety, temperamental woman – a crank. Her thoughts were on others' thoughts – those running across the principal's mind, the chief guest's and others in the staff. Would the principal think she had been careless, couldn't even manage the sports shed and the sports events? The chief guest was already stealing surreptitious looks at his watch, while pretending to scratch himself on the wrist or raising his hand to ward off the sun. Here too Muller knew she had been caught short. She darted forward and handed the guests two cardboard pieces to shield themselves against the sun. They should have thought of a shamiana.

The ladies, the mothers in the audience, obviously thought so too. They cast meaningful glances upwards and delicately wiped their foreheads with floral printed perfumed handkerchiefs. When they were not doing so, they were stealing glances at each other's saris, displaying their own to perfection, pointing out flaws and blemishes to each other and talking about their husbands' transfers, the thieving orderlies, the school exams and the unnecessary fees charged because of the sports day. And they couldn't even arrange the show properly.

"So hot, no?"

"Haan ... and see Mrs. Swain. Just because she is chief guest, she is wearing a Kanjeevaram. In this heat. She must already be steaming."

"See, there. Sambuddha Mukherjee. He is a special guest for the occasion. So sad about his niece, no?"

An elegant shrug of the shoulders. Perspiration was wiped away carefully from faces, so that the make-up remained, caked up to the right degree.

"Sad ... yes. Who knows, really. So many things one hears. That there was some affair-shaffair. Did you get that sari from the exhibition?"

"Yes. But I had wanted one like that. See the one Mrs. Chatterji's wearing. It's nice, no ... it's a Dhakai?"

"No ... a Tangail ... but she wore it before in the party we had at Mishra's ... my sari is also a Tangail ... my brother's sister-in-law gave it when she came. From Calcutta."

Bangles jangled as saris were critically examined. "Haan ... the border is very pretty...."

"Arree. What is special about Tangails are the motifs. It's unique to a weaving family and passed on from father to son ... "

"See the race is starting ... "

The contestants took their place for the 1000-metre. I stood between Cherry and someone else. Cherry was the last to take her place. She swaggered to her place, wiped her hands carefully and bent down. It was almost as if she had already won it; the effort of going around the track thrice was a mere formality. As she took her position, she cast a cursory look at her competition. Her eyes first bulbed up, then she half stood up as she registered my presence among the competitors.

"You are not in the race, Aditi."

I didn't respond. I was looking not at her, but at two other people. One I hoped who would not notice me at least till the race was off and another, whose eyes I prayed fervently would follow me every inch of the race.

But Muller was still in retreat behind her dark glasses, still bent half over her drum, sari pulled over her head. If she was smaller, she would probably have crept into the drum and rolled away. I picked Ma up in the second row, right behind a row of other overly bedecked ladies. She looked pretty in a pink sari, but I did hope she had a clear view of the race. I would have raised a hand to draw her attention towards me as Cherry was already doing, to encourage her supporters, but in my case, circumstances obviously willed otherwise.

I looked at Ma, wishing I could make out whether her eyes were really on me, following my every move anxiously, pointing me out to other parents – that's Aditi, can you see her? Would Ma point me out to Mehta Uncle? If he did finally turn up. The news would be passed around the garden chairs on which they sat and they would look at me in new appreciation, everything bad about me would be forgotten. "Accha . . . we didn't know she was such a good runner . . . "

But Ma too wore dark, moon-sized glasses that covered half her cheeks. And Ma's hands were busy at work keeping her sari in place. It was a light, dainty thing that splayed itself out each time her attention turned elsewhere. I could see its blue border, its careful pleats folding in first, then opening up like petals each time the breeze nudged it.

Would Mehta Uncle come? I had left a message for him with his orderly and had politely requested my parents to see whether he could come. Maybe his opinion of me would change once I won the 1000m in style.

"Get away, Aditi. You are not in the race."

I blinked away my thoughts fast. It was time to concentrate. The sweat was already raining down my forehead but something else was hurting my eyes. The others were nervous too. They were chafing at their places, longing for the announcement to end, for Muller to strike the drum – once, twice and then a final thump, harsh and ponderous. Then we would take off.

Cherry raised a hand, but Muller was not looking her way at all. Her eyes were fixed hard on the drum fearing it too would vanish like the whistle. I pulled my hand out of my pocket. The whistle lay secure inside, its string folded and pinned up tight.

Ma was glancing at her feet, arranging her sari, her fingers grazing her forehead. I knew she too was waiting for someone who had still not come.

The drumbeat sounded the first time. I raised my head, my breath had suddenly caught in my throat. Second thump and we half-squatted, thrusting our heads out, even the sweat froze on our foreheads and then the final beat – DUMMP. We streaked off so fast, so quickly that only I heard Muller's amazed shout – "Aditeee".

The scream rushed past my ears like the wind. The wind whipped hair over my eyes, slapped my cheeks, leaving them smarting with cold. My feet struck the hard earth; I heard the sound pounding into my ears, rhyming with the thudding in my heart. From the corner of my eye, I saw them all, the five of them snapping at my heels. Sometimes a nose dug itself in front or the point of a toe. And Cherry's swinging blue tunic swayed across my eyes like a magician's wand furious at work. She had already taken the lead and had deliberately positioned herself in front, so that I was trapped, not able to edge my way through her side, not able to overtake her.

The sharp white chalk lines marking out the different lanes dissolved into powder. The roar of the crowd sounded like faraway sea waves, all around me I heard the terrible panting of my competitors. Blue dissolved into green, then brown. Mrs. Muller stood starkly marked out, her black and white speckled self, drumstick in hand raised menacingly.

"Get off . . . Get off . . . "

I was conscious of Cherry, and someone else – the three of us running neck to neck. Flash of white shoes, brown elbows, heads jogging furiously, eyes focussed ahead. The competition fell away in degrees, so the sounds now reached me, clearer, sharper than before. I felt a tightening in my chest, heard the scream of my lungs, as my arms urged me forward, my hair stinging my face sharply in protest. I was pushing against an invisible barrier, one I had to break, pushing with my arms, holding my breath, my legs thumping the ground. Go on. Go on. The other girl's breath rushed past me in gusts, the exhausted remains of a scream. Then it was just Cherry and I running the last lap.

In the blurred lines that everything became, I was conscious of Cherry and Muller. Suddenly another image transposed itself in that haze, as if the colours had coalesced to give shape to a definite form – pink in delicate white sandals, someone whose eyes had been always turned away from me. *Look at me, me* – I screamed through aching lungs. *Ma. For once, look at me.* I heard my own loud gasps tumbling out like bricks from the hot oven my lips had turned into. Cherry's head shaking from side to side, her eyes narrowed as she still saw me dogging her. Our shadows merged into a big, bobbing figure – Cherry short and squat; I was squat too but a little bigger. Two bears straight out of Goldilocks.

The blue of Cherry's skirt drifted into a thin red line that stretched like a horizontal band at the very end of my vision – the red tape, which meant the finish was near. *Ma. Look at me . . . me . . . Stop looking for him. Ma.*

Come on . . . Come on . . . The crowds were for me too. The blurred lines were higher. They were standing, the furious claps loud as cymbals. Come on . . . what's wrong with you. I urged myself on, to where the dais was, where the guests sat, where the finish was . . . Cherry still ahead. The wall refused to break down, stayed still in place, its transparent face catching the rays of the sun, glinting in mocking laughter.

In the sudden flash of silence, I heard Muller's voice on the mike – "Cherry Flowers, winner . . . one disqualification . . . "

The cheering hushed. As if the radio had been abruptly switched off. The teachers held on to the red tape, their faces blurred in white, smiles flashed Cherry-wards. Come on . . . come on . . . they were softly urging her on.

The wall stood, indissolute and lasting. I thrust my head forward, taking a last lunge forward. The tape broke. I had surged ahead. *Look . . . Ma . . . Look*. The hush broke a second later, as Cherry moved out of the track, collapsed into the arms of a teacher, who willingly gathered her up in her arms.

I ran along the track, past the crowds on the other side, took a right turn that led inside the corridor. The orange vapour lamps blinked in surprise. I stopped short for the first time, heard the echoes of my running feet ebbing away and the silence that rushed in to fill the gap. Ma, I had left her alone, bereft of company. I should rightfully be there with her just in case Ma was indeed looking for me. *Ma . . . I am sorry . . . Ma*. But even if she were, she would have to put on a strict act because of the other ladies looking on, aghast at what I had just done. I resumed my run, setting myself a greater pace, shrugging off unneeded thoughts.

In the school compound outside, the rickshaws were now coming in, the watchmen were swinging their sticks, directing the vehicles, swatting the flies away, and did not even stop me at the gate. Shops gleamed at me through their decorative glass panels. Horns hooted, tyres squealed furiously, heads turned. But for me the race was not over yet. Stepping over the potholes, sending the pebbles skittering for cover, hearing the sound my feet made on the hard pavement, I could somehow forget how the roaring had abruptly hushed and Muller's harsh voice ominous on the mike. The eyes that would turn not to me, but towards Ma, "That was your daughter, wasn't it, Mrs. Chatterji?" "Why on earth was she running if she wasn't running at all?"

Eyes would roll with hidden meanings, there would be gentle laughter and Ma would blush furiously. "Why can't you be as good as your brother? Your cousins? Why do you embarrass us all the while?" All the while, all the while, as I ran, the words followed too. Circling around my head, over my ears, swinging with my hair over my face.

At the first left, I felt the nudge of a bicycle wheel against my left flank. Moments later, it had moved to the right. I remembered another man on a bicycle not so long ago and speeded up. Women out for their first buys of the morning, stopped and stared, then pointed their fingers at me. Small girls playing hopscotch moved away, other children playing marbles gathered them up, and stood to watch me and the man on the bicycle. The wheel pulled a thread off my socks and I tossed my head and ran on.

The man said something under his breath. I couldn't hear for other words – from Ma, Muller, even Cherry's voice yelping weakly – were still crawling around my ears, nagging me the way a dog pulls ineffectually at one's calves and my breath still rushed out in agonized gasps.

A diagonal turn where the two cows were always tethered. They paused in their rumination and mooed as I passed. The bicycle man teetered for a while as their ropes dangled in his path. I moved past the rickshaw stand, down another left turn. From here, I could see the redbrick building of the YMCA, a naked window open and staring sightlessly. Then a stray bit of sunlight slapped it full on the face, making it gleam. The branches of the mango tree shook as I passed. I caught a glimpse of the black emptiness within the green, as someone parted the leaves and stared. Under the eaves of the attic roof, a shadow huddled. The black cat from the neighbour's was watching me too; it arched its back gracefully and spat with venom on the glass as I came in.

Thamma smiled when she saw me. "I won, Thamma, I won." I was finally able to raise my fist high into the air the way Cherry had done and

Thamma raised her glazed, wintry eyes. I heard her voice following me, soft and gentle as a low late afternoon breeze, the kind that brings the clouds scudding near enough to ruffle the coconut palms. I could smell the sea and salt tears, both at once. I turned the corner of the house only to find the bicycle still there. It slouched against the wall, enjoying the touch of Mohanty's hands on it, as he gave it a brisk, greasy rubdown.

"Back early?"

I didn't answer. I saw Mohanty rise to his feet, wipe his hands on his dirty cloth rag and follow me to the very back of the stairs. He must have been standing right down the ladder, as I climbed in my haste to reach the attic. He must have stooped near the window, his hands cupped around his ears. He must have heard me cry once again in front of the dolls.

The transfers were somehow expected. They appeared in the morning papers the next day. But the night before, a special despatch rider from Bhubaneshwar had delivered the official news, in an envelope sealed with red wax.

What was not entirely expected was that Father was pushed to a somewhat innocuous position – training and development – while Mehta Uncle would hold dual charge for some time, till someone was found to take over Father's place. The news briefly lifted the attention away from me. I thought of writing Father a letter, an anonymous one, detailing all I knew of Mehta Uncle's nefarious activities. But I never did have the time. I never could help Father.

The next morning was also the day of the puja and the day Mohanty was to give his statement to the police.

In the afternoon, soon after the midday paper came out there was a clamour outside the gate. "Why was the orderly claiming he had been shot?"

Two armed guards stood by, freely perspiring under the weight of their weapons and the questions tossed at them.

Mohanty's leg had several bones broken in it. He claimed someone had shot him at close range. He could have been killed. And he had a wife and two children, just about school-going age. Did he know who had done it?

He was silent, tears streaming down his cheeks. "How do I know how this happened? I am a poor man, very poor man."

Seeing the cluster of faces around him, hanging on to his every word, his woes could no longer hold themselves in check. He sat up, directed his wife on how exactly he wanted the pillow placed behind him, pulled the blanket decorously over his bony chest, so that it conveniently slipped away from his plastered leg, and proceeded to tell his story.

"I have always been a very dutifool person, that is why the saheb wanted me in his house. But that house had evil influence – the well, it should have been boarded up. Even the room hidden in the roof, no one even knew it existed. After a long time, they agreed to have a puja . . ."

"What evil influence . . . ?"

Mohanty was confused at the interruption. He paused in mid-flow, his eyes fell on his two children who were staring hard at cameras slung from all kinds of shoulders, and he began once again.

"I am poor so I do duty where they send me. They send me to Sahib's place though everyone knew of the ghost in the well . . ."

"Not on the roof . . ."

"The well was where the bahurani had committed suicide. The roof had a room in it . . ."

"If she had committed suicide, then why was the room in the roof supposed to be haunted . . ."

"Yes, the question is valid. You said the puja was because of strange noises from the roof . . ."

Mohanty looked unhappy, pointed to his leg, wrapped in white gauze peeping from under the blanket, inviting questions.

"The puja was because of the evil influence . . . the ghost was there. I had just gone to make the routine arrangements. Some lights had to be put up . . . "

"Hold on . . . can you stretch that leg out a bit more? Yes, and tell your wife to come and stand behind you. Your children can sit on the bed . . . " And the cameras were set up. Mohanty put on his best smile.

"Don't smile . . . you are in pain . . . right."

At that, he groaned, holding on to his leg. His eyes filled with tears and his wife rushed forward with a glass of water. The next day, that photograph of Mohanty slurping water from a glass, his wife standing behind and the children looking strangely joyful, all eyes fixed on the camera appeared on the front pages of the local paper.

Mysterious shooting in government bungalow

Inquiries are on over the alleged shooting of an orderly in a government bungalow off Cantonment Road. No one has been able to ascertain the exact cause of the shooting. The victim, one Bharat Mohanty, claims the house has been haunted for a long while, and that he was up on the roof to investigate the strange noises that emanated from there from time to time.

A service revolver that the present occupant of the bungalow, Mr. Chittoronjon Chatterji, had reported as missing has been recovered. Mr. Chatterji also explained that the injuries Mohanty sustained were because of his fall from the roof. However, traces of the bullet that was apparently fired from inside the house have been found. Though the police have begun their investigations, it is reported that junior officers are unwilling to take up the case for fear of inviting the ghost's wrath on them.

Meanwhile, the civic administration is seriously taking up the matter of the many government bungalows that dot the city. Most of these are on *Cantonment Road and in the Killa area and date from British times. It is now reported that similar incidents have been reported from other bungalows. The administration has promised to set up an inquiry at once. However, as an immediate short-term measure to assure citizens, the administration has put forward a plan of action. Pujas will be conducted in phases in all bungalows to exorcise evil spirits. The plan is slated to go on course soon. Only then, the civic commissioner claims, a proposal to pull down these bungalows and erect high-rises in their place could be considered.*

Mohanty is expected to be discharged in a day or two. The injury was not serious. The bullet, as the doctors say, slightly grazed him on the shank and he should be fit to even walk out of hospital. Mohanty has however refused to rejoin his former duties, claiming that the ghost had yet to exact its full revenge on him. A case of insubordination has now been slapped against him. Mohanty has a wife and two children (see accompanying photo).

Dear Paul

This is definitely my last letter to you, one that I intend to post also. I wonder why you didn't even bother to write. Maybe you didn't want to be friends with a girl. I am leaving for a new place, to a hostel and I won't give you my address.

My work here is over. The case still has several loose ends (see accompanying diagram) but I suspect that this case too will be closed like all the others I have told you about. Still I do not intend to share my knowledge with the police. One day, when I reveal all this, they will regret their decision.

Coming to the sports day. It went off fine. I came first beating the favourite, Cherry Flowers, but I didn't stay for the prize distribution ceremony. I had reports that an intrusion would soon occur in the attic and this time I was well prepared. By now I had another suspect in my list – besides the man in the mango tree, and the photograph killer, there was Mohanty. There was no reason why he should have been still at home pretending to oil his bicycle when he was supposed to be at my brother's school to bring him back for lunch.

In the attic, I waited for the intruder. I had the gun in place and the whistle ready to blow to call the others in. In the silence, with only a faint buzz as a reminder of the day outside, I heard a distinct crack, the sound of a shoe stepping on dry leaves. The next moment I saw the flash of a grey trouser leg outside the window. It stopped right there, and then it slowly bent. The pleats crinkling, the shank forming a triangle, the knee at its apex, and then a long, gnarled arm like a dry twig moved towards the latch. But I wasn't giving him a chance. I blew hard on the whistle, watching my feet fly over the old cracked floorboards, as I dived forward to shoot him. Things happened very fast. I had barely fired, when I felt the powder hot on my hands, water poured down my eyes but the man was not there. Instead, I heard him scream as he fell. The next sound I heard was the floorboards giving way. One square cut itself up along the edges like a piece of cake and plunged down, falling with a great thud to the floor. The ash and the dust rose through the gaping hole – it seemed as if a volcano had erupted.

The attic was evacuated for repairs. The dolls have been packed up. I hope they will be safe without me. I am moving to a boarding school, not far from Calcutta. Thamma will stay at my Pishi's who lives in a big, old rambling house in Gorcha. I shall look her up on the weekends.

Do let me know if I did the right thing. Will you at least write to me once before I go?

I end as always and now forever with my best regards,

Aditi Chatterji

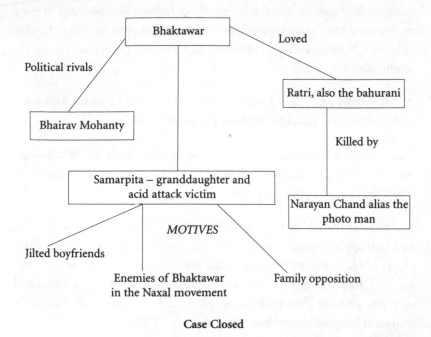

Bhaktawar

Loved

Political rivals

Ratri, also the bahurani

Bhairav Mohanty

Killed by

Samarpita – granddaughter and
acid attack victim

Narayan Chand alias the
photo man

MOTIVES

Jilted boyfriends

Enemies of Bhaktawar
in the Naxal movement

Family opposition

Case Closed

The puja was put off for a brief while. The purohit looked most unhappy; he could neither cancel the whole show nor hike up his rates – that would have been a most un-priestly thing to do. But the dining room had to be cleared up, because a part of the roof had fallen in. Then Mohanty had fallen off the roof and was quickly transported to the government hospital in Father's official Ambassador.

I had made a quiet descent from the attic, trying not to look frightened. Somehow, things had not gone according to plan. The purohit looked carefully at me, but he seemed ill-equipped to deal with the particular kind of evil that had gripped me. He believed Thamma too was affected in some way. She sat by me, merely looking on, smiling once in a while, as I was subjected to a whole range of questions.

The purohit reached some hurried decisions. The auspicious moment had passed – they blamed me for that. Now the potency of the puja would be much limited. The purohit explained that while he could drive away the evil force, he couldn't be sure how far it would go. Sometimes spirits moved away to just the intermediate regions and lingered in trees, on roofs or they might even seek temporary shelter in other houses, which might mean either good business or a loss of reputation in case the neighbours got talking.

"What a relief and a good night's sleep . . . Purohit Moshai's yagna was very effective. He managed to drive the ghost away."

"Pah . . . he's a crook. He puts the wrong mantra. They are in my house now. Running all over the roof, tasting the food, giving us indigestion. Now I will have to get a puja done . . . "

The purohit feared he might find himself in jail on charges of cheating and kidnapping spirits. He flipped the pages of his much dog-eared prayer book, searching for a particularly inspiring, all-purpose mantra. I saw his glance run over me once again. I knew what he saw – a frightened, ugly girl and her ever-smiling, deeply senile grandmother. Finally, he arrived at his pronouncement.

"The ghost will not trouble you again. My puja will ensure that. But sometimes in such a vacuum, other spirits can rush in. There are so many of them, after all. You should board up the room above. Cement it carefully without even leaving a small slit where the spirit can enter. Board up the window, take care of the broken glass pane."

A frown crossed Father's face, he exchanged a worried look with Ma and worked out some hurried calculations. The purohit raised a hand in reassurance. "I suggested a similar thing to Tripathi, two years back. He was then IG, Prisons, now he is some big commissioner in Delhi."

He cleared his throat to convey his meaning. Now his awesome powers were in no doubt. It was obvious Purohit Moshai must have had a hand in Tripathi's elevation.

"Some prisoners who he had had hanged came back to haunt him. He would always see a rope dangling outside his window. The rope would shrivel and then shape itself into a noose, or else loop itself around his neck each time he stepped out. He didn't tell anyone this because they would laugh at him. But he had come to me for consultation. That was when I suggested something like this – to put iron grills all over the windows, put a double lock on the door and all kinds of burglar alarms. After all, he was entitled to claim maintenance expenses from the administration."

Maintenance! The magic word dropped like a coin. Of course, the room could be boarded up, its cracks cemented over, windows boarded over and the administration would pay for it. The purohit swelled in the warm glow of everyone's approval.

Ma stepped forward. I saw the plea in her eyes, the anger that followed as she glanced at Thamma and me was the anger borne of helplessness. Sometimes the way you want things to happen may work out totally differently. "There is also more cause of ashanti that we have . . . "

The purohit had a ready answer to that one too. "I am told there is a good boarding school, somewhere outside Calcutta. They really instil proper discipline, respect for parents, elders, good habits like saying prayers, not stealing. . . ."

And that was how things were decided. And because I couldn't travel by myself, it was arranged for Thamma to visit Pishi for an indefinite stay. But Thamma too was beginning to forget things like rail tickets, her own berth number, her meal times, so it was arranged that a police constable would travel with us. Second class, unreserved.

And what doesn't . . .

List of objects recovered from Aditi Chatterji

A .303 Smith & Wesson Revolver
Paperweights – two: one with antlered deer and another of playing fish
Pen stand with fountain pens
Concise Oxford English Dictionary 1979 edition
Ink bottles
Special scented rubbers
Sharpeners
Old cloth pieces
Sequins
Bangles and bindis
Needles and coloured threads
Dustbins
Two stools – one with a leg missing and the other with half its seat gone
Torch
First Aid Box
Ludo Sets
One badminton racket, two shuttlecocks
Two brooms
Fancy writing pads and decorative envelopes
A desk calendar
A whistle
Letters for someone called Paul

All this, the revolver and the whistle, were packed into two school bags and accompanied Father and me in his official Ambassador to school. Some of the letters I did manage to secrete away. When we reached, the first period was on, the corridors were bare, not even a bored head or two appeared at windows.

Mrs. Hutchinson, the clerk in the office, looked up from her nails resting on her Remington and blinked, "Ah yes, Mr. Chatterji. I will just call Sister Michael."

Father shuffled to the bench. He sat at one end of it, holding on to its arm as if he needed support. High on the wall behind, Gandhi, Nehru and Shastri looked down at Father, while over them all stood a woebegone looking Christ on his cross. Christ's eyes were raised towards the ceiling; he was looking at the fine cobweb lines that crisscrossed each other like birthday party streamers. The door opened and Nabakanta the peon appeared bringing with him the smell of unflushed toilets and the rotten egg smell from the chemistry lab. Mrs. Hutchinson's nose crinkled, she put the glass down and looked at me as if I were the cause for such a foul emanation.

"Such a shame about this all."

I saw Father's eyes shift my way but he looked away as soon as our eyes met. He twiddled his thumbs, looked at the floor and asked it a question, "I hope Principal Madam is not taking a class."

"No, no. She has just gone for prayer. So what are the plans?"

"I will take up the new posting sometime next month."

"Some dislocation?"

"Not much. There are people to help."

"Such a shame, a shame."

"One must accept whatever happens. It is all his doing." And Father unfurled his hands, raised a forefinger towards the cross. Mrs. Hutchinson looked pleased and crossed herself several times.

"Times have been bad. It was good we managed the function well."

There was a pause during which Father returned to thumb twiddling. Mrs. Hutchinson resumed examining her nails. She looked at me, standing on one leg. My other leg was airborne, holding up a loose sock, its ladder stretched into an empty smile. I could do nothing completely well. Mrs. Hutchinson must have picked up my thought-signals for she said next, "Sometimes you never know how children can turn out."

Father's face sank lower; he was now examining the buttons on his shirt. I tapped on the floor, wishing an earthquake would swallow me up. Instead, the door opened a second time and a flurry of white breezed in bringing the same smelly combination – rotten eggs, unflushed toilet, dry leaves and Sister Michael's starched nun's habit.

"Good . . . morning, Sister . . . ," Father stood up, his hand over his mouth – something he always did when he was in an unsure social situation – but Sister Michael had her eyes on me.

"Pull up your socks, child," she said.

I nodded, reluctantly releasing the hands that had been wriggling behind me. The next moment, Sister Michael had bent down and smacked me straight across the knee. It made a sharp, thin noise and it brought everyone's eyes rushing in my direction. The area around my knee first felt cold, but the bones of my face tightened, and a flaming fire spread itself all over.

"Such a shame," Sister Michael then said, looking at me, and at Father, whose eyes alternated between staring at the table and the floor. She put forward the charges against me.

"You were not part of the race at all." I agreed.

"Mrs. Muller said you took her whistle."

This time I made a half-nod. I broadly agreed, but I had my reasons that no one would give much credence to.

"And also the sequins and the needlework box."

My head shook but in the end, all I managed to produce was another nod of agreement. Who would understand that the sequins were meant for the dolls, to give their clothes a new look? Besides, I had only taken some skeins of coloured thread, not the entire needlework box.

"She lies . . . see that, Mrs.Hutchinson, Mr. Chatterji, she lies."

Solemn nods at that profound observation.

"Mrs. Muller says a lot of things have been taken from the sports room."

I denied this – only a whistle. And that had been to ensure that Muller got too busy to notice me.

Father shuffled forward. He held out the piece of paper that catalogued my crimes. The paper looked as if it had been folded, unfolded, refolded many times over. "The list is here, Sister."

Father held the chit of paper between his thumb and index finger. I saw his fingers, squat with square, chipped nails edged with brown because of his habit of taking snuff. His pocket bulged where it held the small rounded tin of snuff. When he was at home or comfortable among friends, he would take it out, knock on its lid with his index finger, jerk a bit of the brown powder onto his palm, where it would lie quiet as a 25-paise coin before he lifted it neatly towards his lips. Today, the tin lay quiet, almost like a guilty child skulking behind a curtain and Father's hands trembled slightly as he held out the paper.

"Here is the list, Sister." His voice was low, his eyes were on the floor and I thought of how he looked on other occasions, when he argued furiously with Mehta Uncle. Especially those times when there seemed no real reason for them to fight. Like the times they argued over things that had happened over 15, 20 years back – the Naxalites or the political goondas, yes, no. I tell you no.

Sister Michael raised her hand to stop him. "I know Mr. Chatterji. You are here to apologize on behalf of your daughter. She should be rightly ashamed of herself. Are you, are you now?"

I could not find my voice. My socks had dragged my voice too, down to my ankles. I drank in small gulps the air around me, but everything had stilled, because they were watching me. So I dragged my head down lower and agreed.

"Thank God for that. You should repent, child. Repent for all that you have done. And thank him . . . Him . . . "

Sister Michael's arm rose in a neat arc, it hovered uncertainly in the air and then rose a fraction higher. The figure on the cross was staring at the finger, hypnotized.

"Thank Him for the nice, ever-forgiving parents he has given you. That they send you to the best school in the city and repent that this is how you repay their kindnesses."

Her starched skirt quivered in righteous indignation. The white pleats shook like a teacher's white cane pointing towards me.

"Sister . . . ," Father was trying to break in again.

With great reluctance, Sister Michael turned towards Father. "Yes . . . yes, Mr. Chatterji, you told me . . . a boarding school would be good. And she will not be such a bad influence on her brother."

Father was using once again his soft voice. Of course, it was my bad behaviour that had led to this – I had humiliated him, embarrassed Ma, the lies that would have to be told on my account, the social hibernation. How could they go to parties and face the inevitable barrage of questions, "What happened that day in the school, Mrs. Chatterji?" and Mehta Uncle's hoarse laugh, "So Aditi evidently takes after her father. Same refusal to face the truth . . . she was never supposed to run , was she?"

The ladies would look on in amusement and as Ma would look away to smile politely to someone who had just come in, they would tug at each other's saris, "Ohhh . . . so this is a Chanderi . . . so lovely, na . . . but you know, I heard something else. That the girl is being asked to leave because of some stealing-wheeling business."

Father continued with his detailed explanation.

"We also arranged for a puja – lot of evil spirits, a ghost . . . "

Sister Michael had begun consulting her watch. She scrubbed its glass face, saw her own face reflected there, and reached a hurried decision, "I think the clocks are running slow . . . I have to be off – there's a leprosy committee meet." She offered her hand to Father. He took three fingers of it in his four brown-edged ones and smiled gratefully.

"Thank you, Sister, for your kindnesses. What can we do? We live with what God has given . . . "

"I would also suggest you arrange for your daughter to meet Father Morden Daniels. He is with the Franciscans, and we know him. He is a trained psychologist." And she swished away, her habit clacking hard against her knees.

Father looked at the floor, all over the room and then with great reluctance towards me. His eyes moved quickly away. I longed to return to the attic once more. But I knew the answer from the sting of tears behind my eyelids. No more attic. It was to be boarded up, sealed forever. Like my own life, packed away into boarding school. No more a nuisance, an embarrassment.

"Go get your things."

Hutchinson nodded, suddenly all understanding. She pressed the buzzer, it burst with a surprised poing into the silence, and Nabakanta the peon came strolling back.

He looked at me with little change of his usual stoic manner. Obviously, the news must have got around. His eyes took in all of me – my head bent, the school belt pulled tight over my tunic, the black spots on my knees, the downcast socks, the shoes turned towards each other commiserating. He stared at all this and raised his eyes to recommence the appraisal but stopped as Father turned to him. Father pointed towards me and ordered Nabakanta, "She has to get her books." Some semblance of normality had at last returned to his voice. I could understand why I had to have an escort. They feared I would decamp with some more things to my boarding school.

I followed Nabakanta down the corridor, the orange lights put up for the sports day glinted down at me, winking at the memory. Nabakanta was scratching his head, finally he found the question he wanted to ask, "You are leaving?"

I looked at the floor tiles instead. Square and gray with black lines running like snakes across them. Nabakanta persisted. "Father is also transferred? Where?"

I refused to answer. He could read the papers if he wanted to. I looked down at my feet moving over the tiles. One foot per square tile. There were eighteen of them in that corridor that ran alongside the school office to where the senior classes began.

"When Tughlak came to the throne . . . ," There was a pause, Tughlak seemed suddenly unsure of himself. But the history teacher had turned her head to watch me pass, several other necks from the front rows also craned towards me. With each step I took, the tiles dum-dummed the same announcement like Mrs. Muller's sports drum. Everyone knows, knows. What you have done. Liar. Thief. Indisciplined. Everyone knows.

At last we took the turn where the middle classes began. Two sections of the eighth standard, one of class seven and then Class VI-B, written in chalk over a blue, louvered door within three steps of which stood the teacher's squat wooden desk. The old ceiling fan that heaved dangerously each time a gust of wind blew through the blue-barred windows, all kinds of birds and insects impaled on the posters that ran along the walls, papering over its coat of soot, undateable fingerprints, inked remarks that refused to be rubbed away.

At my entry, a hush swooped down on the room. The fan still rumbled, two sparrows called 'time' to their squabbles and looked through the window, outside the blue sky stretched away. The teacher's voice cut into the silence. "Fine, take your copies."

I made my legs move again. Every bone shook in rhythm to the fan. They were staring at me. Everyone's eyes rouged over my face, scouring its every feature, as if surprised I wasn't crying. That there was no trace of repentance.

I remembered the dolls, how they had looked on, without any blame, listening to me as I explained to them at least some of my whys.

"I had to run . . . I knew I could beat her."

"Come on, I only . . . really wanted to make everyone happy."

I think I saw the beggar maid blink.

"The medal would have looked nice here. Already this place looks nice."

My eyes located the gun.

"If he comes up here again, I am going to shoot him. I am sure no one wants me up here. They think I am wasting my time."

"I have her history copybook with me." Appu spoke up, holding her hand high over other heads, hoping to draw attention.

"What are you doing with it?" snapped the teacher, as if anything belonging to me would have poison on it. As if fingers would burn from turning the pages because I had smeared acid all over it.

Appu's trembling voice filled the room, "I was doing the essay on 'Why the British could conquer India.'"

I had completed my assignment and Appu had asked for my copy because she hated history.

"Can I take your copy? I will just use a dictionary to change some words and rearrange your points."

And of course, I hadn't refused.

"She completed her assignment." There was a disbelieving note in the teacher's voice.

Appu nodded vigorously, "Yes, Miss."

The stares had come back again. This time I read an unwilling something in their eyes. But the scorn returned once their eyes reached my tight school belt and the run-down socks.

They stared now because two tears had managed to wring themselves out of my eyes and had stopped treacherously where my cheeks rounded to a high.

I went on crying long after the copybooks had been dumped into my bag and when I returned to the office where Father waited for me. He was listening to Hutchinson speechifying about how bad times were. He offered me his kerchief and I cried even more. The kerchief smelt of the snuff he carried in his pocket.

The send-off was something I would always remember. Two vehicles escorted Thamma and me to the station – Sahu's Ambassador and a jeep carrying the suitcases, with a still weepy Mohanty on top, bemoaning the state of his back whenever the jeep sank into potholes or trembled like a gauche schoolgirl every time three waves of speed breakers appeared. The speed breakers were a preventive measure installed by the civic administration during the violence – to stop marauding motorcyclists, violence prone vehicles from making a loose dash towards anonymity.

We moved into the station in a small procession, Thamma and me in the middle of the circle. The two coolies followed behind, wiggly-toed, their hips moving pendulously, our luggage balanced on their heads, Sahu followed, looking oddly different now that he was no longer behind the wheel. I always thought of him seated on his smelly car cushion, its design firmly imprinted on his bottom, his hands fixed to the wheel. Almost as if the car was an appendage he carried along, like an ostrich with its mass of tail feathers. Mohanty wore his sour face; he badly wanted a sympathetic face to pour his sorrows to. And Mehta Uncle stood by the bench waiting for us. His baton twirled aimlessly in the air, looking for an invisible wall to break down. He refused to look at me but it no longer mattered to me.

There were other familiar faces and a very familiar smell too. The smell that had greeted us on our arrival wafted towards us from everywhere, it jostled with other station noises and smells, clamouring to say a final goodbye. I thought of the things I hadn't said goodbye to. The dolls were shut up for ever in the attic, and the one person I would never want to say goodbye to was with me. I took Thamma's hands in my own, felt them clammy and wet. Thamma was not crying, but her hands were giving her away.

"The train's on time . . . thank god."

Thank God. Trains running late, people not being on time, things stepping outside set time limits – all this made Father tense. But now the three parallel lines stretching across his forehead like a tightly strung badminton net eased somewhat.

The tension returned with Bhaktawar's sudden appearance. Before he materialized, the crowd had divided itself into two, like a woman neatly parting her hair. A servant led the way, a hand held out in front, carving out a way for Bhaktawar to advance Moses-like. He dragged his feet as he walked, even the stone tiles of the platform watched, impassive at his painful advance. He came to a stop a metre or so away from Thamma. "I heard you were leaving. I came to give you this . . ."

And he held out a packet, wrapped in old newspaper, pockmarked with oil stains. Probably the servant had helped him pack it, and the wrapping paper had been coaxed away from one of the street vendors.

"It's my autobiography . . . in English . . . ," he drew himself up straighter as he said that.

Thamma turned the packet over and looked at Father, "I cannot read this . . . Aditi can . . . "

No one said a word. They were looking at their feet, everyone thinking the same thought. When would Bhaktawar leave? It was late. Father tapped his watch, adding some musical accompaniment to everyone's thoughts. Its getting late . . . Its getting late.

"Yes . . . Aditi. Smart girl." Then to my surprise, he held his hand out for me. I had no option but to take it. The bones of his hand quivered, thin and easily broken like the twigs discarded by a tree, "Thank you for returning that page. Otherwise I would have forgotten."

I tried to look at everyone from the corner of my eyes but no one was listening. People like Bhaktawar and Thamma usually rambled, their conversations had connections no one could sew together, so who would listen? Father pushed himself in, scratched his forehead as if he wished to erase the frown lines away and said, "Its getting a bit late . . . ," his kindly smile was directed at Bhaktawar.

Bhaktawar tottered obligingly to one side. Father took Thamma by the hand. Soon he would make his way towards the train. "I was just saying . . . " Bhaktawar tried to speak up one last time but Father was jerking his head toward me. The time to move was nearing.

Bhaktawar bent down to touch Thamma's feet. Everyone followed his example, a line formed in front of the bench where Thamma sat. She became the focus of considerable attention. Everyone took their turn, bending low and touching the area around Thamma's feet. Thamma had looked embarrassed when Bhaktawar did that but with everyone else, she was different. She ruffled everyone's hair, patted some heads but her hands with their green veins hovered in the air long after the activity around her had ceased. Then she asked, "Am I going somewhere?"

I heard Ma's soft whine of despair, "Oh God, haven't we been down this road before?" And Father rested a hand on Thamma's shoulder, "I will come to see you in Calcutta. At Torudi's place."

At the thought of meeting her elder daughter again, Thamma's face brightened, "Toru liked the mango acchar . . . "

And Ma cheered up considerably now that the conversation had returned to more manageable areas, "We packed two bottles for Didi."

"Shall we move then?" Father said as the train began to pull into the station, wheels pulling forward reluctant bogies, the stewards hanging half-out of the door, in dreary anticipation of yet another journey.

"AC –1, AC – 1," shouted Father over the sudden din that had fallen over the platform. Only moments before it had been lolling under the high ceiling fans, now benches that had slouched under the benign gaze of dim lamps also came to life. The moths buzzed away in a scared manner, outdone by hurried shouts, feet pattering under heads holding up suitcases, baskets, sacks, everything huddled up in some order, some precariously balanced, others held up by supportive hands following behind.

"Look for 36, 37 – one lower berth, one upper . . . 36, 37 . . . excuse me, sorry . . . "

"Luggage there, below the berth, Bhai Sahab . . . please excuse me . . . old lady here . . . "

I watched Father settling things down, the noise infiltrating that part of me that wanted to remember. Thamma was seated by the window, and she remained there looking outside. She remembered at last what it was she wanted to ask and turned to me, "How long to reach Toru's place?"

"Tomorrow morning, by six, if the train is on time," answered Father instead, pushing the trunk, the holdall right behind under the berth, "Here," he said looking towards me, "this small bag with Thamma's food I am keeping here by this table." He looked around pleased, and the frown had erased itself away, "I will just tell the attendant to keep an eye . . . "

I did not tell him that there was no need for anyone to keep an eye on me. There was little chance of my doing anything on the train.

"You won't get to see much from the window, after a while. Just an overnight journey to Calcutta," he said, parting the curtains, peering through the double-panelled glass. The neon bulb inside the coach winked back at him, and he saw his own face, the hollow in his cheeks unnaturally dark and he hastily turned his head away. I looked out and Mehta Uncle was saying something to Ma. She had been looking downcast, but now she smiled at what Mehta Uncle had just told her. It made my mother look different, radiant like I had never seen her before, but the minute Mehta Uncle moved his head away, she looked like Ma again.

The train jolted, and Thamma and I looked towards Father. The time had come. Father rubbed his hands, looked at the other passengers with their eyes dully focussed on him, everywhere the sound of feet running back to their berths, others seeking a way out.

"I should be going...," he bent down to touch Thamma's feet. And remained staring at her feet for a long while. The light played on his bald spot, smaller than Mehta Uncle's, a shiny patch and black-white hair running away from it. His shoulders heaved and when he raised his head, I saw his eyes were red and a couple of errant silver beads hung on his cheeks. "Why are you crying? Calcutta is so near...," Thamma was saying, even as she rummaged through the tiny red purse she always carried, tucked inside her blouse.

"Here, take this ... eat something in the station ...," and she gave him all the loose change she carried – one 25 paise coin and a one-rupee coin, so new that even the neon bulb paled in comparison. Thamma counted it all over again before giving it to Father. You could not buy much with that but Father and I did not tell Thamma this. Thamma was reassuring him, her crinkled hands on Father's checked shirt. "Don't worry. Aditi is a big girl. She will take care ...," and then everyone looked at me.

"Yes, yes...," Father said and this time I knew the conviction in his voice was genuine.

"I will phone tomorrow, tomorrow ...," he said as he moved towards the corridor. By the time he finished his sentence he was gone. We saw him moments later, standing alone on the platform, amidst the mail stacked in the wheelbarrows, looking as forlorn as the benches. Now emptied of people, the benches looked as resigned as old people watching life pass by. I wished suddenly I had written Father that letter, exposing Mehta Uncle.

The train moved, its wheels at first reluctant, but once it felt the cold steel rails under its feet, it lunged ahead with more enthusiasm, finding itself unfettered, unbound. It took us past the corrugated roofs of the old station, with crows and coolies snatching a breather before the next train came in, before night settled down. Then the slums, the trees hovering over them, the evening making them pull their leaves tight over themselves. Soon they would crouch within their blanket of sleep and while away the night. The road appeared somewhere from behind. I caught sight of the blue Ambassador – my parents were going back home with Bhai. I saw a jeep following them. A flash of a sari appeared in the front and was pulled away in, too quickly. Was Ma travelling back with Mehta Uncle? Doing something that made her smile and be happy, however briefly. I couldn't be sure, really. After all, Mehta Uncle's jeep was not the only one in Cuttack.

The walls of the government bungalows soon appeared, like a curtain dropping over the rest of the city. They hid bungalows just like the ones we stayed in. All had the same sloping rooms, the climbing trees loping over the walls, the cats gleeful in their own company. Did they have hidden rooms in their roofs, a well that was haunted? The dolls had been boarded up. Probably they would remain there, until an explorer decided to dig his way through again. The man in the photo must have been driven away by the strong incense smoke of the puja. The water had been drained out from the well too. The masons would come tomorrow. They would put cement tiles over it.

When I came home for the holidays, I knew I would put my head against the cold stones. Someone inside would still be there, calling out for help, her tears caked into big, dark circles around her eyes. The flag on the temple spire waved a last goodbye. Bhairav Mohanty's house on the hill looked sternly back. The buckets, piled high stood straight and tall, determined never to break down again. Light bulbs flickered to life in some houses and doors began to be slapped shut to keep away the darkness. The train was soon left to itself. Boring its way through the advancing blackness, listening to its own sounds, wheels hurtling over cold steel.

I saw Thamma and me in the dimly lit up window. Thamma was already dozing, her head had fallen to one side, her mouth half-open. I looked much bigger, stronger. I was really a big girl now. And big girls didn't play with dolls. Or talk and play cricket with boys. In the melee and the business of packing up, Paul had slipped into my thoughts like he often did, in a desultory manner. But with Thamma in the train, listening to her as she made that soft noise that was half a snore, or someone laughing in a sudden dream, it was not necessary to think of such things. Of other things too, like how I had managed to keep my initial promise to Paul. Tomorrow – the day we reached Calcutta – would be exactly three months to our first day in Cuttack. I heard the priest's words and Father's too, looking at me in deep sorrow when they said, "One never knows how things will turn out . . ."

Thamma's head turned towards me and dropped onto my shoulder. "Thamma, you want something to eat now?" But Thamma didn't say a word and the train moved on. There were still thirteen hours left to go for Calcutta, that is, if we were on time. Leaning against Thamma, pushing the thought away, I decided to doze a while too.

An Ordinary Ending

A week after I was gone, Father and Ma had a terrible quarrel. It was the night of the house-warming party. The quarrel had something to do with Mehta Uncle. I was just coming to the more interesting bits in Bhai's letter when Sister Thomasina sent for me. She wanted to know if I could meet with Father Daniels when he came around the next Sunday, as was his practice. It meant I would have to forego my visit to Thamma's but would I mind terribly?

I did, but she obviously wasn't asking me. They were keeping an eye on me, surreptitious and obvious like private detectives, waiting for the slightest sign of recalcitrance or indiscipline on my part. I was sure they had put bugs everywhere inside my cubicle and had appointed spies among my classmates to report on me. When I returned, the letter was no longer where I had left it, between the pages of my chemistry book. It was flattering that my methods had now found their imitators.

Father Morden Daniels was a short man, with a very shy paunch. It sat elusive inside his robes and you only saw it peering out, on a second glance. He sat in the room next to the principal and stood up when I entered, a gesture that confused me. He ushered me to a chair, drew the curtains and closed the door and informed me very seriously that all this would help keep things quiet. After all, we were going to have a very serious conversation. I knew why he had closed that second door, the one that led to Sister Thomasina's room. To simply divert suspicion and quell the rumours that abounded about the second door. How Father and Sister crept into each other's rooms through that second door and did things no Father or Sister would have done.

He had a nice table. Under the glass top, there were picture postcards to show everyone that Father Daniels was a much-travelled man. There were other objects d'art strewn around, some with 'Thank you, Father for everything' attached to them. One of these was a particularly mournful looking dog chained to a tree, one of its paws held up a pen stand. There were nice-smelling files on one side of the table. Files that looked as if they were never touched but only served to give a very busy impression.

"So, Aditi, you have made lots of friends, I can see?" he said leaning over the table, his hands folded over his elbows. He was smiling in a way that told me he was trying to be friendly.

I shook my head and then decided I would nod. Just to see his reaction.

"Good . . . Good . . . It's always difficult to make friends in a new place. Many people take time getting adjusted. But Sister Thomasina," he glanced towards the shut second door, but anyone could be behind that, listening through the keyhole, "says you have settled down very well . . . Good."

And when I didn't respond, he drummed on the table with his fingers and said, "Good" again.

I looked at the glass top, at a picture of an upside-down gondola. From my side of the table, it looked like a pretty natty hat turned up against a swirling blue sky. The queen of England stood on her head, tapping a cow under the chin that also stood upside-down. He nodded and pointed, "That's when I was in Venice and that my brother sent me. He is a farmer in Devon."

I nodded and almost said "Good" too. He ran his fingers over the glass top and didn't know where exactly he could stop. He shifted the dog, picked up the pen from its stand and put it back again. He stole a glance at his watch, saw me staring at him through the glass, and realized it was time he got down to business. He began tapping once again, but I saw now that there was a plan to it. He was tapping out the questions he would ask me.

"So, Aditi, since you have settled down so well, I think you must forgotten all your old friends . . . "

I shook my head and then nodded again.

He looked at me. The smile was no longer making an effort to stay on. He was reassured for I was now playing to a set pattern.

"Good... you are extremely well adjusted. I must say, an extremely well adjusted personali-TEE. But one must keep in touch with old friends . . . do you?"

I shook my head, this time meaning it. It didn't matter what Mehta Uncle thought of me. I would take revenge on him when I was older. I had plans of joining the police force. I would shoot him in an encounter, I would file...

"Someone upset you very much . . . no?"

He waited for me to say something. But something had stuck in my throat. How did he know all this? Did he know all that had happened that evening between Mehta Uncle and me?

"By not writing? Paul, wasn't it? Yes, I think his name was Paul."

I nodded, trying to keep from smiling. So he hadn't guessed. He wasn't that smart, after all.

He smiled, "Yes, I can see he was a pretty good friend of yours. Was he a boyfriend?"

I glared at him. I didn't want to have anything to do with boys or men, let alone have a boyfriend. They were hateful, all of them without exception. I wanted to stand up and bawl at him, I HATE MEN.

But of course, that would mean bad manners and a serious breach of discipline. I couldn't afford to disgrace my FAMILY once again.

I shrugged, "No. He was someone I knew in Delhi, for a short while. Just a kid, we played cricket."

"Ah . . . so you played cricket. Were you a batsman?"

"I could have been if the boys would let me. But they were scared I would be too good. So I would always be the Empire."

"The umpire, eh? So you have given wrong decisions sometimes?"

I looked at him in contempt. Did he think I would be so obvious? "No, I read the rule books before I began Empiring seriously. But with Paul, I made a contro ... contro ... doubtful decision. He was run out but I gave him not out."

"Ah ... so the umpire came to his rescue. And he scored a century?"

"No, he got out the next ball. Clean bowled. There was nothing even the best Empires in the world could do about that."

He laughed. He seemed to find it very funny. My lips twitched too. See, I told myself, you can make people laugh.

"But you still became friends?"

"Yes. There was no option. We were thrown together. He was a terrible player and try as I might, I could not really give terribly wrong decisions in his favour all the time."

He was laughing again. Shaking his head, looking at me and saying, "Aditee. Aditee ... "

I wanted to correct the way he pronounced my name. Imagine if someone called him Father Murder Daniels. I was sure he wouldn't like it.

"So Aditi tell me why aren't you playing any sports here?"

I shrugged. Yes, that had been a hard decision. But my feet shook every time I placed them on the block. They refused to start each time the starting whistle blew.

"Who wants to play here? Girls don't like playing cricket – they can't even chase a ball. Then they say, we should change the rules for them ... "

He had begun tapping again even before I was finished. "Nonsense, there's nothing boys can do that girls can't, and do better than them too. Maybe if we talk to your sports teacher, he can get you to start a cricket team. It looks as if you might enjoy that."

I started to shake my head but changed my mind on second thoughts. Yes, it might be fun, especially if I got to bowl and bat, and didn't have to do any fielding. The captain was very much like a king on the field. Queen, I corrected myself.

He got up then, running a hand over his paunch. It had flattened somewhat as if the session with me had depleted it of some mass. "We will talk . . . I will just have a word with Sister Thomasina."

He cast a longing glance towards the closed door. It was standing still. Whoever was behind must have vanished again, in a rush of starch.

"Well, it was nice talking to you, Aditi . . . "

We shook hands and he escorted me to the door. I smiled at him but the moment the door shut firmly between us, I leaned against it to allow myself a big sigh of relief. So that was that. All plain sailing. But he had been a nice man. And despite everything I had been warned about, there had been no inquisition, no beatings with the ruler. He had not even touched me *that* way.

In fact, I almost liked Father Morden Daniels. And those pictures he had on his table. I put one hand into my pocket. The dog with the mournful face sat there, not saying a word.

I think it looks really cool on my table, just where it stands, next to Thamma's photo.

It is a few days after my first session with Father Daniels that I learn about the accident. As with occasions that have a significant impact on one's life, I remember vividly and down to the last detail, the moments that preceded and came after it. I am in class, looking out of the window, watching the breeze rise slowly from under the eucalyptus tree. I hear the flurry of dust and the sound of old, neglected leaves hitting themselves against the white trunk. The breeze rises slowly through the leaves, almost like someone running a comb through a long swathe of hair, leaving it crackling, with a dry fury. It rises to the very top, where a surprised leaf stands upright, unable to shake the breeze away. The tree ooks as if it is holding its breath, waiting to exhale. The next moment I hear the knock that will bring Sister Thomasina into the room, asking for me.

"Miss, can I have a word with Aditi Chatterji, please?"

I rise, reluctant for I am looking still at the tree. It looks spent and exhausted; the breeze is in retreat. I can see it go, beating with its fists on the empty basketball court, raising a last cloud of dust. I follow Sister outside the door. Behind me, the floor screams as chairs, that had been hastily pushed aside when everyone rose at Sister's entry, are pulled in again. I hear the faint swish of differently sized bottoms moving over wooden chair seats, trying to settle down again. I feel Sister's hand on my shoulder.

"Aditi, my dear, you have to be brave."

I feel the same stillness in myself that I had just seen in the tree. It stood outside my classroom window, droopy and depleted, gathering up its strength.

"Your mother, I am afraid she has had an accident."

The breeze is gathering again. Growling under its breath. This time it wastes no time. It strikes at the tree with unleashed venom.

"I am afraid it might be very serious. Be brave, my child. Your father thinks it best you remain here."

The branches flail helplessly at the breeze. The trunk bends too, pleading to be let alone.

I am excused for the rest of my classes. I am allowed to go and see Thamma, my grandmother. Everyone thinks Thamma will be devastated if she is told. But I can see Thamma is puzzled by my sudden appearance. They say Thamma is much the same as usual. No, she doesn't know. We haven't told her. But she looks at me, and I see her frown. Three lines appear as cracks in her porcelain skin. No school, she asks.

No, I left early.

You have eaten? She rubs my forehead, brushes errant flicks of hair away. I feel her fingers, leathery and scratchy on me. I bury my face in her sari. I want to cry but don't. Not because of Thamma but because I can't. Instead I think of the jeep that had followed me for a short while as I made my ignominious exit from the city. A jeep with a woman's sari flying out of its open door.

In the days I wait with Thamma and for news from home, I also manage to finish Bhaktawar's autobiography, *Experiments in half-truths and other stories*. In spite of Thamma's assurances to him, and her insistence in the train that I must read some bits to her, there are some parts it's best to keep her away from. If you ask me, the book was a disappointment. Most magazines had set great store by the book; reviews had touted it as the book that would finally reveal all Bhaktawar's secrets. But in effect the book glossed over the intrigues, the sabotage theories that supposedly broke the back of the Naxalite movement. Even Bhaktawar's descriptions of the family rivalry with Bhairav Mohanty tread over boringly dreary ground. I suppose you couldn't really blame Bhaktawar. The book had evidently been published in a hurry, the publisher possibly was hoping to cash in on the acid attack on his granddaughter, and had severely compromised on quality. The binding gave way even before I reached halfway point.

But the book helped bury an old ghost, one that had long outlived its existence. Bhaktawar confessed his suspicions about his missing books, the ones that Ratri had borrowed, never to return. They had left an untidy gap in his shelves, and a growing emptiness in his heart. For two decades, Bhaktawar wrote, he had borne the loneliness. But the time had come to bury the past, to let go of it, like a broken kite. To wait for death with no regrets.

Ratri was a friend's niece, she was married into a very powerful family but she was lonely. Their friendship, Bhaktawar hinted, had been of a most beautiful kind. Still that couldn't keep the scandal away when Ratri became a frequent visitor to Bhaktawar's house. He lived alone in one wing of the house, and they sat in his study into the late hours, discussing books, music and the future of the country. She borrowed his books, and sometimes within its pages, he would slip in a special letter for her. He liked to think that those letters kept her company in her darkest hours, when the sadness grew too much to hold on.

But in the end, his love had been betrayed. One night, he had waited for Ratri. For hours he had stood by his window watching the rain lash his city, whip it up into a frenzy of emotion. And later he heard of the rumours. That Ratri had disappeared, that she had in fact taken the train out of town, with someone else she had been seeing at the same time. Bhaktawar wrote that he finally forgave her for betraying his love and also for not returning his books. For Ratri too had sustained grievous hurts of her own. Bhaktawar hinted that she had been badly treated by her own family, by someone who constantly cajoled, even bullied her to use her friendship with Bhaktawar, to trap him, to ferret out every bit of information she could about the Naxalites. Narayan Chand had been that kind of man.

I receive a second letter from Bhai and this time manage to read it right to the end though it was patchy with regard to details. I learn it is Mehta Uncle who has suffered the more serious injuries. Everyone, all the eyewitnesses to the accident, said he had been driving much too fast and recklessly.

Ma remains in coma for a full three days when the doctors say anything can happen. The phone call comes the night I wake suddenly, when a minute remains before the phone rings. Somewhere a stray dog barks and then the phone too picks up the sound. I hear the big clock in the hall, the hurried scatter of footsteps, someone looking for a pair of spectacles. The bulb is switched on and I see the end of the door light up in a smile. I no longer fear the worst. I can hear my relatives speak, their voices, soft and urgent. Ma has come out of coma. She will be fine. For the first time, the blame drops away from their eyes. I relax as their gazes rest benignly on me, holding up the not guilty verdict. For all the shame I had heaped on my parents, I could not be responsible for this too. Ma would be in hospital for a few more days and then return home to her old responsibilities.

Things did work out better in a way. Father was readily given a transfer, back to Delhi. He explained to the authorities that he was unable to effectively function in a place associated with unhappy memories. I think he wanted to get Ma away from Mehta Uncle for good and from the place that had brought him nothing but bad luck and ashanti.

Bhai lost a year in school. But I was told that he quickly adjusted to the new school. My counselling sessions with Father Daniels were ended abruptly. He must have been told about the accident and realised he was not up to serious counselling. My classmates put away their sympathy and returned to keeping a watchful distance from me. It had to do with my past – my criminal record that will now forever decide how I am to be treated. You can never put up much resistance once people have made up their impressions.

Mehta Uncle, who lost both legs in the accident, applied for premature retirement from government service.

My plans may have blown up in my face, but that man would no longer trouble us. Bhai and I also began writing regularly to each other. It was tough in the beginning, because unlike with Paul, I could never make up stories with Bhai.

Some 18 years later it looks like, I return to Cuttack. Just days after that terrible cyclone struck large parts of eastern Orissa. I have a bit of time left over between two trains, and am accompanying Bhai as he does a quick tour, trying to desperately assess the damage. Only then will any assistance be forthcoming – from the governments and other powers that be.

The rehabilitation centre appears the hardest hit. Windows in the left wing have been shattered, and the glass panes lie shiny on the ground, the earth's discarded tears. A tree has fallen over, its branches still tattooing a desperate message on a lone unshattered window. The board, with Samarpita's name, hangs askew from two poles, flashing us a lop-sided smile. Other trees in the compound have a bent and crippled look. They too cannot take in the sight of all that destruction.

The nuns who run the centre, open up their hearts readily at the sight of Bhai's notepad and his leaky Reynolds pen. I notice the stain it has left in his pocket. The inmates were giving them a terrible time, the nuns complained. Because more people had to be accommodated, quarrels were now breaking out like summer rash. The nuns said that they had appealed for tents to house the extra people but the government so far had not lifted a finger. Ministers and journalists (and even bureaucrats, one nun added darkly) were only happy in taking an aerial survey of the devastation in the Navy's helicopters.

"Don't worry. I will return soon . . . in a couple of days . . . ," Bhai assures them. Then I hear him making his excuses. Bhai says we have to leave because the train taking me away to Delhi is in two hours' time and there are still a couple of places left to go to.

"If only you had cut out your nostalgia trip, we would have had more time here," he is muttering as we walk out of the gates. A retort rises quickly to my lips but I bite it back because I feel someone watching us. It isn't the nuns — they are already walking back up the driveway. It is someone standing at the very edge of the rough, mud-strewn path. Possibly, an inmate of the centre. Her skin has shrivelled about her, leaving loose flesh flapping around her arms like an elephant's ears. Her hair, silver and brown in places looks unevenly cut. She smiles when she sees she has my attention. Baring her teeth almost in a snarl. I draw in my breath as an old memory stirs uncomfortably alive. Next, I see her hold something up — a discarded leaf. She folds it, places it on her lips and blows into it happily, as if she has found at last her lost whistle.

I try not to make much of this incident. There are already too many things for which I do not have answers. Our old house with the attic looks much diminished, in the manner of men grown old. The Nandas, who are the third family to come after us, do not have very much time to spare. They have come to see their furniture being loaded and taken away to the new flats that have finally been constructed, almost what . . . 18 years after the proposals were first made.

The storm has blown away an entire portion of the roof, exposing the attic for the first time to the elements. But everything about the house either appears shrunken or changed absolutely. The driveway has been tiled over and the unnecessary flowerbeds Ma hated are back. The house without its roof has a terribly deranged look, a madman who has pulled his hair out in frenzy.

The Nandas say they are glad to be moving to a flat. The storm has happened at the right time. The house was haunted. Mr. Nanda's father had committed suicide because voices in the litchi tree had spoken to him.

I leave Bhai to commiserate with the Nandas and move around, to the back of the house. The well had been bottled up, the attic too closed for ever, but the air of misfortune still hangs over the house like a heavy mist. There is a man sitting on his haunches behind the forever unused well. He is weeding the grass and gets up hurriedly, hearing the scrunch of my shoes on the dying leaves. We smile, it seems the easiest thing to do in the face of all that the cyclone has left behind.

"I was just looking around." I spread my hands, wondering why I have to explain things to him, "We stayed here, a long time back."

"I know. Things haven't changed much." We are walking back together, our footsteps evenly matched. I see the ladder still where it first was, leaning against a wall. "I put it back there, best to restore things as they are," he says, his eyes following mine.

"I read your letters," he says next, taking me by surprise. I notice he has changed in the moments we have been walking together. He has blue eyes, as clear as the skies are now, after the clouds of rain have spent themselves. "Maybe you should have posted them. Things might have worked out differently."

I would have liked to linger, to find out how he, the grass weeder with the blue eyes, had managed to find his way into the attic. Just as the man in the old photo once had, just as Mohanty had tried to do before he paid the price. Had he read all the letters, the ones I had hidden

away in the drawer of that old table in the corner, the one with the
stolen desk calendar still on it, showing 1981? Did he really
understand why I had written them in the first place? Possibly, he had
read every one of those letters, even though in places, the greedy rain
had hungrily chomped away words I had painstakingly penned down.
Maybe, like I once had, he too had supplied words on his own, made
up his own letters. His name might just as well have been Paul. But I
cannot wait. Once again, before I can get to the bottom of things, I find
I have to go away. There is a train to catch.

When I meet Bhai for the holidays, I do not tell him all that I have
imagined. It will start everyone worrying again; they will recommend
more sessions with Father Daniels. Instead, Bhai asks after that first letter
he had written me. I do not tell him that I never read it fully, because I
had let it get stolen. I still smarted at that thought. So I change the
subject. "You know something . . . remember, what I too wrote to you.
That I had caught Mehta Uncle and Ma in the drawing room, through a
slit in the wooden floorboards. But you know, there wasn't a slit there
ever, it has a false ceiling of plywood."

Bhai says he has destroyed that letter. He advises me to do the same with
his letter too. "For God's sake, Didi. Stop trying to see things that are
simply not there . . . That were probably never there . . . or who cares . . .
we have to get on with our lives too."

Bhai's vehemence doesn't surprise me. I know I must stop making up stories
to get back at Mehta Uncle. But now I cannot tell Bhai about the bloodstains
also, those red dots falling in a murderous pattern, forming a neat series all
across the attic floor, till they ended near the forever closed trapdoor.

Other things too I understand more clearly now. Because of all that I had
done, Ma had cut herself away from all her friends, and Mehta Uncle
made her happy. I can still see her, laughing gaily in the jeep, her sari
flying into Mehta Uncle's face. One day I hope things will return to
everyday ordinariness. Mehta Uncle and Father will shake hands and
arrange to meet for weekends at the club, or at each other's houses, look
over old photo albums and talk of Koraput, Cuttack, the Naxal menace,

the students' riots, and enjoy Ma's cooking. Because everyone will then be that much older, it won't matter what they did any more. Bhai will join the civil services like he dreams of, travel around the country preparing extensive dossiers for the government. I will probably find something to do . . . maybe write. About all that really happened to Maya, Samarpita and of course, Ratri, the bahurani. Their stories, bound and locked up in a police file, sealed with red wax, all carrying the label proudly, "Closed". Stories that seem somehow unable to break free.

ACKNOWLEDGEMENTS

For this book, I owe all my thanks to: my parents, my sister, Soma and brother Dhruba; Shom Mazumdar, Gyan Pandey, Neena Gupta, Nina Burman and Madhukar Shukla, in whose classes I learnt it was okay to sometimes step out of the box to daydream occasionally; Kiran Nagarkar, who offered kind encouragement at a very early stage; Bhaswati for letting me write for *The Telegraph* occasionally, an immensely confidence-building measure; Pankaj Mishra, for his advice and suggestions that helped immensely; Suguna, who had such immense faith in the book; Padma, whose criticism always made me think differently.

To my friends, to all of whom I am immensely grateful: Angel, Sheba for helping me enjoy work and Dipankar, by all accounts, my oldest friend; Mr. Dave for his faith at a time when any abilities I had were non-existent; Gauraang, for the music he introduced me to; James for his desi doses of wisdom; and for Ajay, for his unquestioning support, for being a sounding board, for being there and for everything else.